MW00812501

# History and Approaches to Heritage Studies

*Cultural Heritage Studies*

UNIVERSITY PRESS OF FLORIDA

Florida A&M University, Tallahassee
Florida Atlantic University, Boca Raton
Florida Gulf Coast University, Ft. Myers
Florida International University, Miami
Florida State University, Tallahassee
New College of Florida, Sarasota
University of Central Florida, Orlando
University of Florida, Gainesville
University of North Florida, Jacksonville
University of South Florida, Tampa
University of West Florida, Pensacola

# HISTORY AND APPROACHES
## TO
# HERITAGE STUDIES

Edited by Phyllis Mauch Messenger and Susan J. Bender

FOREWORD BY PAUL A. SHACKEL

UNIVERSITY PRESS OF FLORIDA

Gainesville · Tallahassee · Tampa · Boca Raton

Pensacola · Orlando · Miami · Jacksonville · Ft. Myers · Sarasota

*Cover*: Meskwaki Historic Preservation Director Johnathan Buffalo discusses construction of Meskwaki wikiups at the Meskwaki Settlement Powwow grounds with Native and non-Native students attending the 2001 University of Iowa Archaeology Field School, specifically organized to address Native American concerns about archaeology. Photograph courtesy of Larry Zimmerman.

This book may be available in an electronic edition.

24  23  22  21  20  19    6  5  4  3  2  1

Library of Congress Cataloging-in-Publication Data
Names: Messenger, Phyllis Mauch, 1950– editor. | Bender, Susan J., editor. |
    Shackel, Paul A., author of foreword.
Title: History and approaches to heritage studies / edited by Phyllis Mauch
    Messenger and Susan J. Bender ; foreword by Paul A. Shackel.
Other titles: Cultural heritage studies.
Description: Gainesville : University Press of Florida, 2019. | Series:
    Cultural heritage studies | Includes bibliographical references and index.
Identifiers: LCCN 2018018126 | ISBN 9780813056180 (cloth : alk. paper)
Subjects: LCSH: Cultural property—Study and teaching. | National
    characteristics—Study and teaching. | History—Study and teaching. |
    Historic preservation—Study and teaching. | Cultural property—Protection.
Classification: LCC CC135 .H57 2019 | DDC 363.6/9—dc23
LC record available at https://lccn.loc.gov/2018018126

The University Press of Florida is the scholarly publishing agency for the State University System of Florida, comprising Florida A&M University, Florida Atlantic University, Florida Gulf Coast University, Florida International University, Florida State University, New College of Florida, University of Central Florida, University of Florida, University of North Florida, University of South Florida, and University of West Florida.

University Press of Florida
2046 NE Waldo Road
Suite 2100
Gainesville, FL 32609
http://upress.ufl.edu

# Contents

# Figures

# Tables

# Foreword

## The Challenges of New Pedagogies of Heritage Studies

In *History and Approaches to Heritage Studies*, the editors Phyllis Mauch Messenger and Susan J. Bender bring together a cadre of well-established heritage scholars who provide a strong baseline for examining pedagogies in heritage. Case studies and theoretical perspectives provide examples of how individuals and institutions can think about transitioning to, and/or creating, heritage studies programs. The chapters range from general issues related to heritage studies, to more focused discussions in feminist pedagogy and Indigenous pedagogies. Many of the authors see the examination of the past through a heritage perspective as a way of addressing social justice issues.

Henry Giroux (2007: 3–4) explains that "many educators have lost a meaningful language for linking schooling to democracy, convinced that education is now about job training, competitive market advantage, patriotic correctness, and a steady supply of labor for the national security state." Giroux (2007: 3–4) also explains that critical thinking is under assault especially in higher education. The strong development of a conservative ideology has shown a deep bias against appeals to reason, dialogue, and secular humanism. Educators have the difficult task of developing an engaged scholarship that has a meaningful critical pedagogy. Students should be able to engage in debate and dialogue related to relevant social problems. They should not only be a part of civic life, but also make a difference in shaping it (Giroux (2007: 5). The teacher's responsibility is about critical education, engaged citizenship, and social responsibility.

In many ways, the development of heritage studies and the recognition of the pursuit of social justice in some form are ways of addressing these issues. They can be attained through cooperative efforts of citizens who believe that all persons are entitled to basic human needs, regardless of economic disparity, class, gender, race, ethnicity, citizenship, religion, age, sexual orientation, disability, or health. Some view social justice as a moral/ethical balance to less-than-effective government-sponsored legal justice. They believe that historical inequities should be addressed and corrected, and those who hold significant power should be responsible to ensure a basic quality of life for all citizens.

By examining social justice issues, I hope that we can reflect on the way our histories are created and the way we live our lives today. Heritage studies has the potential to allow us to recognize the political nature of the past, and it can allow us to challenge colonial injustices and class inequities and permit communities to develop meaningful representations of their heritage. We need to think twice about our traditional heroes, and what we chose to remember, and to think hard about what we are ignoring. The profession of archaeology tends to be a very conservative discipline, and there is a tendency to emphasize what we already know. Questioning what has been omitted and challenging the way the past is created and presented break with the pattern, although this approach is often questioned and met with suspicion. It becomes even more questionable when these new ideas are tied to social causes.

The literature in heritage studies and the pedagogy of heritage has boomed in the past decade with the creation of new journals, and the publication of many new and cutting-edge books. With any new rapid expansion come many new and different perspectives, as well as debate about the direction of a discipline. This volume is quite timely, as it brings together a wide array of scholars and professionals addressing the direction of the field as they work to make heritage studies part of the standard curriculum. By bringing these authors together in one volume, Messenger and Bender provide a meaningful platform to have these very important discussions.

*Paul A. Shackel*
*Series Editor*

## References Cited

Giroux, Henry A.
2007    *The University in Chains: Confronting the Military-Industrial-Academic Complex.* Paradigm, Boulder, Colorado.

# Preface

This volume, *History and Approaches to Heritage Studies*, and its companion volume, *Pedagogy and Practice in Heritage Studies* (edited by Bender and Messenger), had their genesis in two symposia presented at Society for American Archaeology (SAA) annual meetings. At the 77th annual meeting in Memphis, Phyllis Messenger and Susan Bender chaired an electronic symposium, "Lessons from the Trenches: The Pedagogy of Archaeology and Heritage." University Press of Florida editor Meredith Babb expressed interest in a volume on the topic, as did Paul A. Shackel, editor of their Cultural Heritage Series. The following year in Honolulu, Messenger chaired a second symposium, "Lessons from the Trenches II: New Pedagogies of Archaeology and Heritage." In both of these sessions, archaeologists talked about grappling with integrating their work, especially their teaching, into the broader heritage field. Elizabeth Chilton and Larry Zimmerman, who were discussants in the Honolulu session, offered thought-provoking analyses of where we were in the archaeology and heritage enterprise. Participants came away from that session recognizing that we were not alone in trying to rethink and reframe our teaching and learning in archaeology to move beyond seeing ourselves as the authorities in discussions about the past, including stewardship, interpretation, agenda setting, and teaching and learning. Professors Chilton and Zimmerman graciously agreed to write chapters for the project, using their discussions as points of departure.

In the several years that these two volumes have been taking shape, some authors withdrew from the project and others joined it. Paul Shackel's invited chapter on the arc from CRM to heritage became a touchstone for many of the authors as the project developed, and the resulting volumes have profited from each of their contributions. As editors, we have benefited from each of their perspectives and their contributions to the dialogue, which has become more robust as the project developed. All the while, the literature on heritage studies and the pedagogy of heritage has continued to proliferate and provide more connections to the pieces being developed for these volumes. We are grateful to the contributing authors, especially as they continued to revisit their chapters in light of new contributions to this rapidly developing literature.

Even as we pursue more robust understandings of the various connections between archaeology and heritage study, we wish to acknowledge the foundation for this work in the early efforts of the Society for American Archaeology's Public Education Committee, so deftly championed by Edward Friedman and George Smith. Many of the authors in this volume, including its editors, initially met in this context; we were encouraged by Friedman and Smith to develop and expand disciplinary practices that were inclusive of a wider range of audiences and professional statuses than had typically been recognized up to that point. We are grateful for their leadership.

We wish to thank the Institute for Advanced Study and the IAS Heritage Collaborative at the University of Minnesota for providing funding and other support that have enabled the editors to convene for several intensive writing and editing weekends. We also thank the Department of Anthropology at Skidmore College for opening up lab space for one of the weekend work sessions. And we thank our anthropologist spouses for feeding us so well during the writing retreats. A special thanks goes to Lewis C. "Skip" Messenger Jr. for preparing the index for this volume.

# Introduction

## History and Approaches to Heritage Studies

PHYLLIS MAUCH MESSENGER AND SUSAN J. BENDER

In the decades since adoption of the 1972 World Heritage Convention, there has been a growing body of literature about heritage studies. Some scholars discuss the phenomenon of heritage itself, contributing to definitions of heritage and how it is used (for example, Carman 2000, 2002; Fairclough et al. 2008; Messenger and Smith 2010). Others discuss the various methods used to investigate heritage and the ethics and values issues related to heritage (for example, Clark 2006; Little and Shackel 2014; Smith et al. 2010; Sørensen and Carman 2009).

Sørensen and Carman, for example, provide an orientation to heritage as an emerging interdisciplinary field of study, making the case for explicit discussion and critical assessment of heritage methodologies, including "the need for methodological self-awareness" based on case studies (2009: 4). Harrison addresses heritage as an interdisciplinary social phenomenon that needs to take into account relationships with other social, political, and environmental issues. "Thinking of heritage not as a set of tangible 'things', nor as intangible expressions and practices, but instead as relational and emergent in the dialogue between people, objects, places and practices also has implications for how we think about and manage heritage in the future," Harrison argues (2013: 226). Smith (2006) discusses heritage as a process, a series of acts in the present that refer to the past.

A number of authors investigate the positions of stakeholders, the role of human rights and civic engagement, and the importance of values considerations in critical approaches to heritage studies (for example, Chilton and Mason 2010; Hamilakis 2004; Little and Shackel 2014; Logan 2012;

Meskell 1998; Pyburn and Smith 2015; Rubertone 2008; Schofield 2014; Yu et al. 2018). Hamilakis urges archaeologists to create spaces in their teaching practices for critical reflection that allows students to understand how knowledge is generated (2004). Case studies in Schofield (2014) explore the importance of developing practices that involve sharing expertise, listening to community voices, and understanding the depth of feelings that often accompany issues related to heritage. For Little and Shackel, the most basic definition of heritage might be "whatever matters to people today that provides some connection between past and present . . . and it includes the tangible and intangible in culture and nature" (2014: 39). They argue that heritage, civic engagement, and social justice are intertwined and that archaeologists can contribute to new narratives toward those ends (2014: 46–52).

Logan draws connections between cultural heritage and human rights–based cultural practice. "As heritage teachers, we need to reconsider what new knowledge and skills are needed by practitioners in their education if they are to adopt a human rights approach to their work" (Logan 2012: 242). Little argues for archaeologists as scholars "to take seriously both citizenship and the privilege of their positions in order to contribute in a positive way to our society" (Little 2010: 155).

Yu and colleagues introduce the "Toronto Declaration on the Relevance and Application of Heritage in Contemporary Society," while presenting a diverse set of approaches to heritage protection, community involvement, and strategic utilization of expertise (Yu et al. 2018).

Similarly, the authors in this volume and its companion, *Pedagogy and Practice in Heritage Studies* (Bender and Messenger 2019), offer rich perspectives on approaches and practices related to heritage studies. Many of our authors are archaeologists who are deeply committed to the broader frame of heritage studies. They bring their archaeological knowledge and practice to their understanding of and engagement with heritage. Chilton, for example, outlines the various ways that heritage has been defined and implications for how it is used. Her own definition of heritage includes "both tangible and intangible remains of the past and contemporary activities associated with these remains." Shackel adds that "heritage is based on a community's shared values." According to Zimmerman, heritage is "central to identity, to self-esteem, and to daily life." B. Clark (following Smith 2006) discusses how the heritage process can take place through group conversations at a site, talking about what happened here or *could* have happened here (compare Elia et al. 2019; Messenger 2019). K. Clark identifies heritage assets as things from the past that we value enough to carry them into the future.

The authors in this volume offer multiple perspectives on the history of heritage studies and approaches to teaching about heritage. The first three chapters orient readers to changing views of heritage (Shackel, Chilton) and potential influences and disruptors (Franklin). Other authors discuss diverse stakeholders (B. Clark, K. Clark, King, Messenger, Sievert et al., Watkins) and new approaches to heritage education (Croucher and Cobb, Hayes et al., MacDonald, Marciniak, Zimmerman). The companion volume (Bender and Messenger 2019) provides case studies that illustrate how heritage study modifies and enriches archaeology courses and curricula, from modifications of assignments and courses, to considerations of learning theory and assessment strategies to address heritage issues. Taken as a whole, following a "grounded theory" approach as described by Strauss and Corbin (1998), these works contribute to the development of theory related to heritage pedagogy. Strauss and Corbin argue that grounded theories, based on a process that begins with an area of study and allows theory to emerge from the data, are more likely to resemble reality "because they are drawn from data, are likely to offer insight, enhance understanding, and provide a meaningful guide to action" (1998: 12).

Several authors in this volume, including Shackel, Hayes and colleagues, and MacDonald, discuss theoretical and structural shifts taking place as programs transition from public archaeology or disciplinary studies to heritage studies. Chilton analyzes some of the ways that concepts of heritage are being used for framing policies of professional organizations. The chapters by King, Watkins, B. Clark, MacDonald, Sievert and colleagues, and Messenger address the central role that diverse perspectives play in teaching and learning about heritage in respectful and socially engaged ways. Franklin and Marciniak address how new technologies contribute to the shifting field of heritage learning. The transition that Cobb and Croucher describe in the UK context is one that seeks to move from the loss of a funded, unified approach to archaeology and heritage pedagogy to a reassembled approach in which people and things are interconnected and equally affective. They are among several authors, including Shackel and Zimmerman, who discuss the current debates in higher education about teaching critical thinking skills versus skills for professional practice. The impact on heritage, as Shackel describes it, is that "teaching and learning critical thinking skills [as opposed to skill-based programs] . . . allow[s] us to develop more complicated and more inclusive community heritage."

Ethical practices and ethics education are key components of heritage education and are woven throughout the writing in this volume and its companion. Sievert and coauthors discuss the teaching and learning of ethical practices as a critical objective for pedagogy in higher education, especially as they relate to Indigenous and human rights regarding repatriation (see also McGill 2019). Watkins examines ethics and repatriation issues in terms of "teaching Indigenous archaeology." Messenger addresses justice and ethics issues related to heritage through the lenses of gender and class. McGill's (2019) case study on ethics education and assessment of student learning describes how heritage learning can foster complex thinking processes and reflection.

In discussing their teaching philosophies, authors consider their approaches to working with students who learn in different ways, as well as the challenges of teaching in different settings. Watkins discusses the importance of different styles of learning and communicating, which are often culturally specific, and which must be engaged in collaboratively by teacher and learners. He emphasizes the importance of a values-centered approach to teaching Indigenous archaeology and, more broadly, the stories, relationships, and concepts that comprise heritage. B. Clark describes the value of social network theory as a tool for understanding heritage work and teaching in a community context. Community connections such as pairing students and volunteers in fieldwork, oral history projects, or co-created interpretation need to be formalized in heritage pedagogy, she suggests, if students are to learn that heritage extends beyond concern for sites and objects. King describes the challenge of modifying the length and cost of summer field experiences for students who must fulfill their work and family obligations (compare Elia et al. 2019). Franklin offers an educator's perspective on disruptive influences on heritage education, especially technological innovations, such as online learning, and an emphasis on student-centered approaches that allow greater access to information and more specialized learning opportunities. Marciniak presents a detailed case study of how some of the same technological innovations described by Franklin are being used to educate heritage professionals spread across Europe.

Several authors consider current initiatives to develop heritage studies programs, both within a department and across disciplines and colleges. MacDonald discusses how a graduate program in public issues anthropology prepares future practitioners to "articulate with the expanding international field of transdisciplinary studies," focusing on complex contemporary issues, such as global warming or ethnic strife (compare Scham 2019). Both the Canadian program that MacDonald describes and the U.S. program detailed by Hayes and colleagues rely on broad collaboration across academic disciplines and beyond the academy to prepare heritage professionals for work in many settings (see also Shackel, this volume; Pluckhahn 2019). B. Clark and King each describe community-based field programs, both of which have been greatly enriched by the diverse make-up of both students and community participants. They and other authors in this volume grapple with the concept of critical heritage studies, that is, how study of the past can benefit communities today, especially Indigenous and descendant communities.

A number of authors address the theme of perspective in the context of critical archaeology and heritage. Some call it decentering the authority of archaeologists; others discuss the role of multiple stakeholders, who have varied interests and motivations, valid perspectives and points of view, and rich and multifaceted sources of knowledge. Watkins, Sievert and coauthors, and MacDonald all discuss Indigenous archaeology and the complex discourse, consultation, and collaboration that must take place around heritage. Shackel, B. Clark, and King describe complex field programs with diverse sets of stakeholders having potentially conflicting interests and goals. In each case, acknowledging and valuing these differences, and negotiating how they fit into the heritage stories being created as a result of these projects, are critical to reaching mutually acceptable outcomes.

Zimmerman presents an aspirational framework that points toward next steps in the development of a critical pedagogy of heritage. Among the important assessments he makes is that archaeologists would do well to consider why audiences are invested in heritage much more than they are in archaeology, once the hype of *oldest*, *biggest*, and *most mysterious* wears off. Can archaeology really matter? he asks. It can, if we recognize its political nature and use it to challenge colonial and class struggle legacies, and "work with communities to develop meaningful representations of their pasts." He offers a "Trial Hierarchy of Heritage Awareness" as a way to theorize a critical pedagogy of heritage. He suggests that a fruitful approach to teaching about archaeology would be a pedagogy that shows how archaeology can help communities identify elements of their heritage about which they have questions that might be addressed by material culture study. Among other possible benefits would be the ability to challenge deeply rooted, and not always accurate, narratives about their heritage. The key, says Zimmerman, and other authors in these volumes, is to recognize that moving in a continuum—from cultural resource management to public archaeology to critical archaeology to critical heritage—is hard work that requires intentional collaboration with partners and stakeholders in communities. Critical heritage not only allows people to work on projects they helped design, but also helps them learn to craft meaningful public policies that move beyond preservation or repatriation to a place where archaeology matters in people's lives.

## References Cited

Bender, Susan J., and Phyllis Mauch Messenger (editors)
2019    *Pedagogy and Practice in Heritage Studies*. University Press of Florida, Gainesville.
Carman, John
2000    "Theorising a Realm of Practice": Introducing Archaeological Heritage Management as a Research Field. *International Journal of Heritage Studies* 6(4): 303–308.
2002    *Archaeology and Heritage: An Introduction*. Continuum, London.
Chilton, Elizabeth S., and Randall Mason
2010    NSF White Paper: A Call for a Social Science of the Past. SBE 2020: Future Research in the Social, Behavioral, and Economic Sciences. Electronic document, http://www.nsf.gov/sbe/sbe_2020/2020_pdfs/Chilton_Elizabeth_297.pdf. Accessed January 26, 2016.
Clark, Kate (editor)
2006    *Capturing the Public Value of Heritage*. English Heritage, London.
Elia, Ricardo J., Amalia Pérez-Juez, and Meredith Anderson
2019    Teaching Heritage in the Field: An Example from Menorca, Spain. In *Pedagogy and Practice in Heritage Studies*, edited by Susan J. Bender and Phyllis Mauch Messenger, pp. 94–111. University Press of Florida, Gainesville.
Fairclough, Graham, Rodney Harrison, John H. Jameson, Jr., and John Schofield (editors)
2008    *The Heritage Reader*. Routledge, New York.
Hamilakis, Yannis
2004    Archaeology and the Politics of Pedagogy. *World Archaeology* 36(2): 287–309.
Harrison, Rodney
2013    *Heritage: Critical Approaches*. Routledge, New York.

Little, Barbara J.

2010 Epilogue: Changing the World with Archaeology. In *Archaeologists as Activists: Can Archeologists Change the World?* edited by M. Jay Stottman, pp. 154–158. University of Alabama Press, Tuscaloosa.

Little, Barbara J., and Paul A. Shackel

2014 *Archaeology, Heritage, and Civic Engagement: Working toward the Public Good.* Left Coast Press, Walnut Creek, California.

Logan, William

2012 Cultural Diversity, Cultural Heritage and Human Rights: Towards Heritage Management as Human Rights-based Cultural Practice. *International Journal of Heritage Studies* 18(3): 231–244.

McGill, Alicia Ebbitt

2019 Assessing Student Learning in Heritage Studies: What Does It Mean for Students to "Understand" Archaeological Ethics? In *Pedagogy and Practice in Heritage Studies*, edited by Susan J. Bender and Phyllis Mauch Messenger, pp. 50–71. University Press of Florida, Gainesville.

Meskell, Lynn (editor)

1998 *Archaeology under Fire.* Routledge, London.

Messenger, Lewis C., Jr.

2019 Experiencing Antiquity in the First Person through Archaeological Fiction: The Pedagogical Opportunities of BACAB CAAS. In *Pedagogy and Practice in Heritage Studies*, edited by Susan J. Bender and Phyllis Mauch Messenger, pp. 165–184. University Press of Florida, Gainesville.

Messenger, Phyllis Mauch, and George S. Smith (editors)

2010 *Cultural Heritage Management: A Global Perspective.* University Press of Florida, Gainsville.

Pluckhahn, Thomas

2019 The Challenges of Curriculum Change and the Pedagogy of Public Archaeology and CRM at the University of South Florida. In *Pedagogy and Practice in Heritage Studies*, edited by Susan J. Bender and Phyllis Mauch Messenger, pp. 72–93. University Press of Florida, Gainesville.

Pyburn, K. Anne, and George S. Smith

2015 The MATRIX Project (Making Archaeology Teaching Relevant in the XXIst Century): An Approach to the Efficient Sharing of Professional Knowledge and Skills with a Large Audience. In *Sharing Archaeology: Academe, Practice, and the Public*, edited by Peter G. Stone and Zhao Hui, pp. 132–140. Routledge, London.

Rubertone, Patricia E. (editor)

2008 *Archaeologies of Placemaking: Monuments, Memories, and Engagement in Native North America.* Left Coast Press, Walnut Creek, California.

Scham, Sandra

2019 Educating Students about the Modern Realities of Exploring the Ancient Middle East. In *Pedagogy and Practice in Heritage Studies*, edited by Susan J. Bender and Phyllis Mauch Messenger, pp. 112–128. University Press of Florida, Gainesville.

Schofield, John (editor)

2014 *Who Needs Experts? Counter-mapping Cultural Heritage.* Ashgate, Surrey, England.

Smith, Laurajane

2006 *Uses of Heritage.* Routledge, Abingdon, Oxon.

Smith, George S., Phyllis Mauch Messenger, and Hilary A. Soderland (editors)

2010 *Heritage Values in Contemporary Society.* Left Coast Press, Walnut Creek, California.

Sørensen, Marie Louise Stig, and John Carman (editors)

2009 *Heritage Studies: Methods and Approaches.* Routledge, New York.

Strauss, Anselm L., and Corbin, Juliet M.

1998 *Basics of Qualitative Research: Techniques and Procedures for Developing Grounded Theory.* Sage, Thousand Oaks, California.

Yu, Pei-Lin, Chen Shen, and George S. Smith (editors)

2018 *Relevance and Application of Heritage in Contemporary Society.* Routledge, London.

# 1

# Civic Engagement, Representation, and Social Justice

## Moving from CRM to Heritage Studies

PAUL A. SHACKEL

While Cultural Resource Management (CRM) and the federal archaeology program have played a major role in creating a direction for American archaeology over the past several decades, there has been a slow acceptance to developing long-term community heritage projects. The planning process at federal, state, and local levels requires public involvement; however, the involvement tends to be project-oriented, and public involvement ceases with project completion. While Section 106 of the National Historic Preservation Act mandates the recovery and dissemination of the information recovered from important archaeological sites in the name of public benefit, the contribution of the CRM sector to the public or the development of heritage programs has not reached its potential (Praetzellis and Praetzellis 2011: 86–100).

Within the CRM industry there is a growing call for the development of skill-based programs in higher education. This call is part of the larger narrative that is driving the United States economy and influencing higher education. I am not certain that the public will see the full implementation of heritage-based programs in CRM unless we continue our efforts to embed a critical approach in these programs. This chapter outlines the importance of developing civically responsible engagement programs. I argue that a critical approach is important for the development of heritage programs and an inclusive representation in the past as well as in the present. If contemporary CRM training is to work toward the implementation of heritage-based programs, it is important to emphasize a critical pedagogy in degree programs. Moreover, it is necessary to think about inclusion and diversity, past and present, in order for us to promote social justice, present and future.

## Moving toward Heritage Programs

Heritage is based on shared values that people have about culture and their past. Heritage infers integrity, authenticity, and stability, and it is used to clarify the past so that the past can be used in the present. Therefore, heritage is based on a community's shared values, becoming legitimized through a process of formalization and/or ritualization by referring to or recognizing a particular past. By developing a continuum with the past, these traditions reinforce a community's values and behavior. The celebration of this past is important for sustaining identity and a sense of place. Places and events that are commemorated and ritualized become part of a naturalized landscape, and thus, they become reified and part of the local or national public memory (Shackel 2005). Allowing traditionally muted viewpoints to share in the development of heritage makes the process of creating a mutually agreed upon heritage much more complicated, but is necessary. For instance, the meaning of monuments has been contested for a long time (see Savage 1997; Shackel 2003a, 2003b), and whether confederate monuments should remain or be removed from public spaces continues to create considerable dialogue in local communities and on the national level.

I see the rising concern about pedagogy in heritage studies as a result of the growth of community-based archaeology programs. While the nature of U.S. CRM and the federal archaeology program have been influenced by the preservation movement of the 1960s, much of the shaping and rethinking and reinterpretation of modern CRM laws are, in many ways, influenced by the outcomes of the Civil Rights Movement. By the 1980s, archaeologists began to intensify their discussions on ethics, which focused on the conservation of archaeological resources (Fowler 1984) and the rights of descendant groups. Initially, archaeologists were concerned with matters related to American Indian groups, including the issue of reburial (King 1972; McManamon 1992; Winter 1980; Zimmerman 1996). Subsequently, the concerns of other traditionally subaltern groups have been addressed, with these groups becoming a part of the negotiation process of their community and ancestral heritage.

There are several community heritage programs that began as CRM projects, and because of the federal law or through political pressure, they became influential programs that are helping to redefine CRM practices. Projects like the African Burial Ground (LaRoche and Blakey 1997), and the

Cypress Freeway Replacement Project (Praetzellis et al. 2007), among others, make clear and explicit connections between a neighborhood's past and its present, and the heritage programs create an avenue for restorative justice. Incorporating community values into the CRM process is transforming the way we practice archaeology and negotiate the maintenance and/or transformation of tangible and intangible heritage in communities.

Although the above examples provide a nice connection to heritage studies programs, there still exists a tension with CRM. For instance, there has been a growing call from CRM companies and professional organizations for graduate programs to develop and teach attitudes and skills for professional practice in the university curriculum. While these calls also include critical thinking skills (Bender and Smith 2000), such skills sets are sometimes treated as secondary. I believe that the development of skill-based programs has come at a cost of teaching and learning critical thinking skills—the critical thinking skills that allow us to develop more complicated and more inclusive community heritage.

A critical perspective allows us to see the complexity of representation and can lead to the development of an inclusive heritage. Henry Giroux (2007: 3–4) explains how critical thinking is under assault. He notes that the strong development of conservative ideology has shown a deep bias against appeals to reason, dialogue, and secular humanism. "Not only the American public but many educators have lost a meaningful language for linking schooling to democracy, convinced that education is now about job training, competitive market advantage, patriotic correctness, and a steady supply of labor for the national security state" (Giroux 2007: 3). For instance, Stanley Fish (2008: 67) argues that education should be about learning skills rather than "produce active citizens, inculcate the virtue of tolerance, redress injustices and bring about political change." While citizenship and moral behavior should be encouraged, the university is not the place where these values should be learned except when morality includes issues related to plagiarism and cheating, according to Fish. He notes that civic engagement is a political rather than an academic goal.

Some of what Fish (2008: 68) proposes goes against what we work to accomplish in developing a critical heritage curriculum. Fish states that, "as long as respect for the culture, religion, and ideology of the other is a contested ethic rather than a universal one, a university that requires it or attempts to inculcate it is engaged not in educational but partisan behavior."

He explains that while respecting those of other cultures and their values is a particular model of ethical behavior, it may not be the preferred model of some groups, like members of the Aryan nation, who are American citizens. Therefore, these values should not be part of the curriculum.

Yannis Hamilakis (2005: 289) skillfully counters these views. Referring to other social scientists, he explains, "It is a view of education as training in utilitarian technical competences, a view that ruptures the link between knowledge and the self, denigrating the ability to make ethical judgments and develop a wider vision about the world. It is a definition of knowledge as a commodity to be sold and exchanged, rather than as a life-transforming, experiential process; it is the final product now, rather than the process itself that is being valorized. To put it in another way using terms of political economy, knowledge has lost its 'use value' and is seen as having primarily 'exchange value'" (Hamilakis 2005: 289).

In a similar vein, and in a much broader educational context, Harvard University president Drew Gilpin Faust states that the American university is undergoing a crisis of purpose. While many Americans believe that university education should serve the market, this market model conflicts with the idea that "universities are meant to be producers not just of knowledge but also (often inconvenient) doubt" (Faust 2009: 19). Faust recognizes that people need jobs; however, they also seek meaning, understanding, and perspective. She writes that "the question should not be whether we can afford to believe in such purpose in these times, but whether we can afford not to" (Faust 2009: 19). Clearly there is a tension in higher education, which is increasingly being driven by the free market system, and proponents of higher education that believe that education should be more than skill-based needs for the market. While Hamilakis and Faust recognize the free market system and the necessity to train people for jobs, the development of critical thought is important for understanding meaning and the world in which we live.

Although free market capitalist perspectives pervade the discipline of CRM archaeology, there has been a movement in the larger discipline of archaeology to develop such critical thinking skills, which is also an important foundational component for critical heritage programs. Since the 1980s, there has been momentum to reflect critically on how the past has been created. As a result, an objectively neutral past has become more difficult to justify. Therefore, while various strands of heritage studies exist, those scholars who choose to work with communities, rather than on communities, can help to promote a critical heritage perspective (see also both Chilton and Zimmerman, this volume; Kryder-Reid 2019). Those heritage projects that go beyond CRM compliance and promote multivocality have become increasingly visible in the discipline and have shown the benefits of archaeology to the larger public.

## Reinforcing Critical Thinking in Heritage Projects

By engaging communities, we have considerable capability to empower communities whose voices have been traditionally muted. The volumes by Nina Swidler et al. (1997), Joe Watkins (2001), and Kurt Dongoske et al. (2000) are all timely and groundbreaking approaches that show how archaeologists can work with American Indian communities and increase their representation in the national public memory (see also Sievert et al. and Watkins, this volume). Archaeologists also have had to develop a working relationship with non-Indian groups through some trial and error, as illustrated in the case of the African Burial Ground project in New York City (LaRoche and Blakey 1997).

It is imperative to think about the development of engaged programs within the context of higher education in the United States. Perhaps as an outcome of the Civil Rights Movement, there is also a call in higher education to think about representation and community. Many of these heritage projects are developing at the same time that government and business leaders as well as social policy experts are asking universities to assume a greater role in addressing society's increasing problems and meet growing human needs.

New developing programs in higher education are focusing on building and sustaining relationships with neighbors and communities. The Association of American Colleges and Universities (2010) suggests that recent educational innovations to advance civic engagement, such as thematically linked learning communities, community-based research, collaborative projects, service learning, mentored internships, and reflective experiential learning and study abroad opportunities, are all helping students advance toward this essential learning goal. While there is a call for colleges and universities to be active in local and national communities, the experiences of each institution vary considerably (see also both B. Clark and King, this volume).

If heritage scholars, who include archaeologists, are to remain relevant in society, it is important that the discipline participate in heritage building programs. Therefore, engaged heritage scholarship should have a meaningful critical pedagogy (see also Zimmerman, this volume). Students should engage in debate and dialogue related to relevant social problems. These social problems can include topics like representation, race, gender, and labor. Students should not only be a part of civic life, but also make a difference in shaping it (Giroux 2007: 5). Critical reflection offers an opportunity to place the learning experience into a larger context and show the complexity and varied histories that exist. The student should be able to enter into a critical dialogue rather than accept current social and political situations unquestioningly. Students should be afforded the ability to question deep-seated assumptions and myths. Critically evaluating the received narrative about issues of power and hierarchy can lead to recognizing and promoting social justice issues. Students should see their work as part of participating in an unfinished democracy (Ehrlich 2000).

In a similar vein, Michael Nassaney (2009; see also Nassaney and Levine 2009) discusses the importance of developing academic programs that have connections to the wider community. Archaeologists are naturally concerned with developing larger contexts, because it helps us understand where our work articulates with broader historical, social, economic, and/or political issues and democratic values. Understanding the larger context also allows us to reflect on our experience in the community and deepen our understanding of the world and the root causes of social injustices. For instance, if an archaeology project is exploring issues related to race, participants should also understand the development and history of race and racism. They can explore the history of contemporary policies that reinforce these disparities today.

Paul Thacker's (2009) work in Winston-Salem, North Carolina, is an excellent example of where a heritage project is connected to larger social and political issues of the history of race and class. Community leaders invited Thacker and his undergraduate students to work with local residents during the redevelopment of a neighborhood known as Happy Hill. This collaborative work focused on an early schoolhouse that served the African American community and was guided by the following criteria: (1) using collaboration between academic researchers and community members during problem formulation; (2) democratizing knowledge by validating multiple sources of knowledge and promoting the use of multiple methods of discovery and dissemination; and (3) having a goal of social action for the purpose of achieving social change and social justice.

Happy Hill originally consisted of a set of slave cabins and a farmhouse. Because of the strong Moravian influence, the slaves were emancipated in the early nineteenth century, and the area became an enclave for African Americans. One of the important structures that the community wanted to locate was the African American schoolhouse. While the archaeology project did not locate the schoolhouse, community organizers and archaeologists view this project as an important program that helped to democratize the archaeology project. The project revealed an important history that gave the community a deeper connection to the past and the surrounding land. The project placed significant symbolic value on the resources associated with the African American community and it gave this community an important voice in subsequent development in the area. The project also allowed students to work in the diverse surrounding community of Wake Forest, an experience that allowed students to acknowledge white privilege (Thacker 2009: 161).

In another well-known case study, Paul Mullins and Lewis Jones (2011) developed a collaborative research project between Indiana University–Purdue University Indianapolis (IUPUI) and the University's neighboring African American community groups. The project focuses on the former community of Near-Westside that the university demolished in the 1960s as part of its expansion and urban renewal program. Parking lots, buildings, the Indiana University Medical Center, and the IUPUI campus now cover the neighborhood. Many African American members of neighborhood associations have been involved in the research project, and they see archaeology as a way to claim a heritage and develop a community history in an area that has no physical traces associated with the traditional African American community. An oral history project is part of this new collaboration, and the enterprise is seen in the community as something distinct from the university's urban renewal past. The archaeology project directed by Mullins is a unique effort to bring the community and the university together to acknowledge a past that was once deliberately erased from the landscape.

Case Studies of Civic Engagement: University of Maryland

At the Center for Heritage Resource Studies at the University of Maryland, we are in the process of developing several heritage projects that address social inequalities. For instance, in one project, we placed students in the communities surrounding the University of Maryland in Prince George's County. These communities developed during the post–World War II era and served as a suburb for Washington, D.C., with segregated white and black communities. Since the 1970s, white flight has led to accelerated urban decay and the ethnic composition of these communities changed from predominantly white to African American; Latinos now represent the majority population. Students examined the history of housing and reflected on how housing has changed in our lifetime. Racism, immigration, redlining, and white flight are all important issues that led to the browning and graying of American cities and older suburbs, and the increased poverty in these areas is a product of the attack on government programs that serve these populations. A program that makes these issues apparent to the larger community is both political and powerful (Little and Shackel 2014).

One of these communities, Lakeland, sits adjacent to the University of Maryland campus. The community began to develop as an African American suburb around the 1890s. By the early 1960s, the City of College Park received federal support for a flood control project and funding for redevelopment and home renovations. These projects led to the displacement of about two-thirds of the community. A portion of the community's housing was replaced by a mix of subsidized housing and high-density apartments, which are now occupied by University of Maryland students. The other portion of the community was removed and the land was mined for sand and gravel during the 1976 construction of a Washington Metro line. The federal government compensated the larger community by developing this area into a natural recreation area, which is now called Lake Artemisia (Lakeland Community Heritage Project 2016).

Members of the Lakeland Community Heritage Project came to the Center for Heritage Resource Studies and asked for assistance to help them rediscover their community's heritage. The board members from Lakeland discussed their desire for a research project to explore the history of education in the community. The resulting research program revealed that Lakeland opened its first community school in 1903, and in the late 1920s, they received funds from the Julius Rosenwald Fund to establish an elementary school and a high school. From 1928 until 1950, the Lakeland High School served as a regional educational, cultural, and social center for the African American community. Being the only African American high school in the area, it drew people from many different communities to attend school there. Residents and displaced community members recall how the school helped to create a social network, one that still exists today (Lakeland Community Heritage Project 2016).

Lakeland Heritage Days has become a yearly celebration of the community's past, and other events driven by the community members have helped to bring together many members of the Lakeland community, near and far away, to celebrate their past connections and plan for a renewed and viable community. The community heritage project now has a Web page (Lakeland Community Heritage Project 2016), and their community history is published by Arcadia Publishing (Lakeland Community Heritage Project 2009). University of Maryland classes in historic preservation have been held in Lakeland, uncovering more information about the community's history. Additionally, former graduate students have served as board members for the Lakeland Community Heritage Project.

In another example, the Center for Heritage Studies supported a program in Hampden, a working-class neighborhood in Baltimore. The community's history is not part of the dominant narrative of the community. Business interests and developers control the public discourse, which privileges the powerful capitalists, and they often make decisions about interpreting the past without considering the interests of the traditional working-class community. In their heritage project, David Gadsby and Robert Chidister (2011) engaged the local, mainly working-class community with the goal of making working-class history part of the public memory. They held open forums to discuss the needs of the community prior to their research. Bringing the community together and supporting a public dialogue is a way to formulate and promote a more inclusive perspective of the place. The citizens were interested in issues related to women and labor, gentrification, and the history of African Americans in this almost all-white community in a majority black city. As a result of these discussions, the researchers made these issues central to their research design. The goal of their work in labor archaeology has been to make the working-class history part of the public memory of this postindustrial community in Baltimore.

Currently, the Department of Anthropology is working in the anthracite region of northeastern Pennsylvania. The area developed starting in the mid-nineteenth century with coal barons and railroad tycoons dominating the economy and exploiting a mostly foreign-born workforce for the extraction of coal. The coal industry had one of the highest mortality rates of any profession in the United States. Working and living conditions were substandard, and Progressive Era reformers visited the area in 1898 to document the existing work and living conditions. In an 1898 *Century Magazine* article (Rood 1898), they referred to the shantytowns as being a reminder of western life that was common a few centuries earlier, documenting the substandard housing and the lack of sanitation, as well as the malnourished families (Shackel et al. 2011).

The dominant narrative of the region tends to prop up the memory of the coal operators, often at the expense of the workers. One of our first projects was to perform an archaeological survey of a little-known labor massacre in Lattimer, Pennsylvania. The massacre was the culmination of a month-long strike by immigrant coal miners who sought better wages and safer working conditions. They came to the anthracite region of Pennsylvania in order to escape poverty and oppression in their home country; however, they found themselves in the same or worse living conditions than what they had left in eastern and southern Europe. The massacre left twenty-five miners dead, and the incident has nearly been forgotten. Not surprisingly, the event is missing from the official memory of our country, and it reflects the control capital has over the memory of the industrialization of America (Shackel and Roller 2012, 2013).

In 2009, we became committed to help raise the profile of the event with the goal of making it part of the national public memory. We began an investigation of the Lattimer massacre with a survey of the massacre site. The survey results, including bullets related to the battle, stirred many conversations in the community. First, our results and the resulting discussion began to raise the awareness of the importance of working-class heritage and the contributions made by the immigrant laborers.

Figure 1.1. Descendant of a coal miner from northeastern Pennsylvania provides stories about life in a coal patch town as students and faculty listen. Photograph courtesy of Paul Shackel.

Second, our work showed how interested the community is in claiming the history of Lattimer for different political purposes. Hazleton, the city near Lattimer, recently has had an influx of immigrant and first-generation Latinos, and the story of immigrant laborers has been used to justify the way different people view and treat the new immigrants today. Connecting the community's heritage to pro-immigration and anti-immigration sentiment and policies has led to tough discussions in the community. By carrying out oral histories and archaeology in Lattimer, we believe we are awakening the working-class history of the community. Our goal is eventually to place the massacre site and the town on the National Register of Historic Places in order to achieve nationally recognized status by the federal government. We also hope that Hazelton can be a touchstone for a dialogue related to issues about immigration and social justice (Shackel 2013).

The above examples demonstrate critical thinking about a place's heritage, as well as helping a community to expand representation in both the past and the present. As William Logan (2012) explains, heritage professionals need to think about the broader social, economic, and political context of their work. Professionals working at significant places need to understand how their work can potentially have an impact on local communities, Indigenous peoples, and ethnic communities. To follow his lead, I believe that heritage studies can be a way toward developing an inclusive and just past.

## Civic Engagement, Education, and Heritage Studies

While the free market system is calling for more skill-based training, I also believe that an educator's responsibility is about critical education, engaged citizenship, and social responsibility. Our work at the University of Maryland is to deconstruct the knowledge and power of the privileged and rebuild a new paradigm about the past, responding to the needs of the local community. Changing the traditional paradigm creates space for new voices and for new knowledge to be created. It is also important to recognize that, as engaged researchers, we are disrupting the traditional power dynamics in the community. Borrowing from Miguel Guajardo et al. (2008: 8), "We see research as one of the historical hegemonic structures utilized to reproduce the societal inequality, but we understand that we can turn that power around, particularly because of the relationships we have developed through the past generation of work as educators and researchers in this one community."

While the university is being called upon to address the free market needs of industry, which includes CRM, it is also being called upon to address the many needs of communities. Therefore, we cannot ignore the importance of developing a significant critical heritage program, the result of creating a more complex representation of the past in the context of the present. We need to recognize race, class, sex, and other social relationships and aim to historicize them when telling the story of any community. We also need to explore diversity in the past and promote it in the present. The story of a community's heritage is not complete without a representation of a variety of perspectives.

# References Cited

Association of American Colleges and Universities
2010    Civic Engagement. Electronic document, http://www.aacu.org/resources/civi-cengagement/index.cfm. Accessed July 1, 2010.

Bender, Susan J., and George S. Smith (editors)
2000    *Teaching Archaeology in the Twenty-First Century.* Society for American Archaeology, Washington, D.C.

Dongoske, Kurt E., Mark Aldenderfer, and Karen Doehner (editors)
2000    *Working Together: Native Americans and Archaeologists.* Society for American Archaeology, Washington, D.C.

Ehrlich, Thomas (editor)
2000    *Civic Responsibility and Higher Education.* Oryx Press, Phoenix, Arizona.

Faust, Drew Gilpin
2009    The University's Crisis of Purpose. Crossroads essay series. *New York Times,* September 1. Electronic document, http://www.nytimes.com/2009/09/06/books/review/Faust-t.html?pagewanted=all&_r=0. Accessed July 7, 2010.

Fish, Stanley
2008    *Save the World on Your Own Time.* Oxford University Press, New York.

Fowler, Donald D.
1984    Ethics in Contract Archaeology. In *Ethics and Values in Archaeology,* edited by E. L. Green, pp. 108–116. Free Press, New York.

Gadsby, David, and Robert Chidester
2011    Heritage and "Those People": Representing Working-Class Interests through Hampden's Archaeology. *Historical Archaeology* 45(1): 101–113.

Giroux, Henry A.
2007    *The University in Chains: Confronting the Military-Industrial-Academic Complex.* Paradigm, Boulder, Colorado.

Guajardo, Miguel, Francisco Guajardo, and Edyael Del Carmen Casaperalta
2008    Transformative Education: Chronicling a Pedagogy for Social Change. *Anthropology & Education Quarterly* 39(1): 3–22.

Hamilakis, Yannis
2005    Archaeology and the Politics of Pedagogy. *World Archaeology* 36(2): 287–309.

King, Thomas F.
1972    Archaeological Law and the American Indian. *Indian Historian* 5(3): 31–35.

Kryder-Reid, Elizabeth
2019    Do the Homeless Have Heritage? Archaeology and the Pedagogy of Discomfort. In *Pedagogy and Practice in Heritage Studies,* edited by Susan J. Bender and Phyllis Mauch Messenger, pp. 129–147. University Press of Florida, Gainesville.

Lakeland Community Heritage Project
2009    *Lakeland: African Americans in College Park.* Arcadia, Charleston, South Carolina.
2016    Lakeland History. Electronic document, http://lakelandchp.com/history. Accessed September 20, 2016.

LaRoche, Cheryl J., and Michael L. Blakey

1997    Seizing Intellectual Power: The Dialogue at the New York African Burial Ground. *Historical Archaeology* 31(3): 84–106.

Little, Barbara J., and Paul A. Shackel

2014    *Archaeology, Heritage and Civic Engagement: Working toward the Public Good.* Left Coast Press, Walnut Creek, California.

Logan, William

2012    Cultural Diversity, Cultural Heritage and Human Rights: Towards Heritage Management as Human Rights-based Cultural Practice. *International Journal of Heritage Studies* 18(3):231–244.

McManamon, Francis P.

1992    Managing Repatriation: Implementing the Native American Graves Protection and Repatriation Act. *CRM* 15(5): 9–12.

Mullins, Paul R., and Lewis C. Jones

2011    Archaeologies of Race and Urban Poverty: The Politics of Slumming, Engagement, and the Color Line. *Historical Archaeology* 45(1): 33–50.

Nassaney, Michael S.

2009    The Reform of Archaeological Pedagogy and Practice through Community Service Learning. In *Archaeology and Community Service Learning,* edited by Michael Nassaney and Mary Ann Levine, pp. 3–35. University Press of Florida, Gainesville.

Nassaney, Michael S., and Mary Ann Levine (editors)

2009    *Archaeology and Community Service Learning.* University Press of Florida, Gainesville.

Praetzellis, Mary, and Adrian Praetzellis

2011    Cultural Resource Management Archeology and Heritage Values. *Historical Archaeology* 45(1): 86–100.

Praetzellis, Mary, Adrian Praetzellis, and Thad van Buren

2007    Remaking Connections: Archaeology and Community after the Loma Prieta Earthquake. In *Archaeology as a Tool of Civic Engagement,* edited by Barbara J. Little and Paul A. Shackel, pp. 109–130. AltaMira Press, Lanham, Maryland.

Rood, Henry Edward

1898    A Pennsylvania Colliery Village: A Polyglot Community. *Century Magazine* 45(6): 809–821.

Savage, Kirk

1997    *Standing Soldier, Kneeling Slaves: Race, War, and Monument in Nineteenth-Century America.* Princeton University Press, Princeton, New Jersey.

Shackel, Paul A.

2003a    Heyward Shepherd: The Faithful Slave Memorial. *Historical Archaeology* 37(3): 138–148.

2003b    *Memory in Black and White: Race, Commemoration, and the Post–Bellum Landscape.* AltaMira Press, Walnut Creek, California; Roman and Littlefield, Lanham, Maryland.

2005    Memory, Civic Engagement and the Public Meaning of Archaeological Heritage. *SAA Archaeological Record* 5(2): 24–27.

2013 An Historical Archaeology of Labor and Social Justice. *American Anthropologist* 115(2): 212–215.

Shackel, Paul A., and Michael Roller

2012 The Gilded Age Wasn't So Gilded in the Anthracite Region of Pennsylvania. *International Journal of Historical Archaeology* 16(4): 761–775.

2013 Archaeology of Anthracite Coal Patch Towns in Northeastern, Pennsylvania. *International Committee for the Conservation of Industrial History Bulletin* 62(4): 2–4.

Shackel, Paul A., Michael Roller, and Kristin Sullivan

2011 Historical Amnesia and the Lattimer Massacre. *SfAA Newsletter.* May 1. Electronic document, http://sfaanews.sfaa.net/2011/05/. Accessed May 10, 2014.

Swidler, Nina, Kurt Dongoske, Roger Anyon, and Alan Downer (editors)

1997 *Native Americans and Archaeologists: Stepping Stones to Common Ground.* AltaMira Press, Walnut Creek, California.

Thacker, Paul T.

2009 Archaeological Research within Community Service Learning Projects: Engagement, Social Action, and Learning from Happy Hill. In *Archaeology and Community Service Learning,* edited by Michael Nassaney and Mary Ann Levine, pp. 153–167. University Press of Florida, Gainesville.

Watkins, Joe

2001 *Indigenous Archaeology: American Indian Values and Scientific Practice.* AltaMira Press, Walnut Creek, California.

Winter, Joseph C.

1980 Indian Heritage Preservation and Archaeologists. *American Antiquity* 45(1): 121–131.

Zimmerman, Larry J.

1996 Epilogue: A New and Different Archaeology? *American Indian Quarterly* 20(2): 297–307.

# 2

## The Heritage of Heritage

### Defining the Role of the Past in Contemporary Societies

ELIZABETH S. CHILTON

The word "heritage" in current English-language usage means different things depending on the contexts. In the United States, in casual conversation it is most likely to mean one's personal genealogy or ethnicity, but it can also refer to history itself or at least the historical record. One's heritage is something quite personal, even though you may share it with others. Only recently have "heritage studies" and "heritage management" become common parlance in the United States, and even then, these terms are used primarily in academic and professional settings. In contrast, in Europe and Australia, there is a long history of reference to "cultural heritage management," which means roughly the same thing as "cultural resource management" (CRM) in the United States. In this context, the term "heritage" is tied to the inherited identity of a state or nation and controlled by legislation, similar to historic preservation in the United States. In France, French-speaking nations, and some other European contexts, the more common term is "*patrimoine*" or patrimony: "that which is inherited." This too, however, is tied to nationalism and shared cultural identity more than to individual genealogy.

In this chapter, I outline the various ways that heritage has been defined and the implications for how one might approach its management, conservation, interpretation, and/or study. Understanding the evolution of the term and concept of heritage as something distinct from culture allows us to more fully understand the wide range of stakeholders in cultural heritage today and the implications for applying issues of cultural heritage to address broader global challenges, such as social justice and sustainability. Further, being explicit about the self-interests of heritage professionals allows us to understand the power relationships that underlie all evaluations of cultural heritage.

## Defining Heritage

First, it will be useful for the reader if I begin by defining what I mean when I use the term "heritage." I define heritage as "the full range of inherited traditions, monuments, objects, and living environments, and, most importantly, the range of contemporary activities, meanings, and behaviors that are drawn from them" (Chilton and Mason 2010). Thus, it includes both tangible and intangible remains of the past and contemporary activities associated with these remains, including preservation, purposeful destruction, commodification, commemoration, interpretation, repatriation, education, public policy, and tourism (Chilton and Mason 2010). Similarly, the American Anthropological Association defines cultural heritage as "the relevance of the past to contemporary communities and future generations."[1] Heritage can be seen as a set of relationships and references to the past (Harrison 2013: 14), or as Smith put it, "the act of making meaning in and for the present . . . a cultural and social process, which engages with acts of remembering that work to create ways to understand and engage with the present" (2006: 1–2). As such, heritage affects identities and access to power in the present and, thereby, has tremendous implications for the future. Clearly, things like commemoration, destruction, education, and policy have huge impacts on possible future states of individuals and societies (see Harrison 2015).

In the United States, expertise regarding "the past" has traditionally been relegated to the historiographical fields of archaeology and history, and therefore the focus has been on tangible resources—historical archives, buildings, archaeological sites, and artifacts. Each of these types of tangible cultural heritage has its associated heritage experts (archaeologists, archivists, architectural historians, museum professionals, and so on). The growth of the heritage profession in the second half of the twentieth century led to an increasing alienation of nonprofessionals from access to either the objects or the production of narratives about the past (Pannekeok 1998). This represents the birth of "official heritage," by which tangible heritage objects and landscapes were set apart from everyday life (Harrison 2013: 14). The cultural resource management legislation in the United States, for example, while requiring engagement with communities, put the assignation of "significance" squarely in the hands of heritage professionals. Having the expertise with which to argue for this "significance" requires a certain amount of education and technical training. The growth of the profession depended on maintaining full access to such expertise and power, to the point that "saving the past for the future" became more about "saving the past for ourselves" (Spenneman 2011). This self-interest in historical preservation for the sake of heritage professionals has not been widely acknowledged in the United States. In general, the mantra of "saving the past for the future" has been taken as a given, as obvious, and as a value that we need to teach various "publics." The result has been that millions of objects and cultural resource management reports are stored in facilities that are not known or accessible to most people, begging the question as to the public benefits of all of that work.

However, a number of societal changes in the late twentieth and early twenty-first centuries have led to the growth of critical heritage studies as an academic subject and of heritage as a more widely understood concept. These include: (1) adoption of the World Heritage Convention and its focus on "global heritage"; (2) the rise of the concept of "intangible heritage" and recognition for it; (3) postmodern influences on the humanities and social sciences; and (4) community engagement and the democratization of heritage.

## The World Heritage Convention and Universal Value

The World Heritage Convention was adopted in 1972 and its conceptualization reflected "more than a century of monumental conservation in Europe" (Araoz 2013: 146). As Araoz points out, "the philosophical and cultural origins of both the Convention and the modern heritage movement were rooted in the Western conviction that the material existence of certain places is important for having cosmic power or as permanent memory markers of important human events, beliefs, and accomplishments" (2013: 146). The definition of cultural heritage in the Operational Guidelines for the Implementation of the World Heritage Convention includes monuments, groups of buildings, and sites—the so-called tangible culture heritage (UNESCO 2015). The operational guidelines require a demonstration of "Outstanding Universal Value" (OUV) as criteria for World Heritage listing. OUV is defined as "cultural and/or natural significance which is so exceptional as to transcend national boundaries and to be of common importance for present and future generations of all humanity" (UNESCO 2015: 11). Thus, OUV has—by definition—a universalizing goal, which is understandable in light of its historical origins. However, over time there have been increasing critiques of the World Heritage Convention, particularly its tendency to reinforce the voices of the heritage experts over local and descendant communities and to largely ignore cultural heritage beyond the tangible. Also, the universalizing and nationalist outcomes of the World Heritage process have had negative outcomes in terms of social justice. As Ekern et al. discuss, while "cultural heritage can be a unifying force, emphasizing a nation's shared identity, often non-democratic governments . . . force groups to adopt the dominant culture, leading to the destruction of minority cultural identity" (2015: 25). I would argue that, in even more subtle and insidious ways, the nation-state–driven process of nomination to the World Heritage List and the essentializing tendencies of "universal value" have left little room for minority, diasporic, or (in some cases) Indigenous heritage to be celebrated and promoted in any official capacity. In other words, turning World Heritage inscription into a kind of competitive beauty contest (see Cleere 2011; Pyburn 2011) has left little room for the celebration of the diversity of global heritage values and resources.

## Intangible Heritage

Ironically, it was the World Heritage process itself that sparked a global conversation about "intangible heritage." The World Heritage Committee's Nara Document on Authenticity (1994) opened the door for broad discussions of both cultural diversity and the cultural context of heritage values. Gustavo Araoz argues that the Nara Document "challenged long-held Eurocentric criteria for the evaluation of heritage authenticity, asserting that this quality is, instead, dependent on cultural context and expressed in diverse forms throughout the world" (2013: 144). The UNESCO Convention for the Safeguarding of the Intangible Cultural Heritage (UNESCO 2003) called for an acknowledgement of the inextricability of tangible and intangible heritage resources and values, and it called out heritage as the "mainspring of cultural diversity." This was followed by the UNESCO Convention on the Protection and Promotion of the Diversity of Cultural Expressions (UNESCO

2005), which also acknowledged that diversity itself formed the "common heritage of humanity." All of these international documents emphasized the role of diversity in cultural sustainability, shifting the focus away from sites and buildings squarely onto cultural practices and cultural expressions—in short, from the tangible resources to the intangible practices and values.

Even though the UNESCO charters cited above very much represent top-down, "official heritage," they fed into a global conversation about community involvement in both defining heritage values and safeguarding heritage for future generations. This dovetailed with the larger critical heritage studies movement, which called for heritage professionals to move beyond maintaining their expert status as part of the "authorized heritage discourse," a discourse that "privileges expert values and knowledge about the past and its material manifestation, and dominates and regulates professional heritage practices" (Smith 2006: 4). This shift toward greater self-reflexivity and the acknowledgement of power relationships in the creation of knowledge is part of the larger contribution of postmodernism to academia. In archaeology the post-processual critique paved the way for archaeologists to "consider the wider publics and stakeholders" of the past (Chilton 2009: 147). But to what degree has community engagement changed the power dynamics or outcomes of heritage sustainability?

Community Participation—the Democratization of Heritage?

As Araoz points out, the surge in community participation and empowerment came with the 1988 and 1999 revisions to the Australia ICOMOS Burra Charter of 1979,[2] "which established a process that calls for community consultation and input in determining the significance of the place" (2013: 149). The principle of community empowerment has been articulated in several ICOMOS charters since then (Araoz 2013: 149).

More broadly, "community engagement" and "collaboration" have become increasingly popular in archaeology and heritage management. But there is a great deal of variation in the extent to which the community is able to fully effect priority setting (Pannekoek 1998: 8). "Collaboration" runs the gamut from keeping the community informed, to consulting with them, to co-designing projects (see Cowell-Chanthaphonh and Ferguson 2007, and Mullins 2011). The key question is whether the nature of the collaboration has the potential to change the power relationships between the historiographical experts and the heritage communities. Sonya Atalay points out that archaeology relies on Western knowledge systems and, thus, privileges "the material, scientific, observable world over the spiritual, experiential, and unquantifiable aspects of archaeological sites, ancient peoples, and artifacts" (Atalay 2007). Thus, if we start from the sites, the artifacts, the purely tangible forms of heritage, then no matter how much collaboration or consultation there is, we are not going to be able to change the nature of the colonial power relationships (Chilton 2012: 231). This is not to deny the very real expertise that heritage professionals bring to bear in these relationships, but truly sustainable heritage requires deep participation and collaboration by the stakeholder communities themselves.

While I have been, thus far, discussing official heritage, Rodney Harrison (2013: 15) calls our attention to the importance of "unofficial heritage," which includes the values that may surround objects or places but that are not officially recognized by the state. Sometimes the heritage values of the state come into conflict with the unofficial heritage values of communities. This is perhaps inevitable, since heritage values are always assigned by people in the present—they are neither innate nor immutable. As Araoz points out, "This gives rise to the paradox—or perhaps the oxymoron—of the concept of preserving the ability to change" (2011: 58).

## Heritage and the Future

To return to the beginning of this chapter, if one accepts my working definition of heritage as "contemporary activities, meanings, and behaviors" associated with objects, places, and traditions, then heritage is not so much a "thing" to be defined or preserved per se, as much as it is a process. It is a cultural process of "meaning making," the creation of a future through a connection to the past, a means of cultural sustainability and wellness. I have argued elsewhere that "cultural heritage affects all aspects of society and how individuals define themselves in the world" (Brabec and Chilton 2015: 267). Therefore, it is the key to understanding sustainability, adaptation, and resilience to change (Auclair and Fairclough 2015: 3). Auclair and Fairclough note that heritage and sustainability share the most common ground "when both are perceived as being ongoing processes rather than . . . end products . . . and as being people-centred . . . rather than object-oriented" (2015: 9). Culture heritage is the key to the sustainability and resiliency of human societies in the face of environmental change, migration, displacement, and violent conflict. Thus, developing new approaches to the full spectrum of tangible and intangible heritage resources, and engaging stakeholders in ways that allow us to change the nature of power relationships in the present, are critical to the sustainability of human cultures in the face of significant historical and imminent social upheaval and change.

## Notes

1. http://www.americananthro.org/ParticipateAndAdvocate/AdvocacyDetail.aspx?ItemNumber=20528&navItemNumber=592. Accessed March 2, 2018.
2. http://australia.icomos.org/publications/charters/. Accessed March 2, 2018.

## References Cited

Araoz, Gustavo

2011    Preserving Heritage Places under a New Paradigm. *Journal of Cultural Heritage Management and Sustainable Development* 1(1): 55–60.

2013    Conservation Philosophy and Its Development: Changing Understandings of Authenticity and Significance. *Heritage & Society* 6(2): 144–154.

Atalay, Sonya

2007    Multivocal and Indigenous Archaeologies. In *Evaluating Multiple Narratives: Beyond Nationalist, Colonialist, and Imperialist Archaeologies*, edited by Junko Habu, Clare Fawcett, and John M. Matsunaga, pp. 29–44. Springer Press, New York.

Auclair, Elizabeth, and Graham Fairclough (editors)

2015    *Theory and Practice in Heritage and Sustainability: Between Past and Future.* Routledge, New York.

Brabec, Elizabeth, and Elizabeth S. Chilton

2015    Towards an Ecology of Cultural Heritage. *Change Over Time* 5(2): 266–285.

Chilton, Elizabeth S.

2009    Teaching Heritage Values through Field Schools: Case Studies from New England. In *Heritage Values in Contemporary Society*, edited by George S. Smith, Phyllis Mauch Messenger, and Hilary A. Soderland, pp. 147–158. Left Coast Press, Walnut Creek, California.

2012    The Archaeology of Immateriality. *Archaeologies* (Journal of the World Archaeological Congress) 8(3): 225–235.

Chilton, Elizabeth S., and Randall Mason

2010    NSF White Paper: A Call for a Social Science of the Past. *SBE 2020: Future Research in the Social, Behavioral & Economic Sciences.* Electronic document, http://www.nsf.gov/sbe/sbe_2020/submission_detail.cfm?upld_id=297. Accessed January 10, 2017.

Cleere, Henry

2011    The 1972 UNESCO World Heritage Convention. A Success or a Failure? *Heritage & Society* 4(2): 173–186.

Cowell-Chanthaphonh, Chip, and T. J. Ferguson

2007    *Collaboration in Archaeological Practice: Engaging Descendant Communities.* Rowman & Littlefield, New York.

Ekern, Stener, William Logan, Birgitte Sauge, and Amund Sinding-Larsen

2015    *World Heritage Management and Human Rights.* Routledge, New York.

Harrison, Rodney

2013    Heritage: Critical Approaches. Routledge, New York.

2015    Beyond "Natural" and "Cultural" Heritage: Toward an Ontological Politics of Heritage in the Age of Anthropocene. *Heritage & Society* 8(1): 24–42.

Mullins, Paul R.

2011    Practicing Anthropology and the Politics of Engagement: 2010 Year in Review. *American Anthropologist* 113(2): 235–245.

Pannekoek, Frits

1998    The Rise of the Heritage Priesthood or the Decline of Community Based Heritage. *Historic Preservation Forum*, Spring 1998: 4–10.

Pyburn, K. Anne

2011    World Heritage: Universality or Just Globalization? Paper presented at the 76th Annual Meeting of the Society for American Archaeology, Sacramento, California.

Smith, Laurajane

2006    *Uses of Heritage.* Routledge, New York.

Spenneman, Dirk H. R.

2011    Beyond "Preserving the Past for the Future": Contemporary Relevance and Historic Preservation. *CRM: Journal of Heritage Stewardship.* Electronic document, https://www.nps.gov/CRMjournal/Winter2011/view1.html. Accessed January 13, 2017.

UNESCO

2003    Convention for the Safeguarding of the Intangible Cultural Heritage, http://www.unesco.org/culture/ich/en/convention. Accessed March 2, 2018.

2005    Convention on the Protection and Promotion of the Diversity of Cultural Expression, http://portal.unesco.org/en/ev.php-URL_ID=31038&URL_DO=DO_TOPIC&URL_SECTION=201.html. Accessed March 2, 2018.

2015    Operational Guidelines for the Implementation of the World Heritage Convention, http://whc.unesco.org/en/guidelines/. Accessed March 2, 2018.

# 3

## Disruptive Innovations and New Pedagogies in Archaeology and Heritage Education

### A View from 35,000 Feet

M. ELAINE FRANKLIN

> True stability results when presumed order and presumed disorder are balanced. A truly stable system expects the unexpected, is prepared to be disrupted, waits to be transformed.
>
> Tom Robbins 1976: 208

When I first became interested in archaeology, I was a public school teacher living in the Southeast, but my fascination with the human past was located in the American Southwest, specifically in the homeland of the ancestral Pueblo, then known as Anasazi. At that time I wasn't making connections between the archaeological record, the unwritten past, and issues of social justice. That came later. I was simply drawn to the narratives of a people for whom so much was known, yet, at the same time, so little. Archaeologists, some historians, and members of descendant communities possessed a deeper understanding, but I suspected that most Americans knew little more than could be deduced from an image of Cliff Palace in some long forgotten social studies textbook. In time, it became clearer to me that my interest was as much about the making of history as it was about the people and events of the past. It was not so much the "lies my teacher told me" that I found troubling, as it was the truths that were left out.

"Ah ha!" moments like this might be considered the sweet spot in an educator's world because conceptual change requires the introduction of new information that is powerful enough to render the prior understanding unacceptable. French psychologist and philosopher Jean Piaget saw such disruptions, or perturbations, as a means to facilitate the processes of accommodation and assimilation, which he said are central to learning. According to Piaget, new information is assimilated within a paradigm of what we already know and understand about the world. However, when we confront new information that is incompatible with our prior understanding, it leaves us in a state of disequilibrium. In order to restore equilibrium, we are forced to recast our mental models. The more I learned about how history is constructed and appropriated in the present, the less I was able to view it as the objective, often boring, but seemingly benign journey through time that I experienced in high school. I had to recast my mental model.

I begin with this personal narrative in part to introduce myself and contextualize my perspective, but I also use it to introduce the concept of disruption in a way that expands the meaning beyond its very specific usage in the world of business and economics. As used here, and as implied by Tom Robbins in the quote at the beginning of this chapter, disruption is a transformative experience. I have chosen it as the frame for discussing new pedagogies in public archaeology and heritage education because of the pervasive impact that disruptive innovations are having on virtually every aspect of teaching and learning, on every discipline, and on all types of educational institutions, both formal and informal.

Heritage education has been variously defined; some say it refers to both discipline-based content and pedagogical methods, others see it strictly as an approach to teaching about the human past. There are other challenges related to the term beyond the somewhat ambiguous nature of its definition. *Heritage* has been used to identify, or brand, everything from special interest groups (from both the left and the right), to real estate agencies, banks, and subdivisions. In the process, it has been both politicized and trivialized, which might lead to an array of misconceptions for those who are not familiar with heritage education. For the discussion in this chapter, I broadly define it as an inquiry-based approach to learning about the human past that employs multiple sources of information including documents, material culture, oral accounts, and the human and built environment as primary resources. Although I speak of it as an approach, I do not see it as void of content but, rather, rich with content. It is an inclusive human history that is unbounded by geography or the written record (see also Chilton, this volume).

In this chapter, I first provide some clarifying information about the concept of disruption in order to better explain how education in general is being disrupted, and then I look more specifically at the disruptive influences on heritage education.

## Understanding Disruption

The cognitive disruption of an individual is not so profoundly different from the disruptions seen in complex systems. Disruptive innovation models are, to a certain extent, the applying of Piagetian thinking to larger social and economic systems. Educational systems around the globe are currently engulfed in a quagmire of disequilibrium driven by the technological innovations that have, over the last thirty years, put the world at our fingertips. In the United States, there is a deep recognition that this revolution in technology is challenging the ability of traditional models of education to meet the needs of twenty-first-century students and the future they will inherit.

Attempts to modify the traditional models may be inadequate, as the late author and educator Neil Postman pointed out: "Technological change is not additive; it is ecological, which means, it changes everything" (Richardson 2013: 10). In other words, it isn't as simple as replacing older technologies with newer high-tech tools to perform the same tasks. The technological innovations of the last three decades do far more than just help us work faster and more cheaply. They present us with dramatically different options for accessing and processing information, and some would say they are even having an impact on the way the brain is "wired" for learning (Anderson and Rainie 2012).

The term *disruptive innovation* was coined in the late 1990s by Harvard business professor Clayton Christensen. According to Christensen,

> Disruptive innovation is the process by which a sector that has previously served only a limited few because its products and services were complicated, expensive, and inaccessible, is transformed into one whose products and services are simple, affordable, and convenient and serves many no matter their wealth or expertise. The new innovation does so by redefining quality in a simple and often disparaged application at first and then gradually improves such that it takes more and

more market share over time as it becomes able to tackle more complicated problems. (Christensen et al. 2011a: 2)

Numerous examples exist to illustrate how this principle works. When transistor radios were first being produced, they did not seem to pose a threat to the traditional analogue radios because the transistor's sound quality was poor. However, they were portable, presenting the possibility of listening to the radio in a wide variety of places. Portability outweighed the loss of sound quality, and new groups of consumers emerged. Over time, the sound quality improved, prices came down, and the new technology completely displaced the old. Many other examples of technologies that have followed a similar path easily come to mind, from personal computers replacing mainframes, to cell phones outpacing the sales and use of traditional landlines. In every case, the original versions of these technologies were generally of poorer quality than the existing versions; however, they introduced greater accessibility and generated new markets. They did not expand or elaborate on earlier models; they disrupted the earlier models (Christensen et al. 2011b).

## Disruptions in Education

It is not difficult to apply Christensen's definition of disruption to the effect that digital technologies and the Internet are having on education in the early twenty-first century. Distance or virtual learning is not a new concept, televised courses for college credit were available as early as the 1950s; computer-assisted instruction came into use in the 1970s and by the mid- to late 1980s, pioneering work with online learning was being conducted. However, there was little that could be considered transformative in these earlier versions of distance learning. Then, in the mid-1990s, the widespread availability of the Internet had a revolutionary impact on everything from culture, to commerce, to education. As access increased, so did innovations for online instruction. At the K-12 level, this has taken such forms as virtual schools and an abundance of online courses targeted toward homeschoolers or schools that haven't the capacity to offer similar courses on-site. In the 2015–16 school year, the North Carolina Virtual Public School, which is the second largest in the country, reported an enrollment of 36,454 secondary students taking 58,003 courses (North Carolina Virtual Public School 2016). Florida is the leading virtual school provider, with over 200,000 part-time or full-time K-12 students (Florida Virtual Schools 2014).

Virtual and digital options are providing instructional alternatives at the K-12 level but, thus far, would not be considered disruptive because they are typically implemented within existing structures. The situation in post-secondary education is somewhat different. As technological advancements have an impact on the way that work is carried out around the globe, the need for a workforce possessing more sophisticated knowledge and skills has also increased, thus amplifying the need for young people to seek education beyond high school. Complicating this issue is the fact that, as the number of students seeking a postsecondary education is increasing, so is the cost of obtaining a degree. One might argue that this constitutes the perfect storm for disruption. These changing circumstances require a strategic shift away from seeking solutions that enable more students to afford a higher education; the challenge instead is how to make a postsecondary education more affordable (Christensen et al. 2011a; Weise and Christiansen 2014). Students are increasingly concerned with the financial return on their investment in higher education. "Seven in 10 college seniors who graduated from public and nonprofit colleges in 2014 had student loan debt, with an average of $28,950 per borrower" (Institute for College Access and Success 2016). Students are weighing the increasing costs of attending traditional brick-and-mortar institutions against the wages they will be able to earn when they enter the workforce and are justifiably seeking other options. This essentially opens the door to competitors who can provide the goods and services at a more reasonable cost to the consumer. "A disruptive innovation has a couple of key elements or enablers that are particularly salient to the future of higher education. The first is a technology enabler. . . . Online learning appears to be this technology enabler for higher education" (Christensen et al. 2011a: 2–3).

Ten percent of postsecondary students took at least one online course in 2002; in 2008, it was 25 percent. Christensen predicted that this number would grow to 50 percent in 2014 (Christensen et al. 2011a: 31). The reality has varied considerably from the prediction; while the number of postsecondary students taking at least one online course continued to increase, the rate of increase declined. In 2013, a little over 27 percent of students who were enrolled in postsecondary degree-granting institutions took at least one online course (U.S. Department of Education, National Center for Education Statistics 2016).

The second enabler for disruption is a business model innovation (Christensen et al. 2011b). The new business model allows an organization to accomplish the job at a lower price point, or in a more convenient or accessible fashion without an increased cost. Plugging a disruptive innovation into an existing business model never leads to transformation because the existing model uses the innovation in a way that will sustain how it currently operates.

Some of the private for-profit universities were among the first providers of online degree programs; the University of Phoenix began offering online degrees in 1989. The growing need for postsecondary education to become more affordable, coupled with the competition from private online colleges and universities, have increasingly drawn many public institutions into the online arena, and Arizona State University (ASU) is one of the leaders. In 2016, ASU offered more than 100 degree programs completely online, including bachelor's degrees in anthropology, history, geography, and education, as well as numerous graduate-level degrees (Arizona State University 2016). Although ASU entered the online market earlier than other public degree-granting institutions, it is not alone in the field. Oregon State University, the University of Florida, and Colorado State University all offer online bachelor's degrees in anthropology. If ASU and others have a viable business model for their online degree programs and provide a high-quality product, it seems that disruption by private online competitors might be avoided.

Debates over the quality, efficiency, and cost-effectiveness of online learning versus traditional face-to-face instruction tend to resurrect old arguments about the purpose of education. One end of this continuum says that education's purpose is to serve the market by developing a qualified workforce; the other emphasizes education's role in the advancement of knowledge and enlightenment of the human mind (see also Shackel, this volume). Such dualistic arguments tend to force false choices and are rarely useful. Education has moral, intellectual, societal, and self-actualizing dimensions. Polarizing positions, regardless of the argument, are frequently rooted in values and philosophical beliefs, making any advancement difficult. What results from such a dynamic is often nothing more than an endless movement back and forth over the same ground. Or, to borrow another meaty line from Tom Robbins, "Until humans can solve their philosophical problems, they're condemned to solve their political problems over and over again" (Robbins 1976: 332).

While technology is inarguably the primary disrupter in education, the move toward student-centric learning has been identified as a second (Christensen et al. 2011a). This is not a new idea for educators; we have long understood that the construction of knowledge is very much determined by an individual's prior knowledge and privately held beliefs, as well as by physiological factors that can both enable and set limits on what is learned. The need to individualize or differentiate instruction based on the learner's needs is central to an educator's practice; however, doing this thoroughly and well has always presented enormous challenges. Student-centric learning, while an old concept, can now become a disruptor because of the new technologies that make individualized learning a greater possibility.

Many online classes, particularly the earlier ones, have followed a fairly traditional, didactic format. Even though they were online, everything else was much the same as in a typical classroom, with an instructor disseminating information to students who were playing a more or less passive role. In recent years, however, online learning has become a more versatile tool, sometimes used as a stand-alone course, but increasingly seen as a strategy to enhance or complement face-to-face instruction (see also Marciniak, this volume). The flipped classroom is an example of how technology and pedagogical changes can be used together to create a much more student-centered program. The term "flip" refers to a form of blended learning that pairs videotaped lectures, which students view outside of class, with in-class time devoted to problem solving, critical discourse, laboratory experiences, and instructional coaching.

Although this approach was initially used in K-12 classrooms, it is increasingly showing up in postsecondary education. "A number of professors at the University of North Carolina (UNC) at Chapel Hill have experimented with the flipped format, in which professors assign residential students to watch their recorded lectures online and then use the class time for discussion and group work" (Johnson 2013: 20–21). Marcia Roth, a professor in public health at UNC, notes, "With the lecture already under their belts, students ask better, more specific questions; they get more time to spend with their fellow students, applying the information to real-world scenarios and working on softer skills such as adaptive leadership, communication, and problem-solving" (Johnson 2013: 20). Matthew Sayre, an associate professor in the Department of Anthropology at the University of South Dakota, records lectures for his students to watch outside of class, allowing him to devote more in-class time to discussion and problem solving. He points out that such strategies are not necessarily new to archaeologists, explaining that the field school has long been a place where students take material learned in class and apply it in the field (see both Clark and King, this volume; Elia et al. 2019). He emphasizes that this applied kind of learning, including critical thinking skills such as analysis and interpretation, have long been part of the disciplinary training for decades (Sayre 2014).

The transformative effects that disruptive innovations have on learning and the pursuit of knowledge are, perhaps, more profound than just the impact they have on educational systems and institutions. The seemingly limitless capacity to retrieve and publish information afforded by digital technologies and the Internet changes the power structure of education. The individual can now directly access knowledge domains that were previously mediated by "experts," from scientists, to theologians, to gourmet chefs. The challenges and opportunities this presents are considerable. In the following section, I examine some of these in the context of disruptions in heritage education.

## Archaeology and Heritage Education: A Series of Disruptions

Earlier in this chapter, I defined heritage education as I see it. It is a perspective that is heavily affected by my education and experience in the field of archaeology and, particularly, by an anthropological approach to archaeology. Thus, when I reflect on how heritage education is experiencing disruption, I think not only of the impacts seen across education in general, but also of discipline-specific changes that contribute to transformations in practice.

One of these changes was the increased emphasis placed on public engagement in archaeology in the mid- to late 1980s (Selig 2006). The realization that archaeological research had to be relevant to new audiences that were outside the profession in order to remain viable and receive support led, over time, to the development of numerous new programs and products. The existing products and services, such as professional journals and scholarly conferences, were largely too complicated or inaccessible for a general audience. Thus, new less-complex and more-engaging products had to be designed to capture this new market. As interest in, and demand for, these products grew, they became more elaborate, information-rich and, over time, opened up new possibilities for recording, reporting, and interpreting archaeological data. The desire to be relevant to the general public positioned the archaeological profession to be self-disruptive. Christensen would say that an industry cannot disrupt itself, but the transformation that occurred in archaeology over the last two decades might be an exception to that rule.

The second disruptor, which occurred relatively close in time to the new emphasis on public engagement, was sparked by actions outside the profession. The passage of the Native American Graves Protection and Repatriation Act (NAGPRA) in 1990 had an impact on everything from where research could be conducted, to how it could be conducted, and who needed to be involved in the process. NAGPRA might not qualify as a classic disruptor but it seems undeniable that it has had transformative effects on the way American archaeologists conduct research. Consultation, collaboration, and negotiation are not just desired job skills for heritage professionals; they are a necessity (see also Sievert et al. and Watkins, this volume).

Together, the emphasis on public engagement and NAGPRA have, over the last three decades, resulted in the development of new tools and changing practices that could seemingly place archaeology ahead of the curve in terms of educating new professionals. Many of the instructional tools and educational programs that have been designed to engage and inform various segments of the public are highly adaptable to the college classroom, particularly at the undergraduate level. Virtual excavations, agent-based computer modeling of settlement and migration patterns, augmented reality, searchable electronic databases, 3-D computer-generated models of buildings and entire villages, digitized archives—all these and numerous other resources provide a wealth of material for designing highly engaging courses, whether online, blended, flipped, or face-to-face. These tools are ideal for use in project-based learning courses where students, working in collaborative teams, pose authentic questions and have direct access to the data that are relevant to their research. Such courses would be highly student-centric and would require an intellectual investment by the students. If project-based, they would also require collaborative effort and, very likely, the development of effective negotiating skills.

As technological innovations introduce new possibilities in heritage education, they also present new responsibilities and areas of concern. Open access to research data allows users to pose their own questions, analyze what they find, collaborate with others, and construct their own understanding without mediators (historians, teachers, archaeologists, textbooks, and so on) telling them "what happened." This is enormously exciting and, at the same time, somewhat worrisome. As an educator, I embrace this advancement but, also as an educator, I know there are an infinite number of ways that individuals can select and deselect information to reach conclusions that validate preconceived ideas and personal agendas. The challenge with these new capabilities, then, is how to increase the chance that users will think critically about the information they access through the Internet and wisely discern the value of the resources they select (see also Marciniak, this volume). This is a new frontier in heritage education, just as it is in education universally. Disruptive technological innovations can be a democratizing force in heritage education. As stated by Pamela Rutledge, director of the Media Psychology Research Center at Fielding Graduate University, in a survey about the future of the Internet conducted by the Pew Research Center's Internet & American Life Project:

> The ability to act and interact, to synthesize and connect, can radically change an individual's sense of agency. There is a new assumption about participation. It is not just the expectation to participate that we talk about in convergence culture; it is the belief that each person can participate in a meaningful way. Beliefs of agency and competence fuel intrinsic motivation, resilience, and engagement. (Anderson and Rainie 2012: 34)

In education, intrinsic motivation, resilience, and engagement are everything. They are the not-so-secret sauce for success in learning and in life. The past is a contest of stories and, in sharing authority for its construction, history becomes a dialogic practice.

> This contest of stories is a dynamic one that will never sit still to be evaluated once and for all. It is continually being reassessed based on new information, on the integration of new perspectives and, for good or for bad, on the needs and desires of the present. How well we grapple with this contest of stories and construct our own narrative

will depend to a large extent on our intellectual, social, and cultural preparedness. This, then, is the charge for those who work in history education, to learn how to develop and nurture the intellectual skills, as well as the social and cultural understandings that prepare students to become responsible mediators of the human past. (Davis 2005: 175)

## References Cited

Anderson, Janna Q., and Lee Rainie
2012    Millennials will Benefit and Suffer Due to Their Hyperconnected Lives. Electronic document, http://www.pewinternet.org/2012/02/29/millennials-will-benefit-and-suffer-due-to-their-hyperconnected-lives/. Accessed February 14, 2017.

Arizona State University
2016    ASU Online Degree Programs. Electronic document, http://asuonline.asu.edu/online-degree-programs/undergraduate. Accessed September 10, 2016.

Christensen, Clayton, Michael B. Horn, Louis Caldera, and Louis Soares
2011a   Disrupting College: How Disruptive Innovation Can Deliver Quality and Affordability to Postsecondary Education. Electronic document, www.americanprogress.org, www.innosightinstitute.org. Accessed March 20, 2013.

Christensen, Clayton, Curtis W. Johnson, and Michael B. Horn
2011b   *Disrupting Class: How Disruptive Innovation Will Change the Way the World Learns.* McGraw-Hill, Columbus, Ohio.

Davis, M. Elaine
2005    *How Students Understand the Past: From Theory to Practice.* AltaMira Press, Walnut Creek, California.

Elia, Ricardo J., Amalia Pérez-Juez, and Meredith Anderson Langlitz
2019    Teaching Heritage in the Field: An Example from Menorca, Spain. In *Pedagogy and Practice in Heritage Studies*, edited by Susan J. Bender and Phyllis Mauch Messenger, pp. 94–111. University Press of Florida, Gainesville.

Florida Virtual Schools
2014    Florida Virtual School Summary. Electronic document, https://www.flvs.net/areas/contactus/Documents/Florida_Virtual_School_Summary.pdf. Accessed October 15, 2014.

Institute for College Access and Success
2016    Project on Student Debt. Electronic document, http://ticas.org/posd/home. Accessed September 9, 2016.

Johnson, Darve
2013    If I Could be Anywhere. *Carolina Alumni Review.* Electronic document, http://www.carolinaalumnireview.com/carolinaalumnireview/20130304/?pg=20#pg20. Accessed March 15, 2013.

North Carolina Virtual Public School

2016    NCVPS Scorecard 2015–2016. Electronic document, https://ncvps.org/ncvps-scorecard-2015–2016. Accessed September 9, 2016.

Richardson, Will

2013    Students First, Not Stuff. *Educational Leadership* 70(6): 10–14.

Robbins, Tom

1976    *Even Cowgirls Get the Blues.* Houghton Mifflin, Boston.

Sayre, Matthew

2014    Student Initiated Projects, The Flipped Classroom, and Crowdfunding. *SAA Archaeological Record* 14(1): 14–17.

Selig, Ruth O.

2006    SAA Public Education Committee History. Electronic document, https://www.saa.org/publicftp/public/about/PECHISTORY.html. Accessed March 15, 2013.

US Department of Education, National Center for Education Statistics

2016    Fast Facts on Distance Learning. Electronic document, https://nces.ed.gov/fastfacts/display.asp?id=80. Accessed September 9, 2016.

Weise, Michelle R., and Clayton Christensen

2014    Hire Education: Mastery, Modularization, and the Workforce Revolution. Electronic document, http://www.christenseninstitute.org/wp-content/uploads/2014/07/Hire-Education.pdf. Accessed February 14, 2017.

# 4

## Gender, Archaeology, and the Pedagogy of Heritage

PHYLLIS MAUCH MESSENGER

### The Development of an "Archaeology of Gender"

In 1984 Meg Conkey and Janet Spector published their seminal article on the archaeology of gender. In it they called for the application of feminist approaches to archaeological theory and practice. "Feminist scholars conceptualize gender as a complex system of meaning—that is, a social category that lies at the core of how people in particular cultures identify who they are, what they are capable of doing, what they should do, and how they are to relate to others similar to and different from themselves" (1984: 16). It was the first such article to be published, widely read, and taken seriously; it opened the floodgates for development of the literature, theory, and practices related to archaeology and gender. Their article continues to be a touchstone for discussions of gender in realms well beyond archaeology, and it serves as a reminder that uncritical interpretations of gender need to be continually reviewed and critiqued (compare Markert 2016). It also reminds us that issues of gender are embedded in every area of scholarship and public life, including how we engage with, study, and teach about heritage. This chapter offers perspectives on how gender issues related to archaeology have changed both what we learn from the past and how we learn it. It will consider intersections among feminism, gender archaeology, social justice, civic engagement, and heritage studies. It is at those intersections that we can teach and learn about heritage in inclusive and egalitarian ways that will best serve future generations of heritage workers and stakeholders alike.

Nelson and other authors in the *Handbook of Gender in Archaeology* (2006; see also Gero 1996; Sørensen 2000) discuss the use of gender as an entry point for understanding sites, just as Conkey and Spector had described in 1984. It has proven to be a durable approach, leading to fruitful explorations of such archaeological subjects as households, landscapes, public roles, personal and group identities, and even the very concepts of women, sex, and gender. At the same time, these authors and others draw parallels between study of the gendered past and analysis of gender in contemporary practice in archaeology, a field long dominated by male-centered perspectives. Yet gendered aspects of archaeological practice are ubiquitous, once they are named. Some of the categories are work relationships, divisions of labor, communication and cognitive styles, specializations, and normalizing symbolism (Hamilton 2007). While the percentage of women in archaeology-related fields continues to grow, the work for gender equality lags behind. Discussions need to continue on such issues as the gendered nature of acceptable fieldwork techniques, the inherent gender biases in archaeological work, and the marginalization of feminist perspectives in archaeology that stubbornly persist (for example, Claassen 1994; Gero and Conkey 1991; Kehoe and Emmerichs 1999; Nelson 1997; Pyburn 2004; Rizvi and Berg 2008; and Wright 1996). The Society for American Archaeology (SAA) took an important stand on these issues in 2016 with implementation of a new Principle No. 9: "Safe Educational and Workplace Environments" in its Principles of Archaeological Ethics (SAA 2016), addressing harassment based upon sex or gender identity, and related topics. SAA continued to shine a light on gender issues in archaeology at a forum during the 82nd Annual Meeting in Vancouver (Thies and Jones 2017).

Ströbeck (2010: 327–330) discusses an intertwined relationship between Indigenous gender systems and Euro-American feminist and gender archaeological research, arguing that the former informed the latter, while both struggled to break down the norms of male domination in scholarship and perspectives on gender roles as cultural formations. She notes the evolving movement toward the decolonization and empowerment of Indigenous peoples and the continued elaboration of multivocality within archaeological practices (Ströbeck 2010: 338–339). Indigenous feminist scholars (for example, Arvin et al. 2013; Todd 2016) offer cautionary narratives about the need to engage settler colonialism as a still-existing structure that complicates conventional notions of feminism as inclusive and egalitarian. The scholarly work of these authors will provide greater depth and clarity as we continue to engage with the ways in which "class and other kinds of privilege intersect with gender" (Nelson 2006: 2). Similarly, a number of archaeologists write about the relationship of community-engaged archaeology and heritage with current issues of class, privilege, human rights, and decolonization (for example, Bruchac et al. 2016; Franklin and Paynter 2002; Jackson and Smith 2005; Little and Shackel 2014; Logan 2012; Robles García and Corbett 2010; Watkins 2016; see also Clark, King, Shackel, and Zimmerman, this volume; Kryder-Reid 2019).

## Critical Issues in Gender and Archaeology

This chapter explores intersections of theory, practice, teaching, and writing related to archaeology, gender, and heritage. It discusses what feminist archaeologists say about multivocality, multilinear narratives, active engagement, and collaboration to de-center archaeologists' knowledge claims and to open space for community-based management frameworks in today's archaeology and heritage work. Various authors describe feminist discourse and pedagogy as exhibiting an open-ended, democratizing, and relational style (for example, Ashmore et al. 2010). The focus is on the qualities of an inclusive practice, rejecting a position that normalizes traditionally male-constructed meanings and practices by paying attention to the politics of knowledge and the need for reflexivity (Alberti 2006: 424).

The chapter also looks at why the need to discuss gender equity issues in archaeology, and the heritage field more broadly, still exists. Several volumes on women in archaeology celebrate successful careers, but also trace the persistent history of gender bias (for example, Claasen 1994; Díaz-Andreu and Sørensen 1998; White et al. 1999; Williams 1981). As Claassen writes, "One theme running throughout [*Women in Archaeology*] is how women adapt in whatever way necessary to participate in archaeology" (1994: 4), including, for example, taking more jobs in museums and contract agencies, and fewer jobs in academia. Each generation of female students and emerging professionals has the expectation that gender equality has been taken care of, or it is just a "pipeline" issue or a question of numbers (Nelson 2015: 69–70). They assume that sexism and gender bias are stories from the past. Yet, wake-up calls and reminders of the need for continued vigilance keep coming (see Hamilton et al. 2007; Kirakosian and Burkholder 2010; Messenger 2010; Nelson 2006, 2015; Rizvi and Berg 2008; Wylie 2007). "Why are you bothering doing this article [on gendered images in archaeological fieldwork]? It's a non-subject," Hamilton was told (2007: 143). According to Hamilton et al., "Recovering and giving full value to the work of female archaeologists of earlier generations is an essential aspect of writing not just a history of women in archaeology, but *any* history of archaeology, given the marked androcentric bias that has characterized the discipline until recently" (Hamilton et al. 2007: 18).

The stories presented by these authors parallel the findings of a study that focused on characteristics of women leaders in the heritage sector (Messenger 2010).

## Research on Women in the Heritage Sector

Between 2007 and 2010, I carried out research on the experiences of women leaders in the heritage sector, including interviews with a dozen mostly mid-career women whom I perceived to be change agents in archaeology and heritage, to look for common threads in their experiences in education, work, and life. My primary research questions were: (1) "How do women professionals in the cultural heritage sector describe the changing issues they face in their professional lives?" and (2) "What new strategies are cultural heritage professionals using in their teaching, scholarship, and service to respond to changing realities?" (Messenger 2010: 3–4). I used qualitative narrative interviews (Linde 1993), social science portraiture (Lawrence-Lightfoot and Davis 1997), and a constructivist approach to grounded theory (Charmaz 2001; Fassinger 2005; Strauss and Corbin 1998) to develop an explanatory framework linking the events and experiences in my subjects' lives with the changing nature of their heritage work, and with the experiences of others. I wanted to look for common threads in these life stories that might contribute to greater understanding of trends and transitions in how we work, and how we should be teaching and preparing our students for work in heritage fields.

Coding and analysis of interview transcripts identified several core characteristics shared among all my subjects. These included a commitment to social justice and ethical practice, a passion for gender equity, a willingness to de-center authorized narratives and share leadership, a concern for community perspectives and inclusive practices, a respect for interdisciplinarity, and a zeal for teaching and mentoring. These qualities seemed to develop out of formative experiences of exclusion, marginalization, or dislocation, either experienced or witnessed, which contributed to particular practices as professional archaeologists who could thrive in the context of the developing field of heritage (compare Harrison 2013; Nelson 2015; Smith 2006). I began to realize that my grounded theory approach had uncovered a cohort of heritage practitioners who, more or less on their own, had developed their own guidelines, work habits, and teaching practices for what we now call critical archaeology and heritage.

The subjects of my research are all archaeologists or heritage specialists; they represent at least five nationalities. Their work or education has taken place in widely dispersed geographic settings:[1] British Commonwealth countries (3), Latin American countries (3), North America (5); several have a broadly international focus (5). They have worked in one or more of these settings as a primary place of employment: universities (5), heritage sites (3), state or national agencies (4), and museums (5). All have been given pseudonyms in publications and presentations on this research.

In order to put their experiences in dialogue with other narratives of critical pedagogy and critical heritage studies (compare Harrison 2013; Little and Shackel 2014; see also Chilton, Shackel, Zimmerman this volume), I will describe composite portraits drawn largely from four of my research subjects: Barbara and Flora (field researchers and university professors in archaeology and anthropology), Helen (a public sector heritage specialist), and Paula (a community-based archaeologist).

Barbara developed a passion for justice and equity out of childhood and early professional experiences of being marginalized and being exposed to unethical and discriminatory behavior by those who outranked her. She was drawn to study "the people that are invisible, and I became more and more interested in the fact that archaeologists were not interested in ordinary people. They discounted ordinary people, which is also how I began to be interested in gender" (Messenger 2010: 69–70). She strongly believes that scholars and researchers must pay attention to how their work affects the people around them. She pays attention to who *cooks* the food, who *has* food, and who controls the systems that cause inequities of work and resource distribution. She sees this as being "engaged in the world," not living in an ivory tower, and having a kind of "political radicalism." For her, doing archaeology today involves "fair play and honesty" and an ethic based on the "do no harm" principle, rather than "for science" (Messenger 2010: 71). She is committed to providing opportunities for students and colleagues from Indigenous and underserved communities, and preparing her students to be change makers in their lives and work.

Like Barbara, Flora is deeply committed to creating a level playing field for the Indigenous peoples with whom she works (she refers to them as her teachers) and for her colleagues from developing nations. She grew up in a poor, working-class family; her parents instilled in her a respect for "education as the way out" for girls (Messenger 2010: 74). She struggled to find her way through postsecondary education, let alone finishing a PhD. It was during an extended time of living and studying with Indigenous people that she developed an understanding of what her life's work could be. She came to realize that she needed to be the companion, not the leader, even if she had acquired an advanced degree. The aboriginal people she works with should, of necessity, take the lead in deciding what research gets done and who gives permission for use of Indigenous knowledge and materials. "I didn't really understand that people believed what they believe," she says. "They really do believe . . . that we're in this living powerful landscape that can damage us and can help us. It's a whole different way of reading the world. . . . [Now] I see the world in a different way, and I value different things" (Messenger 2010: 76). When her students learn from aboriginal people about their land, she says, "They leave being social justice activists."

Helen has had to create one position after another for herself in the public sector of heritage. She had on-the-job training in archaeology, then learned to apply archaeological techniques to industrial sites and buildings. "I went from being a field archaeologist to being what you might call a preservation person engaging in legal battles and defending archaeology and heritage through the planning system" (Messenger 2010: 79). Later she moved to another position, this time in the policy section of a government heritage agency. "This was a new field, it hadn't really existed before. . . . I tried to get the different professions to work together in conservation." She decided to commission research to make her point that local authorities needed heritage specialists with diverse skill sets (Messenger 2010: 80). Like several other women in my study, Helen expressed frustration that she had not found a strong female mentor to guide her through the emerging field of heritage and the new positions that she had to keep creating for herself. "You have to be passionate and be willing to shape your own direction," she said. "And the people that I've had working for me, you know, who've done best, are the people who actually have a direction and commitment of their own. In heritage, if you wait for the organizations to give you that structure, you're sort of doomed" (Messenger 2010: 82).

Through her career in publicly oriented archaeology, Paula found a way to share the power of place with an entire community, listening to the questions they were asking about their heritage. Like other mid-career women in my study, she talked about the widely held assumptions about gender roles in education and work as she was entering college. "We didn't have many goals as women," she lamented (Messenger 2010: 83). She described how her college professor would not write a letter of recommendation for her graduate school application, and how she took that as a humiliating sign that she wasn't good enough. Nevertheless, she persisted, eventually finished her PhD, and was hired as part of a field crew in the new wave of cultural resource management. She stumbled onto her life's passion during a break from fieldwork, as she listened to an elderly man talk about his life and his connection to the place where they were sitting. "And right then, these are the exact words, I said, 'I wanna work with the public.'" She didn't know exactly what that meant, hadn't heard the term "public archaeology," didn't know anything about historic preservation. But that was the moment she knew what she wanted to do with her life (Messenger 2010: 85). She liked the idea of public service and commitment to a sense of place. Later she was hired as a city archaeologist by people who knew that things around them were important and needed to be studied and protected, because of what they represented in the life of the community. It required paying attention to both environmental and cultural landscapes. What she loves best about her work with the community is the "constant dialogue and reciprocity about the place" (Messenger 2010: 87).

## Implications for Heritage Studies Curricula

Through qualitative and constructivist analysis using grounded theory (as described above), my research identified patterns and commonalities that resonate with the characteristics of critical archaeology and heritage. The life experiences and professional practices of this cohort enabled them to become successful heritage practitioners, without the benefit of the specialized training for heritage professionals that is increasingly available today (compare Cobb and Croucher, Hayes et al., MacDonald, and Shackel, this volume; Kryder-Reid 2019; Pluckhahn 2019). Their impulse to critique and change society was learned, not from theorists of critical pedagogy, but in life's classroom.

What might a heritage studies curriculum look like if it incorporated the life lessons identified by the heritage workers with whom I spoke? How might students, teachers, and community partners engage in teaching and learning about critical heritage issues so that heritage is accessible and meaningful for everyone? A review of key themes and concepts identified by my research interviewees may help to answer these questions.

The first cluster of themes relates to social justice, equity, and ethical practices. It includes racial, class, and gender equity in the workplace (see Rizvi and Berg 2008; Messenger 2010: 33–37). It also includes making heritage and public spaces accessible for all (see Finney 2014; Savoy 2015; Smith 2006; B. Clark, this volume). My informants (and their peers) insist that students and colleagues alike have access to just and equitable work environments. They provide opportunities to read and debate case studies that wrestle with ethical dilemmas (see McGill 2019). They work with colleagues in agencies and policy or cultural organizations to develop and provide meaningful internships and new learning experiences related to heritage issues (for example, Marciniak and Sievert et al., this volume; Elia et al. 2019). They encourage students to take courses that challenge them to engage with other worldviews beyond their own and to think critically and reflexively about what they are learning (for example, King and MacDonald, this volume; Bender 2019; Hayashida 2019; Kryder-Reid 2019; Messenger 2019; Scham 2019), and how they will apply it in their work (see Little and Shackel 2014: 147–153 for a discussion of building peace through heritage).

The second cluster of themes relates to civic engagement, de-centering authorized narratives, and sharing leadership. My informants have found it easier to relinquish the archaeological voice of authority than did their predecessors in a traditionally androcentric field (perhaps it was easier to give up something that never seemed rightfully theirs). They do not uncritically accept the veracity of the Authorized Heritage Discourse (see Smith 2006: 29–34, Harrison 2013: 110–12 for discussions of AHD). They understand that the development of skills in community-engaged research moves scholars on a continuum from research in the public interest to community-based participatory action research, which broadens the participation of underrepresented groups and encourages mutual trust (Office for Public Engagement 2016). Arguably, this also enhances the rigor of research and allows for the development of more accurate conceptual frameworks and culturally appropriate measurement (compare National Science Foundation 2002; Chilton and Mason 2010). Engaged heritage practitioners want all stakeholders to have a sense of shared ownership of heritage, the opportunity to decide what is important to study and preserve, and even the right to decide if aspects of a community's heritage cannot be shared (compare Langfield et al. 2010; Schofield 2014; Smith 2006).

Another important theme that emerged from this study is the value of mentorship. Interviewees work very hard to support their students, both male and female, with mentoring that encompasses both life and work. For them, mentoring experiences have been critically important, yet were often lacking in the early years of their education and work life (compare Nelson 2015: 66–69; Rizvi and Berg 2008). Mentorship sometimes came in surprising forms from outside the field, from the public, or as a result of a negative experience. Almost to a person, my subjects are passionate about providing significant and meaningful mentorship for their students (see also B. Clark, Hayes et al., and King, this volume).

The field of heritage studies is necessarily interdisciplinary. The women represented in this study approach archaeology from an interdisciplinary perspective, drawing on the literature and practices of American Indian studies, art history, cultural anthropology, education, and gender studies (compare Kayes et al. and Watkins, this volume), as well as applied research and practices in the fields of tourism, development, historic preservation, and heritage management, among others (see K. Clark and Sievert et al., this volume). Their language, their scholarship, and their work are consistent with current discussions and theorizing related to critical heritage studies (compare Carman and Sørensen 2009: 22–24; Harrison 2013: 110–113, 192; Smith 2006: 299–308; see also Chilton and Zimmerman, this volume).

Archaeological or architectural preservation of monuments and sites remains important, Logan and Smith tell us, but "they are subsumed within the new field [of Heritage Studies] that sees 'heritage' as a social and political construct encompassing all those places, artefacts and cultural expressions inherited from the past which, because they are seen to reflect and validate our identity as nations, communities, families, and even individuals, are worthy of some form of respect and protection" (Logan and Smith 2010: xiv). Furthermore, according to Harrison, "The newly emerging field of interdisciplinary heritage studies has a clear role to play in commenting critically on new developments in heritage and being more actively engaged with the production of policy and the critical discussion of its function in society" (Harrison 2013: 229).

## Conclusion

The research findings of my study reinforce existing literature on the intersection of archaeology, heritage, and gender, and offer valuable insights into strategies for training a new generation of heritage professionals. These data all point to interdisciplinary, hands-on, community-based experiences that situate archaeology and heritage in the real world and allow participants to be in dialogue with other stakeholders, as essential components of heritage studies curricula. Efforts to eliminate the lingering impact of gender biases and other forms of discrimination in scholarship (for example, what is considered worthy of study or citation) and work environments (from chilly climate to hiring and tenure decisions) must continue as we move toward justice and equity in heritage work.

In his final work on the engaged scholar, educator Earnest Boyer argued that scholarship needs to prove its worth by service to the nation and the world. "The scholarship of engagement means connecting the rich resources of the university to our most pressing social, civic and ethical problems, to our children, to our schools, to our teachers and to our cities" (1996: 20). Similarly, the engaged work of heritage professionals will continue to be refined through theory and practice so that we will be able to make the critical connections between "heritage and other urgent contemporary social, political, economic and environmental issues in the world" (Harrison 2013: 229). The literature of critical pedagogy and critical heritage studies argues for making archaeology matter in people's lives by translating archaeological interpretation into practical elements to help communities, influence public policy, and perhaps even help to build peace and social justice (Little and Shackel 2014: 151).

The heritage professionals described here would agree with these sentiments. They continue to carry out their heritage work and teaching in ways that contribute to the theory and practice of critical heritage studies and critical pedagogy, always remembering that "heritage is a cultural and social process. . . . through shared experiences and acts of creation" (Smith 2006: 307–308). The future of heritage depends on it.

## Note

1. Numbers in each set of categories may total more than total number of respondents (12), as individuals may be included in more than one subset of each category.

## References Cited

Alberti, B.

2006    Archaeology, Men and Masculinities. In *Handbook of Gender in Archaeology*, edited by Sarah M. Nelson, pp. 401–434. AltaMira Press, Lanham, Maryland.

Arvin, Maile, Eve Tuck, and Angie Morrill

2013    Decolonizing Feminism: Challenging Connections between Settler Colonialism and Heteropatriarchy. *Feminist Formations* 25(1): 8–34.

Ashmore, Wendy, Dorothy T. Lippert, and Barbara J. Mills

2010    *Voices in American Archaeology*. Society for American Archaeology Press, Washington, D.C.

Bender, Susan J.

2019    Identity and Heritage: A Faculty Interview on the Use of Image in the Classroom. In *Pedagogy and Practice in Heritage Studies*, edited by Susan J. Bender and Phyllis Mauch Messenger, pp. 179–184. University Press of Florida, Gainesville.

Boyer, Earnest L.

1996    The Scholarship of Engagement. *Journal of Public Service & Outreach* I(1): 11–20.

Bruchac, Margaret M., Siobhan M. Hart, and H. Martin Wobst (editors)

2016    *Indigenous Archaeologies: A Reader on Decolonization*. (First published by Left Coast Press, 2010.) Routledge, New York.

Carman, John, and Mary Louise Stig Sørensen

2009    Heritage Studies: An Outline. In *Heritage Studies: Methods and Approaches*, edited by Mary Louise Stig Sørensen and John Carman, pp. 11–28. Routledge, London.

Charmaz, Kathy

2001    Qualitative Interviewing and Grounded Theory Analysis. In *Handbook of Interview Research: Context and Method*, edited by Jaber F. Gubrium and James A. Holstein, pp. 675–694. Sage, Thousand Oaks, California.

Chilton, Elizabeth S., and Randall Mason

2010    NSF White Paper: A Call for a Social Science of the Past. *SBE 2020: Future Research in the Social, Behavioral & Economic Sciences*. Electronic document, http://www.nsf.gov/sbe/sbe_2020/submission_detail.cfm?upld_id=297. Accessed January 10, 2017.

Claassen, Cheryl (editor)

1994    *Women in Archaeology*. University of Pennsylvania Press, Philadelphia.

Conkey, Meg, and Janet Spector

1984    Archaeology and the Study of Gender. In *Advances in Archaeological Method and Theory*, edited by Michael Schiffer, vol. 7, pp. 1–38. Academic Press, New York.

Díaz-Andreu, Margarita, and Mary Louise Stig Sørensen

1998    Excavating Women: Towards an Engendered History of Archaeology. In *Excavating Women: A History of Women in European Archaeology*, edited by Margarita Díaz-Andreu and Mary Louise Stig Sørensen, pp. 1–28. Routledge, New York.

Elia, Ricardo J., Amalia Pérez-Juez, and Meredith Anderson

2019    Teaching Heritage in the Field: An Example from Menorca, Spain. In *Pedagogy and Practice in Heritage Studies*, edited by Susan J. Bender and Phyllis Mauch Messenger, pp. 94–111. University Press of Florida, Gainesville.

Fassinger, Ruth E.

2005    Paradigms, Praxis, Problems, and Promise: Grounded Theory in Counseling Psychology Research. *Journal of Counseling Psychology*, 52(2): 156–166.

Finney, Carolyn

2014    *Black Faces, White Spaces: Reimagining the Relationship of African Americans to the Great Outdoors.* University of North Carolina Press, Chapel Hill.

Franklin, Maria, and Robert Paynter

2002    Inequality and Archaeology. In *Voices in American Archaeology,* edited by Wendy Ashmore, Dorothy T. Lippert, and Barbara J. Mills, pp. 94–130. Society for American Archaeology, Washington, D.C.

Gero, Joan, and Meg Conkey (editors)

1991    *Engendering Archaeology: Women and Prehistory.* Basic Blackwell, Oxford.

Gero, Joan

1996    Archaeological Practice and Gendered Encounters with Field Data. In *Gender and Archaeology,* edited by Rita Wright, pp. 251–280. University of Pennsylvania Press, Philadelphia.

Hamilton, Sue

2007    Women in Practice: Women in British Contract Field Archaeology. In *Archaeology and Women: Ancient & Modern Issues,* edited by Sue Hamilton, Ruth D. Whitehouse, and Katherine I. Wright, pp. 121–146. Left Coast Press, Walnut Creek, California.

Hamilton, Sue, Ruth D. Whitehouse, and Katherine I. Wright (editors)

2007    *Archaeology and Women: Ancient & Modern Issues.* Left Coast Press, Walnut Creek, California.

Harrison, Rodney

2013    *Heritage: Critical Approaches.* Routledge, New York.

Hayashida, Frances

2019    Making Connections in *Food, Foraging, and Farming.* In *Pedagogy and Practice in Heritage Studies,* edited by Susan J. Bender and Phyllis Mauch Messenger, pp. 198–212. University Press of Florida, Gainesville.

Jackson, Gary, and Claire Smith

2005    Living and Learning on Aboriginal Lands: Decolonizing Archaeology in Practice. In *Indigenous Archaeologies: Decolonizing Theory and Practice,* edited by Claire Smith and H. Martin Wobst, pp. 329–351. Routledge, New York.

Kehoe, Alice Beck, and Mary Beth Emmerichs (editors)

1999    *Assembling the Past: Studies in the Professionalization of Archaeology*. University of New Mexico Press, Albuquerque.

Kirakosian, Katie V., and Jo Ellen Burkholder (chairs)

2010    Gendered Selves: Experiences in and out of the Classroom (Forum). Society for American Archaeology Annual Meeting Program. Electronic document, http://www.saa.org/Portals/0/Final_program.pdf. Accessed October 20, 2010.

Kryder-Reid, Elizabeth

2019    Do the Homeless Have Heritage? Archaeology and the Pedagogy of Discomfort. In *Pedagogy and Practice in Heritage Studies*, edited by Susan J. Bender and Phyllis Mauch Messenger, pp. 129–147. University Press of Florida, Gainesville.

Langfield, Michele, William Logan, and Máiréad Nic Craith (editors)

2010    *Cultural Diversity, Heritage and Human Rights: Intersections in Theory and Practice*. Routledge, New York.

Lawrence-Lightfoot, Sara, and Jessica Hoffman Davis

1997    *The Art and Science of Portraiture*. Wiley, San Francisco.

Linde, Charlotte

1993    *Life Stories: The Creation of Coherence*. Oxford University Press, New York.

Little, Barbara J., and Paul A. Shackel

2014    *Archaeology, Heritage, and Civic Engagement: Working toward the Public Good*. Left Coast Press, Walnut Creek, California.

Logan, William

2012    Cultural Diversity, Cultural Heritage and Human Rights: Towards Heritage Management as Human Rights-based Cultural Practice. *International Journal of Heritage Studies* 18(3): 231–244.

Logan, William S., and Laurajane Smith

2010    Foreword. In *Cultural Diversity, Heritage and Human Rights: Intersections in Theory and Practice*, edited by Michele Langfield, William Logan, and Máiréad Nic Craith, pp. xiv–xv. Routledge, New York.

Markert, Trish

2016    "Nasty Women" and Man the Hunter: Archaeology and Gender Politics in 2016. Electronic document, http://mapabing.org/2016/10/26/nasty-women-and-man-the-hunter-archaeology-and-gender-politics-in-2016. Accessed February 19, 2018.

McGill, Alicia Ebbitt

2019    Assessing Student Learning in Heritage Studies: What Does It Mean for Students to "Understand" Archaeological Ethics? In *Pedagogy and Practice in Heritage Studies*, edited by Susan J. Bender and Phyllis Mauch Messenger, pp. 50–71. University Press of Florida, Gainesville.

Messenger, Lewis C., Jr.

2019    Experiencing Antiquity in the First Person through Archaeological Fiction: The Pedagogical Opportunities of BACAB CAAS. In *Pedagogy and Practice in Heritage Studies*, edited by Susan J. Bender and Phyllis Mauch Messenger, pp. 165–178. University Press of Florida, Gainesville.

Messenger, Phyllis Mauch

2010   *Women as Agents of Change in the Cultural Heritage Sector.* Unpublished EdD diss. on file, Hamline University, St. Paul, Minnesota.

National Science Foundation

2002   Merit Review Broader Impacts Criterion: Representative Activities. Electronic document, https://www.nsf.gov/pubs/2002/nsf022/bicexamples.pdf. Accessed February 19, 2018.

Nelson, Sarah M. (editor)

2006   *Handbook of Gender in Archaeology.* AltaMira Press, Lanham, Maryland.

Nelson, Sarah M.

1997   *Gender in Archaeology.* AltaMira Press, Walnut Creek, California.

2015   *Shamans, Queens, and Figurines: The Development of Gender Archaeology.* Left Coast Press, Walnut Creek, California.

Office for Public Engagement

2016   Public Engagement: A Strategy to Realize Broader Impacts of Research. Electronic document, www.engagement.umn.edu. Accessed October 10, 2016.

Pluckhahn, Thomas

2019   The Challenges of Curriculum Change and the Pedagogy of Public Archaeology and CRM at the University of South Florida. In *Pedagogy and Practice in Heritage Studies,* edited by Susan J. Bender and Phyllis Mauch Messenger, pp. 72–93. University Press of Florida, Gainesville.

Pyburn, K. Anne (editor)

2004   *Ungendering Civilization.* Routledge, New York.

Rizvi, Uzma Z., and Caryn Berg (editors)

2008   *Looking Forward, Looking Back: A Special Issue from the Committee on the Status of Women in Archaeology (COSWA). SAA Archaeological Record* 8(4).

Robles García, Nellie, and Jack Corbett

2010   Heritage Resource Management in Mexico. In *Cultural Heritage Management: A Global Perspective,* edited by Phyllis Mauch Messenger and George S. Smith, pp. 111–123. University Press of Florida, Gainesville.

Savoy, Lauret Edith

2015   *Trace: Memory, History, Race, and the American Landscape.* Counterpoint, Berkeley, California.

Scham, Sandra

2019   Educating Students about the Modern Realities of Exploring the Ancient Middle East. In *Pedagogy and Practice in Heritage Studies,* edited by Susan J. Bender and Phyllis Mauch Messenger, pp. 112–128. University Press of Florida, Gainesville.

Schofield, John, editor

2014   *Who Needs Experts? Counter-mapping Cultural Heritage.* Ashgate, Surry, England.

Smith, Laurajane

2006   *Uses of Heritage.* Routledge, Abingdon, Oxon.

Society for American Archaeology (SAA)

2016    Principles of Archaeological Ethics. Electronic document, http://saa.org/About-theSociety/PrinciplesofArchaeologicalEthics/tabid/203/Default.aspx. Accessed February 24, 2017.

Sørensen, Mary Louise Stig

2000    *Gender Archaeology.* Polity Press, Cambridge, UK.

Strauss, Anselm L., and Juliet M. Corbin

1998    *Basics of Qualitative Research: Techniques and Procedures for Developing Grounded Theory.* Sage, Thousand Oaks, California.

Ströbeck, Louise

2010    Gender and Sexuality. In *Handbook of Postcolonial Archaeology* (World Archaeological Congress Research Handbooks in Archaeology, vol. 3), edited by Jane Lydon and Uzma Z. Rizvi, pp. 327–350. Left Coast Press, Walnut Creek, California.

Thies, Meagan, and Ashley Jones

2017    Creating Safety: Addressing Sexual Harassment and Assault in Archaeology. Sponsored Forum, 82nd Annual Meeting of the Society for American Archaeology, March 30, Vancouver, B.C.

Todd, Zoe

2016    An Indigenous Feminist's Take on the Ontological Turn: 'Ontology' Is Just Another Word for Colonialism. *Journal of Historical Sociology.* 29(1): 4–22.

Watkins, Joe

2016    Looting the Oklahoma Past: Relationships and "Relation Shifting." In *Challenging the Dichotomy: The Licit and Illicit in Archaeological and Heritage Discourses,* edited by Les Field, Joe Watkins, and Christóbal Gnecco, pp. 75–90 University of Arizona Press, Tucson.

White, Nancy Marie, Lynne P. Sullivan, and Rochelle A. Marrinan (editors)

1999    *Grit-tempered: Early Women Archaeologists in the Southeastern United States.* University Press of Florida, Gainesville.

Williams, Barbara

1981    *Breakthrough: Women in Archaeology.* Walker, New York.

Wright, Rita (editor)

1996    *Gender and Archaeology.* University of Pennsylvania Press, Philadelphia.

Wylie, Alison

2007    Doing Archaeology as a Feminist: Introduction. *Journal of Archaeological Method and Theory* 14(3): 209–216.

# 5

## African Americans, American Indians, and Heritage Education

ELEANOR M. KING

The growth in heritage studies over the last fifteen years has begun changing the nature of archaeology, particularly in the public domain. What archaeologists do—discovering and preserving the past for the future—has not altered, but heritage studies have broadened and deepened the framework within which archaeologists work. Increasingly, they must learn to operate meaningfully in a larger, more interdisciplinary context that includes history, environmental sciences, architecture, folklore, anthropology,[1] and other disciplines. Heritage per se is not a new concept. It has roots not only in these constituent disciplines but also in the practical concern of officials entrusted with preservation on public lands. A basic assumption behind setting aside these spaces is that safeguarding the world's natural and cultural heritage is necessary to inform the future—an echo of the archaeologist's creed. It is no wonder, then, that heritage studies initially focused on combining disciplinary forces to preserve the physical remains of the past in public and other spaces. Problems of heritage interpretation (for example, Silberman 2010), real estate development (for example, Fleming 2010; Wallis and Gorman 2010), and other practical issues continue to be central to heritage discussions (King 2014). However, heritage has recently migrated from practice to academia, and heritage as a concept has expanded to include intangible as well as tangible aspects of the past (King 2014; see also Chilton, this volume). The result has been a rich florescence of theory focused on memory, tradition, values (Carman and Sørensen 2009; King 2014, 2016b), and the commemoration of places and events in the public imagination (Shackel 2005; see also both B. Clark and Shackel, this volume).

Key to contemporary discussions of heritage is the idea that heritage is the core of our identities. "To know who you are, you need to know who you were," according to Chilton (2013). Heritage is the story we tell about ourselves—who we are and where we come from, both individually and collectively (King 2014; King and Epstein 2015). It can help define identity, not only locally, regionally, and nationally (Smith et al. 2010), but also internationally, for diasporic communities (King 2014). Because heritage encompasses intensely personal, social, and cultural connections to a shared past (King 2014), it is entangled in issues of power (Chilton 2013; Shackel, this volume). After all, whose story are we telling (King 2014)? Whose past are we investigating (King and Epstein 2015)? Whose are we preserving (Smith et al. 2010)? If "heritage is based on shared values that people have about culture and their past" (Shackel, this volume), then what happens when different values exist or that past is disputed (for example, Chirikure and Pwiti 2008; Herrera 2013)? In short, who owns the past (Smith et al. 2010) and who gets to interpret it?

Traditionally, the answer to these questions has been "the local or national majority," in the sense of the group within a region or country that controls the most wealth, power, and prestige. In other words, those with the greatest access to resources and rewards used to prevail, as they had the political clout to enforce their choices. Nowadays, however, that picture has become more complicated. The Native American Graves Protection and Repatriation Act (NAGPRA) of 1990 and similar laws in other countries challenged the premise of majority rule and began giving voice to the previously voiceless—Indigenous communities whose heritage was often the one under discussion (see also Sievert et al., this volume). Across the world, countries are becoming increasingly diverse due to transnational labor migration, war, and other forces (King 2016b). The recent influx of over 1 million Syrian refugees into Europe demonstrates how fast these demographic changes can happen. In addition, the rapid development of the Internet has facilitated interaction across borders and cultures (see also Marciniak, this volume). One has only to peruse that brave new virtual world to see how fluid, multivocal, and contested identities have become. As Shackel (this volume) points out, it is no longer possible to answer questions about heritage in a way that privileges one group over another, or one strong voice over the "traditionally muted" ones, even though the process of reaching a consensus might be complicated.

These changes are especially evident in the United States, where U.S. Census projections suggest that the European American majority will become a numerical minority by the mid–twenty-first century (Colby and Ortman 2015; King 2016b). That means that the museums, landmarks, parks, and other public and private spaces that enshrine our view of who we are will not reflect the actual American population, and neither will the people who work in those places. Unable to recognize themselves in heritage spaces or practitioners, future citizens are unlikely to care deeply about saving the past for the future. To engage them, the concept of local and national heritage must become more inclusive than it is now, and this change must translate to both places and faces (see also Nunnally 2017; Hayes et al., this volume).

The challenge of diversifying heritage spaces is perhaps the easiest to address. In the United States, several federal agencies, notably the National Park Service (NPS), are already focused on ensuring that a more diverse range of heritage is included in current preservation efforts (Baker et al. 2009; Kaufman 2004). The NPS's Second Century Commission, assembled in anticipation of the agency's 2016 centennial, addressed this issue directly. Remarking on declining numbers of visitors to national parks and the preponderance of middle-class European Americans among them (Chen et al. 2009: 1, 11; see also Johanson 2013; Taylor et al. 2011), Commissioner Maria Hinojosa suggested that it was not enough to welcome nontraditional visitors when they showed up: "The National Park Service must find ways to invite new publics into the parks" (Baker et al. 2009: 22). The same could be said of all heritage spaces. "Everyone should be able to walk in the footsteps of our history" (Baker et al. 2009: 17).

One way of captivating new publics is to capture a greater range of sites. Broadening this net plays to the strength of archaeologists, as they are often the ones who identify and investigate heritage places. This approach does not call on them to modify existing practices beyond increasing the diversity of what they investigate, and current trends suggest such a change is already under way. A growing number of graduate students choose to focus on African American or other underrepresented archaeologies. At the same time, archaeologists are increasingly incorporating public outreach and community involvement in their project planning. As Connor (2013: 29) notes: "Culture and identity do not exist in isolation. Place and community connect identity with culture" (cited in King 2016a, 2016b). To those familiar with place-based educational theory (see Sobel 2013), this view of heritage and community comes as no surprise. Having community members participate in the investigation of their own heritage ensures a more balanced representation of the past (Shackel, this volume). It can also rally the community (Bohlin 2011) and affirm its collective identity (Holtorf 2010; Shackel, this volume), thereby giving members a greater stake in preservation. Co-creation of knowledge and memory (Bollwerk et al. 2015), or involving the community in all stages of the project and its outcomes, can be an especially powerful form of outreach (for example, B. Clark, this volume). By incorporating a diverse range of viewpoints into our narratives, especially Indigenous ones, we reach a more complex and nuanced historical understanding (Lane-Kamahele 2016: 121, cited in Nunnally 2017). Many countries are now progressing toward just such a more inclusive "official heritage" (Chilton 2013), although most are still far from agreement.

The second challenge, people recognizing themselves in heritage practitioners, has proved more intractable. Despite recruitment efforts by universities and national agencies in the United States, for example, recent statistics show that practitioners remain overwhelmingly European American (for example, American Anthropological Association [AAA] 2016; U.S. Forest Service [USFS] 2013; NPS 2010, 2015). While we can hope that the inclusion of a more diverse range of heritage in national repertoires will attract more diverse specialists in the future (Chilton 2013), that remedy will take some time. We need the new perspectives offered by different voices now, not only to round out our views of the past, but also to help identify the heritage worth saving.

It is also unclear how well this site-focused approach will work alone, as the root of the problem lies in heritage education—how we attract, select, and groom the next generation of specialists. It is only recently that heritage studies have been defined as an interdisciplinary academic domain (Harrison 2010). Most university programs remain in their infancy and very few are associated with specific heritage degrees, all of them at the graduate level (King 2014; see also Hayes et al. and MacDonald, this volume). It is too early to tell, then, how these new curricula will affect heritage education and awareness overall. Students today generally still enter into heritage careers by going through traditional programs in affiliated subjects, such as archaeology and museum studies, followed by on-the-job training. Unfortunately, these are precisely the types of majors that are failing to attract a diverse population. The remainder of this chapter addresses the lack of practitioner diversity from the perspective of archaeology in the United States, outlining the scope of the problem and suggesting some remedies, with special attention to two underrepresented groups, African Americans and American Indians.

## Defining the Problem

Statistics from a sampling of federal agencies and professional organizations demonstrate the lack of diversity among heritage practitioners in the United States and underscore the scope and nature of the problem. As of the U.S. Census in 2010, less than 73 percent of both the population and the labor force[2] were European American (Humes et al. 2011: 4). During that same period (2008–2011), statistics collected by federal agencies and professional organizations show that this group disproportionately occupied heritage positions, from cultural resource management (CRM) firms to universities to local, state, and federal governments, despite attempts to rectify the situation.

In FY 2010, the total workforce of the U.S. Forest Service (USFS) was 86 percent European American, while the Bureau of Land Management (BLM) registered 84 percent in the same category (USFS 2013). That same year, an Equal Employment Opportunity report from the NPS showed that a total of 82.5 percent of all NPS employees, both permanent and seasonal, were European American/White. This finding suggests that most ethnic minorities were underrepresented in the parks (see Table 5.1),[3] a situation that had persisted for the previous three fiscal years (NPS 2010). Additionally, many of the ethnic minorities employed at the NPS were not in supervisory or managerial positions, which remained dominated by European Americans (NPS 2010: table A3-1), particularly in the four highest-paid employment categories (NPS 2010).[4] Significantly, when it came to heritage-specific positions such as archaeologists, historians, or museum curators, the proportion of European Americans in the NPS was even higher, over 90 percent (NPS 2010: table A6).

The numbers from different professional organizations frequented by heritage practitioners, specifically archaeologists, are equally dismal. A comparison of membership surveys made around the same time as the 2010 Census indicates that an overwhelming number of people in these orga-

Table 5.1. Comparison of FY 2010 National Civilian Labor Force and National Park Service workforce compositions

| Race/Ethnicity | National Civilian Labor Force totals | | | NPS Workforce totals | | |
| --- | --- | --- | --- | --- | --- | --- |
| | Female | Male | All | Female | Male | All |
| Black or African American | 5.7% | 4.8% | 10.5% | 2.9% | 4.1% | 7.0% |
| American Indian or Alaska Native | 0.3% | 0.3% | 0.6% | 0.8% | 1.7% | 2.5% |
| Asian | 1.7% | 1.9% | 3.6% | 0.8% | 0.8% | 1.6% |
| Native Hawaiian or Other Pacific Islander | 0.1% | 0.1% | 0.2% | 0.2% | 0.5% | 0.7% |
| White | 33.7% | 39.0% | 72.7% | 30.7% | 51.8% | 82.5% |
| Hispanic or Latino/a | 4.5% | 6.2% | 10.7% | 1.7% | 3.1% | 4.8% |
| Two or More Races | 0.8% | 0.9% | 1.7% | 0.4% | 0.5% | 0.9% |
| *Totals* | *46.8%* | *53.2%* | *100.0%* | *37.5%* | *62.5%* | *100.0%* |

Source: Humes et al. 2011: 4; National Park Service 2010: Table A1.
Notes: While American Indians/Alaska Natives and Native Hawaiians/Other Pacific Islanders are represented in the NPS at a higher rate than in the general workforce, these employees are mostly craft workers (National Park Service 2010: 69, and Table A3-1).

nizations, too, were European American (see Table 5.2). Superficially, the percentages among anthropologists seem more in sync with the general population; only 73.8 percent of AAA members self-identified as "White." Scholars in this discipline, however, tend to feel such antipathy toward racial classifications that many regularly refuse to put down their ethnicity or simply mark "other." It is likely, then, that the actual percentage of European Americans in the AAA was higher, based on trends in the rest of the data.[5] Even without knowing absolute numbers, the data in Table 5.2 show that the total number of non-"White" or mixed ethnicities in the AAA came to less than 19 percent, whereas in the national labor force it was 27.3 percent during the same time period (AAA 2011).

In archaeology-focused organizations, the picture was even worse. In assessments of member needs conducted by the Society for Historical Archaeology (SHA) in 2008 and the Society for American Archaeology (SAA) in 2010, the majority of members answered the question on ethnicity,[6] and most self-identified as "White/European origin." In the SAA, all other ethnicities, including the category of "other," comprised only 16.3 percent of the total (SAA 2010). In the SHA, the contrast was even more striking—non-European American categories combined accounted for less than 10 percent of the membership (SHA 2008). These figures are troublesome, particularly for the SHA, whose "disciplinary foundations" lie in "the archaeology of Af-

Table 5.2. Summary comparison of membership survey data from three professional organizations

| Ethnicity | AAA | SHA | SAA | National Civilian Labor Force |
|---|---|---|---|---|
| Black/African origin | 2.5% | 0.8% | 0.2% | 10.5% |
| American Indian/Alaskan Native | 1.4% | 1.6% | 1.1% | 0.6% |
| Asian | 4.8% | 0.9% | — | 3.6% |
| Pacific Islander | — | 0.1% | — | 0.2% |
| Asian/Pacific Islander | — | — | 1.7% | — |
| White/European origin | 73.8% | 90.7% | 83.7% | 72.7% |
| Hispanic/Latino/a | 6.2% | 2.4% | 5.8% | 10.7% |
| Two or More Races/Multiracial | 4.0% | — | 2.7% | 1.7% |
| Other | 7.3% | 3.5% | 4.8% | — |
| Totals | 100% | 100% | 100% | 100% |

Sources: AAA 2011 Membership Survey data (as of 2/25/2013); SHA Members Needs Assessment Survey 2008; and SAA Members Needs Assessment Survey 2010.
Note: The rates for the SHA have been adjusted proportionally to total 100%, because people self-identified in several categories rather than just using "Other," so the actual total = 102.7%.
— = Not applicable.

rican American lifeways" and those of "other disenfranchised members of our society" (Joseph 2016: 3). One would expect a discipline founded on diversity to exhibit the most, not the least, diversity among its researchers.

Since that time, these trends appear to have continued, despite the efforts of federal agencies and professional organizations alike to increase diversity. In response to reports by the National Parks Second Century Commission (Baker et al. 2009; Chen et al. 2009; Rogers et al. 2009) that emphasized the importance of increasing employee diversity in the parks, the NPS launched an initiative on cultural diversity. It established the Office of Relevancy, Diversity and Inclusiveness (NPS 2016b) to encourage "diversity as a practice that allows employees to develop in an inclusive environment," and to offer supportive programs to effect such a transformation (Brian Joyner, personal communication 2016). The NPS now also has programs devoted to diversity recruitment and support, and its Web pages deliberately feature a diverse array of individuals, from visitors to park rangers (for example, NPS 2016a; Brian Joyner, personal communication 2016). Similarly, the USFS has implemented a Multicultural Workforce Strategic Initiatives Program aimed specifically at recruiting students of diverse backgrounds (USFS 2013). These programs are in their early days, however, and such recruitment shifts take a long time to develop and document. From 2010 through

2015, the last year analyzed, the percentages of minorities in the NPS have fluctuated slightly without changing significantly (NPS 2015; see also Table 5.1).

The story is similar among the professional organizations. The 2016 AAA membership survey reports the same basic numbers as the 2011 one did, showing, if anything, slightly less diversity (see Table 5.2). The numbers for AAA archaeologists, available in 2016, reveal even greater disparities, similar to those reported earlier by the professional archaeological organizations, and most likely this represents the continuation of an earlier trend.[7] The SHA, meanwhile, commissioned its Gender and Minority Affairs Committee to look into the issue of discrimination within the organization. The committee reported its findings to the board, and the organization has since made a concerted effort not only to encourage diversity but also to combat racism actively, both within and outside the organization (Flordeliz Bugarin, personal communication 2016). The SHA has sponsored antiracism workshops at its annual meetings and has adopted a multipronged Diversity Initiative that includes reaching out to non–European American communities to teach them about the potential relevance of historical archaeology and its findings to their lives and, hopefully, to recruit new practitioners (Joseph 2016). In the SAA, the most recent developments concern the emergence in 2013 of the new Queer Archaeology Interest Group (QAIG), representing another minority whose voices have also been largely absent in traditional archaeology.

While steps such as these are promising, they are not sufficient to address the whole problem of diversity among heritage practitioners. Ultimately, both the professional organizations that support archaeologists and the federal, state, and local agencies that employ them depend on the education sector to produce new recruits. Nonacademic institutions can provide scholarships, internships, and summer programs that help spur students on to heritage careers, but colleges and universities are the ones largely responsible for attracting, training, and mentoring future professionals. Unfortunately, judging by current statistics, their programs so far are failing to attract a diversified group of students. This is especially true for archaeology, a subject that has the potential to reveal otherwise hidden truths about our diverse past that mainstream history has not recorded. It should by all rights entice people of underrepresented backgrounds to become archaeologists, yet fails to live up to its potential. The following section examines why.

## The Problem within Archaeology

Archaeology can offer people an important way to reclaim and elucidate their heritage. It is also a unique, interdisciplinary hybrid of the humanities and STEM (science, technology, engineering, and math) disciplines, including both the natural and the social sciences. Additionally, it promotes critical thinking (Hamilakis 2004; Shackel, this volume), an important objective at most universities. One would think, then, that archaeology would be appealing to a broad constituency and esteemed by every academic administrator. The reverse, however, is more often true. Why? Recent experiences at Howard University, a Historically Black College and University (HBCU), suggest that the reasons lie in a subtle mix of barriers that include misperceptions of the field, finances, and programming issues.

### Misperceptions

Archaeology occupies an ambiguous place in contemporary society: it is universally recognized yet relatively unknown. While almost everyone could give a definition of what they think archaeology entails, from the erroneous ("dinosaurs," "looking for treasure") to the accurate ("digging," "exploring the past"), they usually do not see it as a versatile STEM science that combines a variety of methods and approaches. Even less do they think of it as relevant to their lives (see also Zimmerman, this volume). As one Howard student put it while reflecting on a recent archaeological experience, "I did not know how much archaeologists contribute to history and our assessment of the culture" (King 2008: 226). Indeed, the discipline is often viewed as dilettantish and out of step with the contemporary world. This same student had previously thought that archaeology was reserved for "older, white men" in khakis digging in exotic places (King 2008: 226).

There are few archaeological role models visible in the media. Television abounds with doctors, lawyers, nurses, detectives, businessmen, and even forensic scientists, but archaeologists tend to be overlooked, aside from the occasional special on public networks or the Discovery Channel. The shows that do include them often provide bad or inaccurate examples (for example, the National Geographic Channel's "Diggers"; King and Epstein 2015; see also Watkins, this volume.) In movies, archaeology is generally exoticized, placing it outside the experience of most people (King and Epstein 2015). As for social media, they are self-selecting platforms; despite the best efforts of archaeologists to promote themselves through Facebook, Twitter, blogs, and other venues, their reach is restricted to those with a pre-existing interest in archaeology. Most people therefore have few opportunities to correct their misperceptions of the field.

To many working in predominantly European American universities, the consequences of this invisibility or undervisibility may seem slight. Undergraduate and graduate programs teem with eager young apprentices ready to learn the craft. However, in places that serve a different population, the consequences of these misperceptions can be dire. Effective 2015, the anthropology major at Howard University was cut, despite the high profile and quantifiable successes of the program's archaeology component, which had been featured in news reports, the alumni magazine, and promotional materials (for example, Hamilton 2006; Howard University Office of Sponsored Research 2010). Archaeology students also consistently won first prizes based on their fieldwork in the annual Undergraduate Research Symposium of the College of Arts and Sciences. When discussing the cuts, senior administrators indicated that they viewed archaeology as nonessential "enrichment." African American audiences echoed the same sentiment during presentations I made with students on archaeological fieldwork. The curricula at other HBCUs further support the perceived irrelevance of archaeology to this community. In 2010 when the decision to cut Howard's program was made, only 10 out of 102 HBCUs offered any archaeology at all. Of those, only Howard offered specific classes beyond the introductory course, although four others had classes that incorporated archaeology in their history programs.[8]

Misperceptions about archaeology are not confined to African Americans, but cut across generally poor, disenfranchised populations. Among American Indian nations, the problem is compounded by a generalized mistrust of the archaeological community arising from previous conflicts over NAGPRA and other issues (see related discussions in Sievert et al.; Watkins, this volume). In addition, specific spiritual beliefs often preclude any involvement in archaeological projects. In this climate it is difficult to argue that archaeology can offer people a unique way to reclaim and elucidate their undocumented past.

## Finances

The financial realities of higher education also play a role in deterring minorities from archaeology. Since the recession of 2008, many students find themselves unable to secure hitherto routine educational loans, often because of their parents' credit status. More than a few Howard students have dropped out of college in the last few years due to that problem, as well as to rising tuition costs. Those who are first-generation-in-college have the added pressure of making certain their families' expenditures are well invested. As tuition and other costs become ever more expensive, many students do not feel they have the leisure to experiment with unproven career paths. They perceive the financial constraints as pressure to choose courses of study, such as pre-med, that lead to readily identifiable employment. Exacerbating this pressure is the current "utilism" or "needs and scarcity-driven behavior" (Sahlins 1996: 397) in higher education that emphasizes technical training for specific jobs rather than big-picture or critical thinking (Hamilakis 2004; Shackel, this volume). Misperceived as they are, the fields of archaeology and anthropology (archaeology's umbrella subject in the United States) seem even more esoteric in this climate. Indeed, they often feature prominently in lists of impractical majors put forth by politicians and pundits.

Contributing to this image problem is the fact that few students are exposed to archaeology at the precollegiate level. While they may touch on it in a history class, they rarely engage with archaeology (see White 2019). The increased focus on mandatory testing has all but squeezed out the few archaeology programs that once existed. "Heritage" as a concept is not specifically taught except in the generic sense of what we as a group of people may have inherited from the past. With the exception of history, heritage fields are thus largely unavailable to students until they get to college. Unfortunately, freshmen are often required to declare their majors when they first register—before they have been academically exposed to archaeology and other heritage fields. While students may change their majors at a later date, finances dictate they do so cautiously, to avoid delaying graduation. Accumulating more expenses does not make sense, especially when students know that securing a job after college will take time. They may therefore be averse to exploring domains in which they might otherwise thrive, such as archaeology, turning instead to more familiar fields. For the same reason, students who discover a passion for archaeology over the course of their college studies may be disinclined to pursue it.

## Programming

If we are to answer the questions raised at the beginning of this chapter about who owns the past and whose past we are preserving, we first need to ask, "Whose past are we teaching?" Since the 1960s, university programming in archaeology, like that in most disciplines, has evolved to make room for increasingly diversified points of view. The concomitant growth of historical archaeology during that time has driven home, too, the importance of focusing on a wider range of time periods than the traditional prehistoric past taught in many U.S. programs. Universities now offer coursework in historical archaeology, the archaeology of gender and ethnicity, and the archaeology of specific ethnic groups. However, it is not enough to offer the odd topical class; we need to weave diversity into the very fabric of what we do, from introductory to specialized courses. Otherwise we relegate it to being an afterthought rather than an integral part of the archaeological perspective—an elective rather than a core concept. Archaeologists have become better over recent years at consulting communities about fieldwork and working collaboratively with them to co-create knowledge. This process allows all the parties involved to become more actively engaged with the past and its interpretation. Perhaps it is time we do something similar for curriculum development as well.

Adding urgency to this issue is the deep-seated belief among many minority ethnic groups that high-achieving members have an obligation to "give back." It is not enough for students to achieve personal success; they must use it to the advantage of their communities. This ethic is so strongly rooted among African Americans that at Howard "community service" is a significant category in faculty promotion, and the image of the "activist scholar" is widely touted on campus. That is another reason, beside finances, why the more familiar disciplines like law or medicine are so popular. Not only do they lead to readily identifiable jobs, but to intuitively obvious ways of giving back to the community. Lawyers can defend the unjustly accused; doctors can open inner-city clinics. What can archaeologists do? If students do not recognize themselves in the archaeology being taught, they fail to understand that it could help their communities by giving voice to a voiceless past. After all, for many disenfranchised groups not traditionally represented in the history books, archaeology is one of the best ways of telling their stories and reclaiming their heritage.

Addressing these concerns in the classroom is not enough, however. Most archaeologists would probably agree that they were first seduced into the profession through fieldwork, with its heady combination of physical, intellectual, and even interpersonal challenges. You can study a stratigraphic diagram all you want; nothing beats feeling those layers slip through your fingers. There is a special wonder that comes to students when they experience that visceral connection to their own past. Touching it leaves an indelible impression; studying it reaffirms who and what they are. While field schools today incorporate a wide variety of subject areas and time periods, there are still too few that target the concerns and interests of specific minority groups. Such hands-on training, in conjunction with a more focused academic program, is vital. It serves not only to interest students in archaeology initially, but also to stimulate them to pursue it—or related heritage fields—as a career.

While there is no single template for devising archaeology programs that will better attract diverse students, the one we implemented at Howard offers some insights as to how targeted programming can work.

## The Howard University Archaeology Program
## and Warriors Project Archaeology

As previously mentioned, Howard's Anthropology Program is now defunct. Neither major nor minor remained as of the end of the 2014–15 academic year, although the program's faculty members still offer a few anthropology classes through the various departments in which they have taken refuge. Before its closure, however, the program was situated in the Department of Sociology and Anthropology[9] and trained undergraduates in a full four-field approach to the discipline that was both academic and applied. In fact, Howard was the only HBCU to do so. When I originally joined the Howard faculty in 2001, students could only minimally specialize, due to a dearth of professors and of classes beyond the introductory level. Over time, however, my colleagues and I managed to shape the Anthropology Program into one that focused increasingly on African American heritage.

Heritage, as in all of the tangible and intangible things we inherit from a common past, is a unifying theme on Howard's campus, where classes focus on the African American experience from the initial diaspora to the present day. Disciplines and courses across the university stress the contributions that people of African descent have made. Prominent is their story in the New World, where resistance and resilience enabled these forced immigrants to develop a new and vibrant culture from the ashes of the many old ones they carried with them. This quintessentially American story of immigrants' triumph against all odds helps ground students at Howard and other HBCUs and prepare them for a world outside the campus that is often still hostile. By "re-membering" they counteract the "dismemberment" caused by the Middle Passage and slavery (Thiong'o 2009).

The research of all four faculty members in anthropology was heritage-related, so marrying archaeology to the theme of recapturing the past was a natural step. Two of us were archaeologists, the third a bioarchaeologist, and the fourth a linguist interested in African legacies in the New World. We extended the reach of the more traditional coursework by converting classes such as "Method and Theory in Archaeology" into focused discussions of Africa and the African Diaspora. Even in general classes such as "Introduction to Archaeology," for example, we augmented the usual methods and "stones and bones" coverage with more diverse examples, including specific discussions of African American archaeology. We supplemented formal classes with internships and independent studies that allowed students to delve more deeply into specific topics that interested them. Central to this effort were field projects that encouraged participation by a wide variety of students, not just the best and the brightest, as well as student research. The latter generally took place after the fieldwork ended, as independent studies leading to presentations at professional conferences, such as the annual meetings of the AAA, SAA, and SHA. Typically, students would make the same presentation, often a poster, in the annual college research symposium, where, as noted, they consistently won first place, sometimes sweeping second and/or third place as well in the same competition.

Due to its longevity, the field project that reached the most students was the Warriors Project Archaeology (WPA) program I directed in the Southwest. This program had the added benefit of involving another important group of underrepresented students—American Indians, specifically the Apache. It developed as part of a larger National Park Service initiative, the Warriors Project, which since 2002 has encouraged African Americans and American Indians to discuss their mutual past on the frontier. WPA research centered on the interaction between the Buffalo Soldiers, the African American regiments of the U.S. Army created after the Civil War, and the Apache, specifically the Warm Springs band, during the last of the Apache Wars in the late 1870s. The program comprised two subprojects, one in the Guadalupe Mountains National Park in Texas from 2004 to 2006, and the other in the Gila National Forest in New Mexico from 2008 to 2011. Our research focused primarily on documenting the camp and battle sites associated with the two warring groups and the interaction of both soldiers and warriors with nonmilitary Anglo and Hispanic pioneers. We also examined the different ways each group used the landscape (King 2016a).

While the research was productive, the main purpose of the WPA was student training. The goal was to take students who had never before been in the field and actively expose them to archaeology related to their heritage. Participants included African American undergraduates, primarily from Howard, and American Indian students, mostly Apache. From the beginning, the project partnered with the Mescalero Apache Tribe, whose students joined us every year. In the last year, two San Carlos Apache students also participated. Added to the mix were European- and Hispanic American as well as international students and staff. The crew typically ranged from high schoolers to graduate students, with the occasional middle schooler from Mescalero (King 2016a). Training focused on survey—an important component of CRM jobs—and excavation, using a variety of approaches from metal-detection to ground-penetrating radar to test pits.

The exposure to field life was just as important to students as the professional training was. Field schools were short, averaging two to three weeks. Project personnel lived together in remote housing and everyone rotated camp duties such as cooking and cleaning. This isolation, typical of many field schools, helped the group bond, but, to avoid overwhelming the students, workweeks were broken up with visits to nearby towns and archaeological or historic sites. The WPA program covered all student and staff expenses, including travel to and from the field school, local transportation, and meals both in camp and in town (King 2016a).

Although students were the mainstay of the project, another aspect was community involvement. Mescalero archaeologists and representatives from our government partners (the NPS and USFS) regularly augmented our ranks, as did other visitors, including volunteers, professional archaeologists, and officials from other agencies. In addition, Mescalero tribal members ranging from elders to children visited the project midseason every year. In the last few seasons, archaeologists from the White Mountain Apache Tribe joined them, as well as representatives from the Fort Sill and San Carlos Apache Tribes. These visitors were important to the basic training as they offered additional knowledge about the area we were investigating—geological, botanical, zoological, and historical. The Apache visitors in particular had a wealth of information on local plants and animals and their traditional uses (compare Herr 2013). For the non-Apache students, it was an eye-opening introduction to cultures very different from their own. For the Apache students, it was an opportunity to showcase their history. They also found it reassuring to touch base with their families and friends after being immersed among strangers (King 2016a).

The program altogether was very successful in reaching diverse students and encouraging them to pursue archaeology. During seven years of fieldwork, fifty-five students participated, of whom forty-seven, or 85.5 percent, were members of ethnic minorities (see Table 5.3). Of these forty-seven, one was already pursuing a master's degree, eight went on to graduate school in archaeology, four went to graduate school in anthropology, and one received his doctorate in history.[10] Some of those archaeology students worked in cultural resource management or cultural heritage while they were studying, as did two additional Mescalero participants. Several students were already on this trajectory before participating in the WPA program, but it is clear from their comments and recollections that the program spurred them on. As a Howard alumna wrote from her graduate program at New Mexico State University, "My experience . . . was truly enlightening. I am modeling my professional career on what we have done in the . . . [Warriors] Project. I am going to be a historical archaeologist and continue this kind of work" (Linsey Richbow, personal communication

Table 5.3. Warriors Project Archaeology outcomes

| Ethnicity | Total participants | Archaeology grad school | Related grad school | Work in cultural heritage |
|---|---|---|---|---|
| African American | 30 | 7 | 5 | — |
| Apache & other American Indian | 13 | 1 | — | 4 |
| Hispanic or Latino/a | 3 | — | — | 1 |
| Filipino-American | 1 | 1 | — | 1 |
| *Total ethnic minority participants* | *47* | *9* | *5* | *6* |
| European or European American | 8 | 2 | — | 1 |
| *Total participants* | *55* | *11* | *5* | *7* |
| *% of ethnic minority participants* | 85.5% | 19.1% | 10.6% | 12.8% |
| *% of total participants* | 100.0% | 20.0% | 9.1% | 12.7% |

*Source*: Courtesy of the author.

*Note*: There is some overlap between archaeology graduate school and cultural heritage work, as at least three of the graduate students also worked in CRM and/or in NFS summer internships (one American Indian, one Filipino-American, and one European American). Factoring in this overlap, the total % of ethnic minority students involved in heritage-related studies or work = 38.3%; the total number of student participants overall involved in such work = 38.2%.

— = Not applicable.

2007). In all, 34 percent of the non–European American students engaged in heritage-related studies or work after the program.

Perhaps most exciting were the sixteen students among them who chose to return to the program or to participate in another field school I run in Belize (King 2016a). Most of these "repeats" were from Howard, but one San Carlos Apache student joined us in Belize in 2012. She was so impressed by the experience, which she said opened new worlds for her people (Twila Cassadore, personal communication 2012), that she obtained money from her tribe to return the following year on another project with three other San Carlos students. Among the WPA students who pursued additional fieldwork, eight participated in three or more field seasons, often moving from field student to supervisor in the process.

The overall results of the Howard programming were dramatic. Before we began emphasizing fieldwork, very few students experienced the field and even fewer went into archaeology as a career—I know of only three who did from 1990 to 2005. Between 2005 and the closure of the program in 2015, we sent six students for master's degrees or PhDs in archaeology specifically, while five more pursued advanced degrees in related fields. Another student transferred from Howard but has since matriculated for a

PhD in archaeology. Thus, we more than doubled the number of archaeologists we produced.

## Lessons Learned

While many lessons could be drawn from the Howard Anthropology Program and the WPA, four stand out in terms of creating hands-on heritage programs that will appeal to diverse students. First, students must participate in archaeology/heritage that is directly relevant to them. As one Howard student noted, "Working on [this project] placed me face-to-face with the realities of my history." The power of this connection cannot be overstated, precisely because, as noted, heritage is so central to our individual and collective identities. Being able to touch their own heritage helps students realize that, in the words of another Howard student, "history and culture are not distant, intangible concepts that . . . can only be access[ed] in books or on Google."

Second, field seasons need to be short in order to attract students of varied backgrounds, especially low-income or younger students. (The same may apply to other forms of apprenticeship and internship.) A shorter season has several advantages. To begin with, it allows even modestly funded projects to cover expenses for students who cannot pay their own way. It also takes less time away from summer jobs so that students can pursue both opportunities. Even so, several Howard students backed out of Warriors Project Archaeology at the last minute because they ultimately could not afford the time off. Among the Apache students, the conflict was even more noticeable. Most of those who joined the program were high schoolers because college-age students could not leave their jobs. This issue could be resolved with subsidies that pay students to work, like those available through the National Science Foundation's Research Experiences for Undergraduates (REU) program. However, these grants mandate longer research periods, usually at least ten weeks, and there are other advantages to a shorter field season. For students who have never been out of a city or far from home, two weeks will generally meet their quotas for nature, heritage, and close-quarters living with strangers. The shorter time span makes for a manageable first adventure, particularly for younger students. REUs also assume that students are adequately prepared to move from dependent to independent research in a single season, that is, from working on someone

Figure 5.1. Student participants Alina Epstein (Richard Montgomery High School, *left*) and Linsey Richbow (Howard University, *right*) share a screen during the Warriors Project Archaeology program in the Guadalupe Mountains National Park, 2006. Mixing ages can help unify diverse groups. Photograph courtesy of Eleanor King.

else's ideas to working on their own. In reality, however, many students need more stepping-stones, which shorter field seasons provide (King 2016a).

Third, cultivating academic and age diversity in field schools and other practical learning situations has wide-ranging benefits. It gives students a more realistic sense of their own talents and limitations. As many project directors know, the academically gifted do not necessarily make the best fieldworkers or practical learners, while students who seem the least "serious" academically often flourish in the field due to its hands-on nature. In another vein, high schoolers in the WPA program learned that college students did not necessarily know or do everything better than they did. Often, the younger students had a better understanding of the environment and a surer grasp of excavation technique. Suddenly, college seemed more attainable. Having graduate students also in the mix similarly showed the undergraduates and younger students that advanced training might be possible. These realizations helped participants gain perspective on themselves and also unified the group, as members came to depend on each other.

The fourth and final lesson from the Howard experience is that mentoring is critical to the success of any heritage program, especially in hands-on specialties like archaeology. Although many field situations do not allow for one-on-one mentoring, it is especially important when the environment, the people, and the work are unknown to students. Close mentoring relationships help students unaccustomed to the very idea of archaeology become bolder in their investigations. Given the lack of role models among heritage practitioners, mentoring is particularly critical for helping minority students forge a career through uncharted terrain. Many of the Howard graduates who are pursuing advanced degrees have been lucky enough to find good mentors in their respective institutions. Nevertheless, several continue to touch base with us at Howard because, as they are fond of saying, they know we have their backs; alumni have repeatedly commented that it was individual mentoring by the entire faculty, not just one member, that helped them obtain their undergraduate degrees and decide on their careers.

Conclusions

Preserving the past to inform the future will require energetic collaborations across disciplines as well as reimagined programming. It will also demand greater inclusiveness. If we are to educate both future professionals and the public to care about our shared heritage, then we need to make sure that the net we spread is wide. That goes for both the heritage we want to preserve and the practitioners we want to encourage. While we have made some progress in diversifying the sites we protect, we still have not succeeded very well in recruiting a diverse group of heritage professionals, especially archaeologists, despite the best efforts of national agencies and university programs.

Several factors contribute to the lack of current practitioner diversity, requiring a multipronged approach. Professional organizations and federal agencies are best placed to remedy public misperceptions of the role of archaeology and heritage. They can also help address the cultural and financial barriers for potential students, who do not view heritage studies as a viable career option. These groups have the collective clout to counteract incorrect popular images and put forth accurate information. They also have the capacity to reach out to underrepresented populations at a young age; Project Archaeology and other precollegiate programs are perhaps our most effective means of doing so (King and Epstein 2015). The focus on diversity recruitment among federal agencies entrusted with cultural heritage also promises to have an impact in the long term. Paid internships and grants targeting underrepresented students can go a long way toward mitigating financial constraints.

A core issue remains programming, however, and it is here that individual archaeologists in academia can have an impact. Archaeologists have generally failed to promote the relevance of archaeology in universities (Hamilakis 2004), and they have not been entirely successful at developing programming that appeals to a wide range of students. The experiences of the Howard Anthropology Program and the WPA, however, provide insights into these problems and possible solutions, which can be generalized to other heritage programs.

First, universities should institute more targeted programming, focusing on the specific heritage of the people we want to attract. While many institutions will need to remain broad in scope to cater to all comers, they can make their offerings more deliberately inclusive. Centering entire programs around issues such as social justice (Shackel, this volume) and the meaning of heritage can also help diversity programming by exposing differences and incongruities in our views of the past.

Second, hands-on activities like internships and fieldwork should be key to any archaeological programming. As Howard field projects routinely became part of the anthropology major's canon of study, they attracted even students not primarily interested in archaeology. Some of them switched their concentration as a result. Most commented in retrospect that being exposed to field-based inquiry is what made them interested in pursuing graduate studies—even in unrelated fields.

Third, short field seasons are a must for both financial and pedagogical reasons. No archaeological or other heritage program is going to attract diversity unless it has adequate funding to support students, especially for fieldwork. Besides paid internships, one way to make this happen is via a shorter field season, as it still gives students time to earn summer funds. In addition, a shorter season allows more tentative students to try archaeology without the heavy commitment many traditional field schools demand. It can help them transition more gradually, too, from dependent to independent learner. If we are to get serious about supporting diversity, we need to develop funding that will cater to this kind of field experience rather than to the usual model.

Overall, archaeologists need to pay better attention to pedagogy than they have been willing to do in the past (Hamilakis 2004). Besides exposing students to hands-on learning situations in a way that will most attract and benefit them, we need to take into account different learning styles and cultural backgrounds (Connor 2013; Johnson 2012; King 2008, 2016b; Reetz and Quackenbush 2016; Scheuerman et al. 2010; Watkins, this volume). We should use pedagogies that address the needs of the multicultural classroom (Connor 2013) while building on students' existing cultural knowledge (Scheuerman et al. 2010). Only by consciously confronting these issues will we be able to reach a wider range of students and ensure their future participation in archaeology and other heritage-related fields (King 2016b). The Howard experience suggests that a part of this approach should be strong mentoring throughout a course of study. These efforts need not necessarily be coordinated, but mentoring should be the basic principle informing faculty-student interactions. Such sustained mentoring helps steady students on their course through heretofore-unimagined territory and gives them the benefit of advice from different points of view.

In sum, as we seek to include students of diverse and academically varied backgrounds in archaeology and heritage studies, we need to pursue diversity on many different levels. The necessity of diversity in content is a given. Diversity in pedagogical approaches is also needed, however, and promises to help revitalize our programs more generally, as we seek to accommodate a range of learners. The bottom line is that, if we do not devote conscious and sustained effort to these issues, we are dooming ourselves. The power balance is shifting. On the one hand, neither heritage studies nor archaeology has a future without diverse voices claiming their stake. On the other hand, working to widen our circle will ensure that exciting, fresh ideas and perspectives become an ongoing reality.

## Acknowledgments

Thanks to Phyllis Messenger and Susan Bender for inviting me to be part of their 2013 SAA symposium and this book. The NPS, the USFS, Howard University, Indiana University of Pennsylvania (IUP), and the Ladder Ranch all provided funding, expertise, and/or material support to Warriors Project Archaeology (WPA). The following individuals were especially helpful: Fred Armstrong, Gorden Bell, Charles Haecker, John Lujan, Pat O'Brien, and Jan Wobbenhorst from the NPS; Christopher Adams and Larry Cosper from the USFS; Steve Dobrott from the Ladder Ranch; and Beverly Chiarulli from IUP. Richard Thomas and Daniel Ginsberg (AAA), Karen Hutchison (SHA), Meghan Moran and Alyssa Barnett (SAA), and Barbara Little, Brian Joyner, and Katrina Reyes (NPS) helped me locate statistics for their respective organizations. My thanks go to them and to the crews of the WPA, as well as to Phyllis Messenger, Steve Epstein, and Alina Epstein, who not only edited but also helped me rethink my logic in several places. Any errors remaining are my own, however. Finally, I wish to salute my Howard colleagues, Flordeliz Bugarin, Arvilla Jackson, and the late Mark Mack, whose different ideas and teaching styles helped shape my own. Mark, this one's for you.

## Notes

1. In the United States, of course, archaeology is a part of anthropology, but in other parts of the world, the disciplines remain separate.

2. That is, 72.4 percent of the total population and 72.7 percent of the total labor force.

3. Lack of diversity in the NPS, it should be noted, extends to gender as well; males predominate in all categories except Asian (NPS 2010).

4. European Americans comprised 81.4 percent of all officials and managers, and 86 percent on average in each of the top four employment categories (Senior Executive Service through GS-13).

5. In addition, the rates for the AAA reflect not just archaeologists, but other practitioners.

6. Over 55 percent of the SHA membership responded to the survey, and, of that total, 97.8 percent answered the question on ethnicity. For the SAA survey, 47.6 percent of the membership responded, and, of those, 97.4 percent responded to the question.

7. Numbers of archaeologists for the 2011 AAA survey were not available.

8. These four include Jackson State University, North Carolina A & T State University, North Carolina Central University, and Oakwood University.

9. It is now the Department of Sociology and Criminology.

10. The figures in Table 5.3 include not only Howard students, but also two students from IUP (one of them already in graduate school there) and a student who transferred from Howard but has since gone on for her PhD.

# References Cited

American Anthropological Association (AAA)

2011    Membership Survey. On file with the American Anthropological Association. Accessed February 25, 2013.

2016    AAA 2016 Membership Survey_Subfield_Race. Excel table on file with the American Anthropological Association, Arlington, Virginia.

Baker, Howard H., Jr., J. Bennett Johnston, Linda Bilmes, James J. Blanchard, Milton Chen, Rita Colwell, Sylvia Earle, John Fahey, Belinda Faustinos, Victor Fazio, Jr., Carolyn Finney, Denis P. Galvin, Maria Hinojosa, Sally Jewell, Tony Knowles, Stephen H. Lockhart, Gretchen Long, James McPherson, Gary B. Nash, Sandra Day O'Connor, Jerry L. Rogers, Peter M. Senge, Deborah A. Shanley, W. Richard West, Jr., Margaret Wheatley, E. O. Wilson, Loran Fraser, and Rosemary Peterne

2009    *Advancing the National Park Idea.* National Parks Second Century Commission. Electronic document, http://www.npca.org/assets/pdf/Commission_Report. PDF. Accessed February 20, 2013.

Bohlin, Anna

2011    Idioms of Return: Homecoming and Heritage in the Rebuilding of Protea Village, Cape Town. *African Studies* 70(2): 284–301.

Bollwerk, Elizabeth, Robert Connolly, and Carol McDavid

2015    Co-Creation and Public Archaeology. *Advances in Archaeological Practice* 3(3): 178–187.

Carman, John, and Marie Louise Stig Sørensen

2009    Heritage Studies: An Outline. In *Heritage Studies. Methods and Approaches*, edited by M. L. Stig Sørensen and J. Carman, pp. 11–28. Routledge, New York.

Chen, Milton, Stephen H. Lockhart, Gary B. Nash, Sandra Day O'Connor, and Deborah A. Shanley

2009    Education and Learning Committee Report. *Advancing the National Park Idea.* National Parks Second Century Commission. Electronic document, http://www.npca.org/assets/pdf/Committee_Education_Report.PDF. Accessed March 25, 2013.

Chilton, Elizabeth

2013    Discussion Comments for "Lessons from the Trenches II: New Pedagogies of Archaeology and Heritage." Paper presented at the Society for American Archaeology 78th Annual Meeting, Honolulu.

Chirikure, Shadreck, and Gilbert Pwiti

2008    Community Involvement in Archaeology and Cultural Heritage Management. An Assessment from Case Studies in Southern Africa and Elsewhere. *Current Anthropology* 49(3): 467–485.

Colby, Sandra L., and Jennifer M. Ortman

2015    Projections of the Size and Composition of the U.S. Population: 2014–2060. *Population Estimates and Projections.* Current Population Reports. P25-1143, issued March, United States Census Bureau. Electronic document, https://www.

census.gov/content/dam/Census/library/publications/2015/demo/p25-1143.pdf. Accessed February 22, 2016.

Connor, Sloan

2013    Transforming Multicultural Classrooms through Creative Place-Based Learning. *Multicultural Education* 21(1): 26–32.

Fleming, Arlene K.

2010    Heritage Values, Public Policy, and Development. In *Heritage Values in Contemporary Society*, edited by George S. Smith, Phyllis Mauch Messenger, and Hilary A. Soderland, pp. 101–112. Left Coast Press, Walnut Creek, California.

Hamilakis, Yannis

2004    Archaeology and the Politics of Pedagogy. *World Archaeology* 36(2): 287–309.

Hamilton, Kerry-Ann

2006    Opening New Doors . . . Digging Enhances Degrees. *Howard Magazine* 14(2): 18–21 (Winter).

Harrison, Rodney

2010    What is Heritage? In *Understanding the Politics of Heritage*, edited by Rodney Harrison, pp. 5–42. Manchester University Press, Manchester, UK.

Herr, Sarah

2013    In Search of Lost Landscapes: the Pre-Reservation Western Apache Archaeology of Central Arizona. *American Antiquity* 78(4): 679–701.

Herrera, Alexander

2013    Heritage Tourism, Identity, and Development in Peru. *International Journal of Historical Archaeology* 17: 275–295.

Holtorf, Cornelius

2010    Heritage Values in Contemporary Popular Culture. In *Heritage Values in Contemporary Society*, edited by George S. Smith, Phyllis Mauch Messenger, and Hilary A. Soderland, pp. 43–54. Left Coast Press, Walnut Creek, California.

Howard University Office of Sponsored Research

2010    *Howard University's Partnership in the Desert Southwest Cooperative Ecosystems Study Unit.* Brochure prepared for the Cooperative Ecosystems Study Unit Network National Meeting, Washington, D.C., June 22–24.

Humes, Karen R., Nicholas A. Jones, and Roberto R. Ramirez

2011    Overview of Race and Hispanic Origin: 2010. *2010 Census Briefs.* Electronic document, http://www.census.gov/prod/cen2010/briefs/c2010br-02.pdf. Accessed March 2, 2013.

Johanson, Mark

2013    Missing in US National Parks: Minorities. *International Business Times*, September 9. Electronic document, http://www.ibtimes.com/missing-us-national-parks-minorities-1403613. Accessed May 27, 2015.

Johnson, Jay T.

2012    Place-based Learning and Knowing: Critical Pedagogies Grounded in Indigeneity. *GeoJournal* 77: 829–836.

Joseph, J. W.

2016    President's Corner. *Society for Historical Archaeology Newsletter* 49(2): 2–4.

Kaufman, Ned

2004    Cultural Heritage Needs Assessment: Phase I. Draft, April 8. Electronic document, http://www.cr.nps.gov/crdi/publications/PhaseIReport.pdf. Accessed February 26, 2013.

King, Eleanor M.

2008    Buffalo Soldiers, Apaches, and Cultural Heritage Education. *Heritage Management* 1(2): 219–241.

2014    Heritage and the Underrepresented: The Perspective from Howard University. Paper presented at the 79th Annual Meeting of the Society for American Archaeology, Austin, Texas.

2016a   Crossing Boundaries: Archaeology across Cultures and School Levels. Paper presented at the 117th Annual Meeting of the Archaeological Institute of America, San Francisco.

2016b   Systematizing Public Education in Archaeology. *Advances in Archaeological Practice* 4(4): 415–424.

King, Eleanor, and Stephen Epstein

2015    Where Are We Going? The Impact of Project Archaeology on the Profession, Past and Future. Paper presented at the 80th Annual Meeting of the Society for American Archaeology, San Francisco, California.

Lane-Kamahele, Melia

2016    Indigenous Voices. In *A Thinking Person's Guide to America's National Parks*, edited by Robert Manning, Rolf Diamant, Nora Mitchell, and David Harmon, pp. 117–126. George Braziller, New York.

National Park Service (NPS)

2010    *Equal Employment Opportunity Program Plan. Accomplishments for FY 2010 and Updates for FY 2011.* Report from the Equal Employment Opportunity of the National Park Service, Department of the Interior. Electronic document, NPS_MD715_Accomplishments_FY2010_Updates_FY2011_Masterfile (Rev 121710). pdf. Report on file with the National Park Service.

2015    2010–2015 Total Workforce. Report on file with the National Park Service.

2016a   Frequently Asked Questions. Electronic document, https://www.nps.gov/aboutus/faqs.htm. Accessed July 18, 2016.

2016b   Office of Relevance, Diversity and Inclusion. Electronic document, https://www.nps.gov/orgs/1244/index.htm. Accessed July 18, 2016.

Nunnally, Patrick

2017    National Parks: Can "America's Best Idea" Adjust to the Twenty-first Century? *Open Rivers: Rethinking Water, Place & Community, 7: 107–114.*

Reetz, Elizabeth C., and William Quackenbush

2016    Creative Collaborative Learning Opportunities for Indigenous Youth with Archaeology-based Environmental Education. *Advances in Archaeological Practice* 4(4): 492–502.

Rogers, Jerry L., Carolyn Finney, James McPherson, and W. Richard West, Jr.

2009    A Different Past in a Different Future. Cultural Resource and Historic Preservation Committee Report. *Advancing the National Park Idea.* National Parks Second Century Commission. Electronic document, http://www.npca.org/assets/pdf/Committee_Cultural_Resources.PDF. Accessed February 22, 2013.

Sahlins, Marshall

1996　The Sadness of Sweetness: The Native Anthropology of Western Cosmology. *Current Anthropology* 37(3): 395–665.

Scheuerman, Richard, Kristine Gritter, Carrie Jim Schuster, and Gordon Fisher

2010　Sharing the Fire: Place-Based Learning with Columbia Plateau Legends. *English Journal* 99(5): 47–54.

Shackel, Paul

2005　Memory, Civic Engagement and the Public Meaning of Archaeological Heritage. *SAA Archaeological Record* 5(2): 24–27.

Silberman, Neil Asher

2010　Technology, Heritage Values, and Interpretation. In *Heritage Values in Contemporary Society*, edited by George S. Smith, Phyllis Mauch Messenger, and Hilary A. Soderland, pp. 63–73. Left Coast Press, Walnut Creek, California.

Smith, George S., Phyllis Mauch Messenger, and Hilary A. Soderland

2010　Introduction. In *Heritage Values in Contemporary Society*, edited by George S. Smith, Phyllis Mauch Messenger, and Hilary A. Soderland, pp. 15–25. Left Coast Press, Walnut Creek, California.

Sobel, David

2013　*Place-based Education. Connecting Classrooms and Communities.* 2nd ed. Orion Nature Literacy Series. Orion, Great Barrington, Massachusetts.

Society for American Archaeology (SAA)

2010　SAA Needs Assessment. Electronic document, https://ecommerce.saa.org/saa/staticcontent/staticpages/survey10/index.cfm. Accessed February 28, 2013.

Society for Historical Archaeology (SHA)

2008　Member Needs Assessment. Survey on file with the Society for Historical Archaeology.

Taylor, Patricia A., Burke D. Grandjean, and James H. Graman

2011　*National Park Service Comprehensive Survey of the American Public 2008–2009. Racial and Ethnic Diversity of National Park System Visitors and Non-Visitors.* Natural Resource Report NPS/NRSS/SSD/NRR-2011/432. Electronic document, http://www.nature.nps.gov/socialscience/docs/CompSurvey2008_2009RaceEthnicity.pdf. Accessed March 1, 2013.

Thiong'o, Ngũgĩ wa

2009　*Something Torn and New. An African Renaissance.* Basic Civitas Books, New York.

U.S. Forest Service (USFS)

2013　PowerPoint presentation by the U.S. Forest Service, based on research of the MD-715s. Document on file with the U.S. Forest Service.

Wallis, Lynley A., and Alice C. Gorman

2010　A Time for Change? Indigenous Heritage Values and Management Practice in the Coorong and Lower Murray Lakes Region, South Australia. *Australian Aboriginal Studies* 1: 57–73.

White, Charles S.

2019    Archaeology in School: Tapping into Histories and Historical Inquiry. In *Pedagogy and Practice in Heritage Studies*, edited by Susan J. Bender and Phyllis Mauch Messenger, pp. 30–49. University Press of Florida, Gainesville.

# 6

# Learning NAGPRA and Teaching Archaeology

APRIL SIEVERT, TERESA NICHOLS, K. ANNE PYBURN,
AND JAYNE-LEIGH THOMAS

One objective for pedagogy in higher education that should cut across all disciplines is the teaching and learning of ethical practice. Burgeoning research on the scholarship of teaching and learning at the college level provides fertile spaces for cultivating research about how ethics are framed, practiced, and conveyed within a wide expanse of disciplines. Ethics awareness has developed especially in the context of recognizing the effects of colonialist perceptions and biases in scientific practice. Specialists in anthropology, archaeology, and museum and heritage studies are no strangers to defining ethical principles, and then addressing what we think students need to grasp (Bender and Smith 2000; Hamilakis 2004; see also McGill 2019). Perhaps this is nowhere more apparent than when considering pedagogy designed to convey issues of Indigenous and human rights concerning repatriation in general, and appreciation and compliance with the Native American Graves Protection and Repatriation Act (NAGPRA) in particular. In this chapter, we explore the state of teaching and learning related to NAGPRA in the context of ethics pedagogy and the preparation of scholars and future professionals for culturally engaged archaeology that looks beyond repatriation as loss, to an archaeology in which repatriation is one vital step in reconfiguring how archaeology and collections are meaningfully understood.

The past few decades have seen nothing less than a revolution in archaeology, paralleling the expansion of heritage studies. The addition of relativist critiques that challenged the positivism of "traditional" nineteenth-century science laid the groundwork for a more engaged and ethical professional practice, such that contemporary archaeology is a very different science from anything preceding it. In fact, philosopher of science Sandra Harding (2014) has said that the discipline of archaeology is leading the way to the future of science, blazing a trail to collaborative research that the rest of the sciences will have to follow. The question becomes, where did the path to collaboration originate? It can be argued that post-processual approaches, including feminist perspectives (see also Messenger, this volume) and the development of the World Archaeological Congress (WAC), have brought the discipline from its concerns with simply studying the past into its modern social contexts of seeing how the use and interpretation of the past affects the present and its myriad stakeholders. Adding considerations of historicity, materiality, and memory to the useful scientific equipment of deductive reasoning, replicability, and verifiability developed during the so-called "new" archaeology of the 1970s has equipped the discipline with multiple ways of knowing and understanding both the past and the present.

In 1990, the United States Congress passed the Native American Graves Protection and Repatriation Act (NAGPRA—Public Law 101-601; 25 U.S.C. 3001-3013) to restore control over ancestral remains, funerary objects, sacred objects, and objects of cultural patrimony to federally recognized tribes in the United States. The new emphasis on social justice as a challenge to the absolute priority of science was occurring in many intellectual communities, including the growth of cultural and ethnic studies departments, so the timing of the law was no accident. The intent of NAGPRA legislation was manifold: to recognize rights of Indigenous people over their ancestral heritage and curtail the practice of removing Native American human remains from burials without consulting descendants, to treat these remains and objects with respect, to consult with living descendants about possible cultural affiliation and preferred treatment, and to repatriate remains to appropriate federally recognized tribes (Trope and Echo-Hawk 1992). NAGPRA did not spring from a vacuum, resulting from wider activism and dialogues about Indigenous rights in the United States. Prior to passage of the legislation, the Vermilion Accord, drawn up during the WAC Intercongress in 1989, addressed finding common principles about which scientists and Indigenous people of North America could agree, and suggested that mutual understanding and respect were possible (Zimmerman 2002: 91).

Many archaeologists have acknowledged that recognizing the significance of the cultural and historical context of science is not the same as

April Sievert, Teresa Nichols, K. Anne Pyburn, and Jayne-Leigh Thomas rejecting the value of replicability and verification. Yet many American archaeologists continue to present issues of repatriation in terms of a false dichotomy between science and religion in their research and teaching (Lippert 2005; White Deer 1997), mistaking science as unwaveringly objective on the one hand, and religion as purely ideological on the other. Neither perspective is helpful, and the perception has perpetuated a system of interaction founded on distrust and dismissiveness. As we consider the lessons and skills that students will carry with them into the professional world, these repeating oversimplified dichotomies must be confronted and deconstructed in the classroom (see also Watkins, this volume), as well as in the lab, the repository, and the field.

## What Does NAGPRA Do?

Since 1990, thousands of material objects and individuals have been repatriated to recognized Indigenous tribes across the United States through the process delineated by NAGPRA. Thousands more have not (U.S. Government Accountability Office 2010; Riding In 2012). The legislation impelled archaeologists and biological anthropologists to reconsider and justify how ancestral remains contribute to research for the "common good." It also called for the institutional guardians and repositories holding these ancestral remains and cultural objects to consider their treatment of the traditional "owners" of that heritage and how the Euro-American heritage model often fails to accommodate different systems of knowledge and belief (Carman and Sørensen 2009: 16–17). As the international framework of heritage-related policies created by UNESCO and other initiatives expands, NAGPRA has implications for another countries' treatment of "cultural property" and for Indigenous communities calling for mechanisms to support international repatriation (Harrison 2013: 110); these are underscored by the contradicting principles of preserving heritage of "outstanding universal value" for the benefit of an imagined global community while protecting local understandings of intangible heritage and cultural rights (Logan 2012; Turtinen 2000). Despite over twenty-five years in existence, NAGPRA remains both controversial and poorly understood (Cryne 2010; Nash and Colwell-Chanthaphonh 2010). Scientists in many cases remain unclear about the process of compliance, and uncertain how they might redirect research into new and fruitful work *with and for* Native Americans as opposed to *about* Native Americans. By returning control of religious objects to tribes, NAGPRA is fundamental to religious freedom and tribal sovereignty (Riding In 2012; Tsosie 2012). It also emphasizes the need for archaeologists and bio-anthropologists to democratize knowledge and the process of knowledge creation. For scholars, the act opens a door to new and productive types of scholarly collaboration, by rescuing scholars from the "culture wars" pitting science against religion and by supporting consultation and collaborative effort. Before NAGPRA, even scholars wishing to repatriate human remains to descendant communities would have fought against university regulations and lack of funding. Unfortunately, much of the rhetoric about NAGPRA and science has focused unconstructively on negative outcomes, and collections disposition is seen in terms of loss—loss of control, collections themselves, job opportunities, research potential, and academic freedom (Buikstra 1983; Joyce 2002; Kakaliouras 2012; Larsen and Walker 2005).

Changes to the legislation in 2010 extended tribal rights to thousands of collections of human remains that had been designated culturally unidentifiable (either because of poor record keeping or by virtue of greater antiquity, thought to obscure biological and cultural links with modern people). NAGPRA altered the process of research on ancient North America significantly by conveying to descendant communities proprietary rights over the remains of ancestors, many of whom have been curated and researched at museums and universities for over 100 years, and by encouraging new and productive partnerships with descendant communities through the consultation provisions of the law and new sources of government funding. The NAGPRA process requires developing specific protocols and policies for handling human remains and working closely with tribes, whose perspectives on science, biological anthropology, archaeology, curation, and repatriation are as highly varied as those among scientists (Neller 2004; Zimmerman and Branam 2014).

Scientists are accustomed to working within ethical frameworks for research on living subjects monitored by institutional review boards (IRBs), but IRBs provide neither oversight nor guidance for research on deceased individuals (Bendremer and Richman 2006; Colwell and Nash 2015; Joyce 2002). Consultation of the type required by NAGPRA essentially extends the provisions of informed consent to descendant communities. Archaeologists and bio-anthropologists whose research focuses solely on human remains may have relatively little experience with human subjects' protocols, and graduate programs do not always touch on these issues. While students and professionals are encouraged to define the benefits of their research to the public and to stakeholders as part of their "broader impacts," Joyce questions "how often [do] archaeologists ask what harm [they] might do?" (2002: 100). Museum studies programs similarly need to encourage emerging professionals to more carefully "weigh the consequences of their choices, not only on human remains as if they exist in a social vacuum, but how their actions will impact the cultural and spiritual well-being of the living, too" (Colwell and Nash 2015: 14).

From the perspective of universities and museums, compliance with NAGPRA legislation is crucial because failure to comply can result in civil penalties and place funding from governmental agencies in jeopardy. At its extreme, poor handling of NAGPRA reporting has led to criminal investigation, as in a case involving the University of Nebraska (Niessel 2011: 838), which ultimately resulted in the return of the remains of over 1,700 individuals to a tribal coalition. Penalty avoidance is the worst rationale for repatriation. Understanding the foundation and spirit of the law in terms of human rights and restorative justice should be what spurs archaeologists and anthropologists to recraft their research directions to include Indigenous directives and to dedicate time and energy into building the relationships that are necessary for not only respectful and satisfying repatriation, but also for engaging in new kinds of collaborative scholarship. The ability to both comply with the legislation and continue to develop research on ancient North America is contingent on having a population of mentors and educators in the scientific community able to work with tribal representatives to develop socially conscious and ethically informed research directions, and to not only include, but take direction from, Native American scholars and specialists in the development of new scientific research. Museums and universities that hope to continue curation of human remains also have an ethical mandate to recognize that few individuals in their collections could freely give consent and that they should therefore seek consent from "a nested set of communities, expanding outward from kin to clan/village to tribe to regional tribal consortia to inter-tribal coalitions" (Colwell and Nash 2015: 14).

From both institutions and federally recognized tribes, NAGPRA compliance requires educated personnel who can negotiate the process of documenting and researching collections for possible repatriation, researching cultural affiliation, consulting with tribal professionals, and handling remains and materials. Rather than reducing job prospects for biological anthropologists, there may be an increasing number of positions available in doing the work that NAGPRA generates. Unfortunately, there appears to be only a small pool of qualified professionals who understand and appreciate both scientific and tribal needs sufficiently to direct NAGPRA implementation projects, or to develop participatory research that speaks to both contemporary Native Americans and traditional scientists. Watkins (2010: 56) writes, "I think instead that we merely choose to create 'graduates'—people who we can hope can go on and do better than we can. And yet we don't mentor them enough; we don't give them the abilities to deal with situations that they will have to face in order to become administrators, in order to become the people who can control the process through which we can protect the heritage that it is up to us to protect."

Watkins (2010: 52) suggests that archaeologists' and biological anthropologists' tendency to think of Native American cultures as either extinct or as vestiges of the past creates a roadblock to effective compliance as well as ethical research. This problem is particularly serious in states without tribally owned land and tribal presence.


Archaeology as an Ethical Science

To address the needs of the next generation of archaeologists to, as Watkins states, "go on and do better than we can," biological anthropologists, bio-archaeologists, and archaeologists need to upgrade their understanding of science and rethink the way in which scientific research principles are implemented and taught. Forsman (1997: 110) suggests that archaeologists need to communicate their findings in a way that is less technical and more personal: "This might necessitate placing more priority on people and their beliefs and understanding of the world than on our scientific values." This is beautifully said, but understanding people's values and beliefs is a scientific goal of archaeology, and archaeologists are most remiss when they fail to apply this goal to the present as well. Furthermore, as Sandra Harding has pointed out, inclusion of diverse perspectives can only enhance research designs and interpretations of data (2014). In fact, archaeologists are equally

April Sievert, Teresa Nichols, K. Anne Pyburn, and Jayne-Leigh Thomas remiss in their failure to understand the impact of their own values and beliefs on their professional practice.

Hanna (2003) emphasizes that repatriation is often painted as a simple controversy between "science" and "religion" in both academic and public perception, a false dichotomy that is not helpful (Pyburn 2007). Professional archaeologists, a growing number of whom are members of Indigenous groups, participate in a wide variety of religions. Teachers at institutions of higher education may often avoid discussions of religion and spirituality, which delegitimizes a wide variety of value systems and can dehumanize how students approach the broader world (Forsman 1997). The intellectual heritage of all groups includes ways of knowing that overlap with any definition of science. Empiricism is not imperialism; scientific ethics require that archaeologists recognize that varied forms of verification and qualitative understandings always coexist. This is not to say that science is the same as religion, but that scientists are not without cosmology, nor are Indigenous cultural experts prone to substitute belief for verification.

It appears that biological anthropologists have been slow to incorporate NAGPRA into the mainstream in graduate theses and dissertations. Data collected from ProQuest about topics of dissertations reveal that out of 360 theses in physical anthropology between 1990 and 2014, 50 percent mention "Native American" in keywords or other delineators. "NAGPRA" is mentioned as a delineator in only 3 percent. Anthropologists who argue that their work may be relevant to Native Americans may not be doing an adequate job of relating NAGPRA to their work, starting as graduate students and continuing the practice into professional positions. The January 2015 *SAA Archaeological Record* was a special issue titled "NAGPRA and the Next Generation of Collaboration," encouraging professionals young and old to think about the growing opportunities to work with Native Americans and to counter the unfortunate widely held view among archaeologists that NAGPRA is "paralytic" (Altschul 2015). The SAA Executive Board and Committees on Native American Relations and Repatriation worked together on this issue to explore how NAGPRA-related consultation can lead to new forms of archaeological research that are mutually beneficial to researchers and Native American communities (Gonzalez and Marek-Martinez 2015). As Dorothy Lippert states, while NAGPRA has exposed "deficiencies in how the profession relates to tribal people . . . at the same time, the laws pushed us forward and made us stronger" resulting in new ways of working together and understanding the lives of the ancestors (2015: 38). That issue, however, mentioned little about how to teach those new perspectives on research.

## The "Learning NAGPRA" Project

In 2014 and 2015, researchers from Indiana University received National Science Foundation funding through their Cultivating Cultures of Ethical STEM initiative for two phases of a project to study how repatriation is taught and learned, and to work toward interventions to improve the resources available. The "Learning NAGPRA" project seeks to identify and understand the challenges to preparing professionals for work related to NAGPRA and repatriation by comparing approaches to ethics at research universities with those at tribal-serving institutions. The project hopes, in collaboration with tribal colleges and participants, to look beyond traditional Euro-American pedagogy, toward methods that speak to both Indigenous and non-Indigenous students. The first year focused on background research and project planning and aimed to understand the perspectives and priorities of students and educators in learning and teaching about ethics and, more specifically, NAGPRA in anthropology and museum studies–related programs. For the most recent news about our research results and ongoing work, we suggest you visit our website (Learning NAGPRA 2017).

A core component of the grant through its first three years is the Learning NAGPRA Collegium, a workshop format that brings together graduate students, educators, museum professionals, tribal cultural specialists, and members of professional organizations to discuss and then create educational methods and materials for particular audiences in different disciplines and at all stages of career. The collegium setting, drawing from the scholarship of teaching and learning, is designed to create collaborative spaces where participants can evaluate information and brainstorm paths forward for teaching and learning about NAGPRA. The first two Collegium meetings were held at Indiana University in Bloomington, Indiana, while the third and final Collegium meeting was hosted by the Institute of American Indian Arts (IAIA) in Santa Fe, New Mexico.

At the first Collegium meeting in August 2015, twenty-five participants (see Figure 6.1) gathered and discussed guiding values in their current work

Figure 6.1. Participants from the 2015 Learning NAGPRA Collegium (listed alpha-
betically): Daryl Baldwin, Miami Tribe of Oklahoma; Nicky Belle; Felipe J. Estudillo
Colòn, Laguna Pueblo, assistant professor of museum studies, IAIA; Carlina de
la Cova, assistant professor, University of South Carolina; Crystal DeCell; Brian J.
Gilley; Jessica Harrison; Ricardo Higelin Ponce de León; Katherine Kearns; Desireé
R. Martinez, Gabrielino (Tongva); Dru McGill, North Carolina State University;
Teresa Nichols; K. Anne Pyburn; Jennifer Meta Robinson; Rebekah Ryan; Jessie
Ryker-Crawford, White Earth Chippewa, associate professor of museum studies,
IAIA; April Sievert; Vickie Stone; Jayne-Leigh Thomas; Davina Two Bears (Navajo),
PhD candidate, Indiana University; Velma K. Valdez; Joe Watkins; Carrie V. Wilson;
Teresa Wilson; Larry J. Zimmerman, Indiana University–Purdue University India-
napolis/Eiteljorg Museum. Photograph courtesy of Indiana University.

of professional associations and tribal governments, crucial gaps in methods of teaching and outreach, barriers and frustrations experienced working with repatriation, the primary target audiences for NAGPRA education,
and educational materials for those different groups. These discussions,
held in both small groups and as a collective whole, addressed how particular gaps, problematic concepts, misunderstandings, and confusion pervade
both university systems and many sectors of the public. The next two Collegium meetings in 2016 and 2017 were structured into working groups as
we worked collaboratively to develop the methods, format, and content for
educational materials.

Faculty from the Museum Studies Program at the Institute of American Indian Arts participated in the first Collegium and are acting as senior
consultants over the three years of the second phase of the grant. IAIA has
developed three successive courses on repatriation in response to student

interests and professional goals. It is essential that university students (and faculty) have more exposure to the priorities and pedagogies designed by Indigenous educators and scholars. An idea repeated throughout the first Learning NAGPRA Collegium was how to improve cultural competency, which is necessary for both understanding why NAGPRA exists and how to carry out fundamental aspects of NAGPRA compliance, especially consultation. As Paulette Steeves (2015) argues, Indigenous voices in academia can help "counter traditional American epistemologies of agnotology" or "ignorance-making" (2015: 127; Proctor and Schiebinger 2008: vii). Proctor and Schiebinger describe this ignorance making as generated though mechanisms such as "neglect, secrecy and suppression, document destruction, unquestioned tradition, and myriad forms of inherent (or avoidable) culturopolitical selectivity" (2008: vii). Similarly, a Collegium participant highlighted fear as an impediment to both required consultation and collaboration. Relationship building between universities and tribal institutions, between Native American scholars and diverse student populations are important avenues for reducing ignorance and fear while increasing cultural competency and collaborative opportunities.

Research Design and Results

After reflecting on Chip Colwell's important 2010 survey of tribal repatriation workers (Colwell-Chanthaphonh 2012) and the Society for American Archaeology's 2015 survey of members about their views and activities relating to repatriation (Alonzi 2016), project staff administered two online survey questionnaires targeting students and educators in anthropology and museum studies–related programs. The student surveys were sent to department chairs and directors of undergraduate and graduate studies to be redistributed to their students, while educator surveys were sent directly to professors who taught topics such as professional ethics, American archaeology, osteology, museum curation, and human rights. Two rounds of surveys were sent out to 226 anthropology-related programs and 91 museum studies–related programs. Along with these surveys, project personnel have been conducting in-person and phone interviews with educators, students, and repatriation professionals on similar themes.

As Ann Kakaliouras (2008; 2014) has suggested, if a balanced discussion of repatriation is not a fundamental part of physical biological anthropology and archaeology courses, educators perpetuate the attitude that skeletal remains are "specimens," and repatriation can only mean a threat to science and a loss of information. Drawing on the "NAGPRA at 20" symposium participant surveys, students and educators were prompted to respond to two open-ended questions: "Who benefits from NAGPRA, and what are those benefits?" and "Who is harmed by NAGPRA, and what are those harms?" (Keller O'Loughlin 2013: 230). Student respondents (n=894) wrote detailed answers to those paired questions. Sixteen percent feel that NAGPRA is an effort to balance the pursuit of knowledge and the right of Native American communities to give or deny consent/access to certain research questions or research methods. But 20 percent felt that NAGPRA has negatively led to losses in scientific knowledge. Those respondents then varied on whether that loss of knowledge most harmed Native American communities, the scientific profession or specific types of researchers, or the general public. Exemplary quotes include:

NAGPRA harms everyone, including Native Americans. By allowing a vocal minority to determine what is done with human remains in this country, we are seriously hurting our capacity to perform scientific inquiry on the lives of people living in North America in the past. . . .

When remains are reinterred without proper study, everyone misses out on potentially very valuable information about human evolution, human behavior, health, and disease.

The harm can be the claim that anything and everything is ancestral. . . . Everyone benefits from learning the history of human kind as one collective.

The unequal distribution of benefits from that knowledge was not discussed in that theme of responses.

Another troubling narrative seen in some student responses was the perception that having limits on research is incompatible with rigorous scientific inquiry. For example, one student explained that NAGPRA harms science because "researchers are limited by what the native peoples agree to let them do." Disallowing research on archaeological discoveries exacerbates the reality that the archaeological record will always be a puzzle with missing pieces, because not all materials or human remains are preserved and available to be excavated, the student response indicated. Another respondent argued that scientific knowledge in general is harmed by the outcomes of NAGPRA, stating that "repatriation can lead to materials becoming inaccessible for further research. As far as archaeology is a science, this destroys the reproducibility of research carried out on repatriated materials, which necessarily erodes the credibility of data generated from them."

This construction of repatriation deplores the loss of restudy for verifying findings and claims that it erodes the scientific value and the credibility of data generated from human remains. The attitude is ironic given that archaeological excavation, by destroying archaeological context, effectively precludes replication and verification as well. While reburial may preclude future research of specific types, the ability to form respectful relationships through consultation opens the door for tribes and institutions both to build trust and to consider permissible research and even continued curation with appropriate protocols determined on a case-by-case basis (Kakaliouras 2014; Neller 2004).

Those narrower constructions focusing on loss and limitation reflect the variety of student experiences in learning about appropriate research protocols for limiting harm to others. In answer to the open-ended question, "In your coursework, what have you learned about the ethics of working with human subjects?," about 7 percent of students (out of 976 respondents) felt they had received little to no instruction on the topic. An additional 1 percent had not yet covered the topic in class but anticipated doing so. This is an encouragingly high number, but there are still students interested in receiving guidance or more guidance on these issues. As anthropology and museum studies focus on people, living or dead, instructors discussing research and research design can do an even better job that goes beyond briefly mentioning that universities have IRB processes that may or may not apply to specific kinds of investigation. With more and more tribal governments creating their own IRB processes for research in their communities, students need to learn how to take into account the multiple perspectives, priorities, and power relationships connected to their research at early stages in the development of a research design.

Multiple responses showed recognition of, and interest in, resources coming from a wider variety of perspectives. When asked open-ended questions about what resources or materials would better equip them to handle issues related to ethics or NAGPRA, several students emphasized the importance of having Native American voices in the classroom—as authors of required class readings, guest lecturers, or professors. Some students suggested that Native American perspectives were beneficial because they provide different insights into the cultural importance of the law and its practice than do university and museum professionals. Others wanted more information about how the process of consultation and repatriation works from the tribal side, so they could learn more about relationship building, a finding that bodes well for future collaborative work.

Many respondents viewed case studies as helpful educational materials, echoing the findings of other scholars studying the teaching of ethics (Card 2002; Colwell-Chanthaphonh et al. 2008; see also McGill 2019). A few respondents suggested that reading or hearing the experiences of tribal members who participated in the consultation process would help clarify how the process worked for the various parties involved. More diverse and up-to-date case studies would help students gain a better sense of best practices while emphasizing that cookbook-type, standardized approaches do not cope well with wide diversity in tribal histories and cultural practices (Neller 2004; Zimmerman and Branam 2014). Students were eager to break down the "us or them" conversations and talk about creativity and collaboration in community controlled research or curation. As part of the survey, students were asked about their interest in courses or internships relating to archival research, community-based participatory research, conflict resolution or mediation, consultation, curation, and grant writing. Over 65 percent of students (out of 959 responses) were interested in educational opportunities to learn about or participate in community-based participatory research. Atalay (2012) emphasizes that community-based participatory research (CBPR) will play an important role in the future of archaeology, because it asks researchers to consider the relevance and benefits of their work for different audiences, stakeholders, and participants. CBPR pedagogies are still relatively new, but "training that is self-reflective and self-critical" is essential to preparing professionals to practice (Atalay 2012: 113). Pedagogies to prepare students to be responsible for NAGPRA-generated work should likely follow suit.

In our survey responses, 12 percent of undergraduates and 32 percent of graduate students had experience working on NAGPRA-related tasks in their research, work, and internship experiences, more than we initially expected. Although the tasks they worked on varied, students who had

NAGPRA experience were much more likely to be extremely interested in a job with NAGPRA duties compared to those who did not have NAGPRA experience as a student (38 percent vs. 23 percent). Furthermore, only one student (0.4 percent) who had worked on NAGPRA-related tasks was extremely disinterested in a future job dealing with NAGPRA, whereas 4 percent of students without that exposure would not consider that a viable job option. While some educators expressed concern in interviews about how and at what levels to include student learners in ongoing repatriation efforts, it appears that greater knowledge of NAGPRA has positive benefits in dispelling fear among students about NAGPRA-related jobs and jobs working with Native American communities. Only 27 percent of students without NAGPRA experience were extremely interested in jobs working with Native American communities, compared to 45 percent of students who had NAGPRA experience. As students gain first-hand experience working with communities or see their professors engage in more collaborative, engaged research, they see more possibilities for their disciplines and their future work.

Based on preliminary results, educators and students agree that both undergraduate and graduate students benefit from learning about NAGPRA, but the context and depth of that educational content varies with level. For undergraduate students, an anthropology major does not guarantee what type of employment they will hold later in life. NAGPRA on the undergraduate level can be used as part of larger learning goals relating to Native American history and contemporary culture, the history and theory of anthropology and museum studies, human rights and the rights of indigenous peoples, and considerations of the ethics of research on marginalized communities. In other words, it is broadly transferable. Teaching about NAGPRA can then be seen as creating informed citizens with a more ethical and humanistic consciousness, similar to how heritage studies can encourage students to reflect on the issues of civic engagement and social justice (Little and Shackel 2014). Graduate students in comparison are more likely to become practitioners who will actively encounter repatriation or NAGPRA-related work. This group needs to gain deeper knowledge of the process of NAGPRA compliance and tribal consultation and to hear a variety of perspectives from tribal and museum repatriation professionals and cultural specialists.

After surveying students and educators nationwide, we conducted a pilot study to assess in specific classrooms how learning about NAGPRA as a case study may help students build their understanding of human rights with respect to the histories of Native American tribal nations, along with the skills to consider the viewpoints of many stakeholders in order to find common ground. This comparative study looks at courses in five universities across the United States, at schools with varying levels of Native American student populations, with teachers writing reflections and students answering short questionnaires before and after taking the course. This study should allow us to see student transformations over a semester and provide a guiding model as we further develop NAGPRA-related educational materials, plan to distribute those to instructors, and identify how to assess their impact.

## Conclusion

As the Learning NAGPRA project moves forward, we see the need for enhanced discussion and preparation for students in anthropology, cultural heritage, historic preservation, museum studies, and cultural resource management. NAGPRA is one facet of much broader cultural resource management legislation, tribal preservation and reclamation efforts, heritage studies, and works toward democratizing theories and methodologies. Whether or not students later go on to professional careers in these fields or are simply informed and engaged U.S. citizens, the history and spirit of NAGPRA has much to teach. Even for those educators who are resistant to engaging with NAGPRA, the law exists and will continue to exist, such that their students will be required to know what NAGPRA compliance entails. It will prove necessary to emphasize the importance of true consultation on matters of repatriation, along with the potential for collaboration inherent in relationship building.

Archaeology is at a crucial point in its disciplinary evolution, and although NAGPRA involves sensitive, complex issues, it also represents a mandate for interested and interconnected parties to sit down together to decide what the future could look like for scholarship and practice in heritage fields. On the one hand, this promises to create energized and interdisciplinary new directions in heritage studies. On the other hand, if educators continue to ignore NAGPRA or present it solely as detrimental to research, they are doing themselves and their students a disservice by ignoring opportunities to reconnect the resources they steward to the communities who care deeply about them and could offer either improved interpretation or more meaningful questions to explore. Negative approaches to repatriation in the classroom will likely discourage students who are eager to engage with the social justice aspects of the social sciences and explore the human-centered histories in the humanities. They may also propel students to seek research opportunities outside of the United States, but many communities worldwide are aware of NAGPRA and are considering their own needs to reclaim control of their cultural objects and narratives.

The Learning NAGPRA project includes multiple participants to define, think through, and suggest more effective educational materials for teaching ethics. The process of exploring what to teach in these broad discussions, particularly in the collegium context, reveals, in some sense, how to teach. First, educators need to allow emotion into the classroom and create safe spaces for their students to work through difficult issues. Second, tough topics should not be exclusively discussed with graduate students; undergraduate students in a variety of majors can benefit from learning more about the challenges of living in a multicultural, settler-colonial society. Third, students are interested in, and educators should require the inclusion of, multiple perspectives that will be respectfully and honestly considered. And fourth, one of the best methods of including those diverse perspectives is to find ways to introduce immediate and personal experiences.

Improved education on NAGPRA and the thoughtful ethical considerations of working with human remains may help scientists overcome barriers to developing research and creating progressive relationships with tribal partners. With NAGPRA compliance acting as a vehicle for collaboration, can we be optimistic that the enhanced dissemination of knowledge will transform the fields of biological anthropology and archaeology and allow for more participatory and inclusive research? Perhaps, but knowledge as "content taught" does not substitute for pedagogy that encourages thinking critically about how anthropology as a discipline has stirred or stymied the development of new approaches to collaborative scholarship. Merely teaching how to comply with the law, while inarguably useful, will be insufficient to produce the next generation of archaeologists, biological anthropologists, and other heritage professionals.

## Acknowledgments

The Learning NAGPRA project is supported by NSF grants 1449465 and 1540447. Thanks to Jennifer Meta Robinson, Katherine Kearns, Jessie Ryker-Crawford, Felipe J. Estudillo Colòn, the First Nations Educational and Cultural Center and Social Science Research Commons at Indiana University, Brian J. Gilley, Davina Two Bears, Ricardo Higelin Ponce de León, Adam Crane, Dru McGill, Joseph Stahlman, Heather Williams, Nicholas Belle, Crystal DeCell, Yarí Cruz Rios, Jennifer St. Germain, and Alicia Adelman.

## References Cited

Alonzi, Elise
2016     SAA Repatriation Survey Analysis. *SAA Archaeological Record* 16(4): 15–20.
Altschul, Jeffrey H.
2015     From the President. *SAA Archaeological Record* 15(1): 3.
Atalay, Sonya
2012     *Community-Based Archaeology: Research with, by, and for Indigenous and Local Communities*. University of California Press, Berkeley.
Bender, Susan J., and George S. Smith (editors)
2000     *Teaching Archaeology in the Twenty-First Century*. Society for American Archaeology Press, Washington, D.C.
Bendremer, Jeffrey C., and Kenneth A. Richman
2006     Human Subjects Review and Archaeology: A View from Indian Country. In *The Ethics of Archaeology: Philosophical Perspectives on Archaeological Practice*, edited by Chris Scarre and Geoffrey Scarre, pp. 97–114. Cambridge University Press, New York.
Buikstra, Jane E.
1983     Reburial: Why We All Lose—An Archaeologist's Opinion. *Council for Museum Anthropology Newsletter* 7(2): 2–5.
Card, Robert F.
2002     Using Case Studies to Develop Critical Thinking Skills in Ethics Courses. *Teaching Ethics* Fall 2002: 19–27.
Carman, John, and Marie Louise Stig Sørensen
2009     Heritage Studies: An Outline. In *Heritage Studies: Methods and Approaches*, edited by Marie Louise Stig Sørensen and John Carman, pp. 11–28. Routledge, New York.
Colwell-Chanthaphonh, Chip
2012     The Work of Repatriation in Indian Country. *Human Organization* 71(3): 278–291.
Colwell-Chanthaphonh, Chip, Julie Hollowell, and Dru McGill
2008     *Ethics in Action: Case Studies in Archaeological Dilemmas*. Society for American Archaeology Press, Washington, D.C.

Colwell, Chip, and Stephen E. Nash

2015    Repatriating Human Remains in the Absence of Consent. *SAA Archaeological Record* 15(1): 14–16.

Cryne, Julia A.

2010    NAGPRA Revisited: A Twenty-Year Review of Repatriation Efforts. *American Indian Law Review* 34(1): 99–122.

Forsman, Leonard

1997    Straddling the Current: A View from the Bridge over Clear Salt Water. In *Native Americans and Archaeologists: Stepping Stones to Common Ground*, edited by Nina Swidler, Kurt Dongoske, Roger Anyon, and Alan Downer, pp. 105–111. AltaMira Press, Walnut Creek, California.

Gonzalez, Sara, and Ora Marek-Martinez

2015    NAGPRA and the Next Generation of Collaboration. *SAA Archaeological Record* 15(1): 11–13.

Hamilakis, Yannis

2004    Archaeology and the Politics of Pedagogy. *World Archaeology* 36(2): 287–309.

Hanna, Margaret G.

2003    Old Bones, New Reality: A Review of Issues and Guidelines Pertaining to Repatriation. *Canadian Journal of Archaeology/Journal Canadien d'Archéologie* 27(2): 234–257.

Harding, Sandra

2014    Postcolonial Science and Technology Studies: Issues and Challenges for Feminism. Public lecture, Mellon Foundation Sawyer Seminar Series in Science and Technology Studies, Indiana University, Bloomington, November 29.

Harrison, Rodney

2013    *Heritage: Critical Approaches*. Routledge, New York.

Joyce, Rosemary

2002    Academic Freedom, Stewardship and Cultural Heritage: Weighing the Interests of Stakeholders in Crafting Repatriation Approaches. In *The Dead and Their Possessions: Repatriation in Principle, Policy and Practice*, edited by Cressida Fforde, Jane Hubert, and Paul Turnbull, pp. 99–107. Routledge, New York.

Kakaliouras, Ann M.

2008    Toward a "New and Different" Osteology: A Reflexive Critique of Physical Anthropology in the United States since the Passage of NAGPRA. In *Opening Archaeology: Repatriation's Impact on Contemporary Research and Practice*, edited by Thomas W. Killion, pp. 109–129. School for Advanced Research Press, Santa Fe, New Mexico.

2012    An Anthology of Repatriation: Contemporary Physical Anthropological and Native American Ontologies of Practice. *Current Anthropology* 53(S5): S210–S221.

2014    When Remains are "Lost": Thoughts on Collections, Repatriation, and Research in American Physical Anthropology. *Curator: The Museum Journal* 57: 213–223.

Keller O'Loughlin, Shannon

2013    Moving Forward from the Last Twenty Years: Finding a New Balance. In *Implementing NAGPRA: A Critical Analysis of the Intent, Impact, and Future of the*

*Native American Graves Protection and Repatriation Act,* edited by Sangita Chari and Jaime M.N. Lavallee, pp. 223–238. Oregon State University Press, Corvallis.

Larsen, Clark Spencer, and Phillip L. Walker

2005    The Ethics of Bioarchaeology. In *Biological Anthropology and Ethics: From Repatriation to Genetic Identity*, edited by Trudy R. Turner, pp. 111–119. State University of New York Press, New York.

Learning NAGPRA

2017    Learning NAGPRA: Resources for Teaching and Training. Electronic document, http://learningnagpra.indiana.edu. Accessed June 10, 2018.

Lippert, Dorothy

2005    Remembering Humanity: How to Include Human Values in a Scientific Endeavor. *International Journal of Cultural Property* 12(02): 275–280.

2015    Repatriation and the Initial Steps Taken on Common Ground. *SAA Archaeological Record* 15(1): 36–38.

Little, Barbara J., and Paul A. Shackel

2014    *Archaeology, Heritage, and Civic Engagement: Working Toward the Public Good.* Left Coast Press, Walnut Creek, California.

Logan, William

2012    Cultural Diversity, Cultural Heritage and Human Rights: Towards Heritage Management as Human Rights-based Cultural Practice. *International Journal of Heritage Studies* 18(3): 231–244.

McGill, Alicia Ebbitt

2019    Assessing Student Learning in Heritage Studies: What Does It Mean for Students to "Understand" Archaeological Ethics? In *Pedagogy and Practice in Heritage Studies*, edited by Susan J. Bender and Phyllis Mauch Messenger, pp. 50–71. University Press of Florida, Gainesville.

Nash, Stephen E., and Chip Colwell-Chanthaphonh

2010    NAGPRA after Two Decades. *Museum Anthropology* 33(2): 99–104.

Neller, Angela J.

2004    The Future Is in the Past: Native American Issues in Archaeological Collections Care and Management. In *Our Collective Responsibility: The Ethics and Practice of Archaeological Collections Stewardship*, edited by S. Terry Childs, pp. 123–135. Society for American Archaeology, Washington, D.C.

Niessel, Zoe E.

2011    Better Late than Never? The Effect of the Native American Graves Protection and Repatriation Act's 2010 Regulations. *Wake Forest Law Review* 46(4): 837–865.

Proctor, Robert, and Londa L. Schiebinger

2008    *Agnotology: The Making and Unmaking of Ignorance.* Stanford University Press, Stanford.

Pyburn, K. Anne

2007    Uma Questão Nada Simples. *IPHAN, Revista do Patrimônio Histórico e Artístico Nacional* 33: 25–35.

Riding In, James

2012    Human Rights and the American Indian Repatriation Movement: A Manifesto. *Arizona State Law Journal* 44: 613–624.

Steeves, Paulette

2015    Academia, Archaeology, CRM, and Tribal Historic Preservation. *Archaeologies* 11(1): 121–141.

Trope, Jack F., and Walter R. Echo-Hawk

1992    The Native American Graves Protection and Repatriation Act: Background and Legislative History. *Arizona State Law Journal* 24: 35–78.

Tsosie, Rebecca

2012    NAGPRA and the Problem of Culturally Unidentifiable Remains: The Argument for a Human Rights Framework. *Arizona State Law Journal* 44: 809–905.

Turtinen, Jan

2000    *Globalising Heritage: On UNESCO and the Transnational Construction of a World Heritage*. Stockholm Center for Organizational Research, Stockholm.

U.S. Government Accountability Office

2010    Native American Graves Protection and Repatriation Act: After Almost 20 Years, Key Federal Agencies Still Have Not Fully Complied with the Act. Report GAO-10-768, July. U.S. Government Accountability Office, Washington D.C.

Watkins, Joe

2010    Wake up! Repatriation Is Not the Only Indigenous Issue in Archaeology. In *Bridging the Divide: Indigenous Communities and Archaeology into the 21st Century*, edited by Caroline Phillips and Harry Allen, pp. 49–60. Left Coast Press, Walnut Creek, California.

White Deer, Gary

1997    Return of the Sacred: Spirituality and the Scientific Imperative. In *Native Americans and Archaeologists: Stepping Stones to Common Ground*, edited by Nina Swidler, Kurt Dongoske, Roger Anyon, and Alan Downer, pp. 37–43. AltaMira Press, Walnut Creek, California.

Zimmerman, Larry J.

2002    A Decade after the Vermillion Accord: What Has Changed and What Has Not? In *The Dead and Their Possessions: Repatriation in Principle, Policy and Practice*, edited by Cressida Fforde, Jane Hubert, and Paul Turnbull, pp. 91–98. Routledge, New York.

Zimmerman, Larry J., and Kelly M. Branam

2014    Collaborating with Stakeholders. In *Archaeology in Practice: A Student Guide to Archaeological Analyses*, edited by Jane Balme and Alistair Paterson, pp. 1–25. Wiley, Chichester, West Sussex, UK.

# 7

## Teaching Indigenous Archaeology
## to Multiple Constituencies

JOE WATKINS

In 1952, C. W. Weiant of Hunter College, New York, wrote: "Archaeologists, by and large, have been too much engrossed with the problems of their own specialty to give much thought to pedagogy" (1952: 251). Not surprising to say, I expect that same statement might be made about the majority of the people who teach archaeology in a college or university setting. In many (most?) circumstances, the only requirement for teaching archaeology is the advanced degree: occasionally an M.A. for undergraduate programs and a PhD for graduate programs. However, as the popularity of archaeology increased during the heyday of the Indiana Jones movies, so too did the number of introductory archaeology classes. Because these classes offer the opportunity for instructors to provide students of wide-ranging backgrounds with the basics of archaeology's ways of providing insights about the human condition, it is imperative that those who reach the largest number of students do so in effective and innovative ways.

Pedagogy is a foreign word to many college instructors, unless the instructor has at least a passing background in education theory. I admit I don't have such a background, and would venture to guess that the majority of college instructors have very little (if any) background in education theory (see also Zimmerman, this volume). Most of my information has been picked up from Carol Ellick (my wife and colleague) or from others along the way as I've taught college and graduate classes.

I was fortunate, however, to be part of a project convened in Wakulla Springs, Florida, February 5–8, 1998 (Bender and Smith 1998: 11), resulting in a broad examination of the state of teaching archaeology (see Davis et al. 1999 and Lynott et al. 1999 for additional thoughts on teaching archaeology). Anne Pyburn and George Smith's successful National Science Foundation grant entitled "Making Archaeology Teaching Relevant in the XXIst Century" (MATRIX) allowed the creation of teaching modules and more background on teaching pedagogy and style (see Pyburn and Smith 2015 for information on the MATRIX project). Bender and Smith's *Teaching Archaeology in the Twenty-First Century* (2000) laid out the project from start to finish.

I write specifically about teaching archaeology in this chapter, but archaeology is only one discipline within the broader heritage field. Other aspects of heritage that are represented deal with interpretation, public outreach and education, heritage tourism, heritage preservation and conservation, site management, museum studies, creative industries, architectural heritage, historical towns, cultural landscapes, and other fields of inquiry aimed at helping the public relate to their own and others' heritage. "Heritage management" is a global industry that can have a significant impact on local and regional areas.

## Learners and Learning

While it may seem obvious, "learning" does not happen without collaboration between the instructor and the students. Instructors can lecture until they are blue in the face, and students can scribble notes that capture the high points of the lecture, but true learning doesn't occur unless both groups become actively involved in helping the other. For many university instructors in archaeology, the current staple lecture includes a PowerPoint presentation with lots of pictures and text used to illustrate the points the instructor thinks are important. While such lectures are so much better than the "old" days of droning lectures interrupted occasionally by the metallic click of slides being changed, many students do not respond well to being lectured "at."

Students have a tendency to learn in ways that are somewhat individualistic, but those styles of learning may be broadly generalized. Richard Felder (1996: 18) describes learning styles as "characteristic strengths and preferences in the ways [students] take in and process information" and discusses the Myers-Briggs Type Indicator of individual personality types, Kolb's Learning Style Model, the Herrmann Brain Dominance Instrument, and the Felder-Silverman Learning Style Model. In an article on "how teachers teach to students with different learning styles" (Harr et al. 2012: 142), the authors recognize that it is "important for both teachers and students to know that they perceive, process, and communicate information in unique ways" (Harr et al. 2012: 145).

But in spite of the widespread discussion of learning styles, the concept does get debated in education literature. In "The Myth of Learning Styles," Cedar Riener and Daniel Willingham (2010) say that "belief in learning styles is not necessary to incorporating useful knowledge about learning into one's teaching" (2010: 33). The authors place the difference in student outcomes on individual ability and background knowledge rather than on learning styles, concluding with: "Students differ in their abilities, interests, and background knowledge, but not in their learning styles. Students may have preferences about how to learn, but no evidence suggests that catering to those preferences will lead to better learning" (2010: 35).

Cornel Pewewardy (2002) notes that Native American students tend to reflect more than mainstream students prior to offering an answer. Because of this connection between this behavior and the culture of Native Americans, these students may not attempt to answer unfamiliar questions for fear of not performing well. Teachers who do not understand these values and resulting attitudes may perceive Native American students as lacking interest and motivation. However, Price, Kallam, and Love (2009) warn teachers against using a "one-size-fits-all" approach to teaching such a culturally diverse group as American Indians, instead encouraging the use of teaching styles and strategies that can lead to greater success for American Indian students.

In addition to being concerned with learning styles, it is important that an instructor involved in teaching classes to diverse students be aware that there are cultural influences that also impact a student's success in academic situations. A student might be an auditory learner, but his or her culture might frown upon asking questions out of a perception that to ask questions might insult the instructor's ability to adequately present the information without misunderstanding. The concepts of high and low context and direct and indirect communication styles are rarely taught or discussed in anthropology courses, but once students are made aware of these culturally influenced differences in human interaction, many students (and even instructors) better comprehend the ways that background cultural issues influence student success. In this regard, American Indian students can sometimes be perceived as inattentive or unprepared in a classroom setting because of their tendency not to speak up or to question academic experts or "superiors." I nearly flunked out of my first year of graduate school before I understood that questioning the experts was not only allowable, but expected. Price, Kallam, and Love (2009) recast "direct" and "indirect" communication styles into "linear" and "circular" communication in relation to American Indian students. The terminology seems more fitting when one considers what has been applied to the conception of time among various groups. More often, Western cultures generally perceive time to be linear, and in linear communication, people get directly to the point, saying exactly what they mean and what they want you to believe. Tribal cultures have been described as perceiving time to be cyclical and circular, and circular communication often occurs "around" the subject to allow the listeners to come to their own conclusions. However, as with indirect communication, problems arise when the speaker and listener are communicating in different styles.

Alison Wylie (2005), writing about the Reno Workshop that led to the development of the Society for American Archaeology's (SAA's) Principles of Archaeological Ethics, draws attention to the use of this method of communication by Leigh Jenkins Kuwanwisiwma, a member of the Hopi Tribe of Arizona. Midway through the first session of the workshop, Kuwanwisiwma identified a number of ways in which the whole issue of resource protection is framed in terms that are fundamentally at odds with tribal values. He drew no particular lesson from this account, but left it to the assembled archaeologists to think through its implications for the issues they had been discussing. Later that afternoon, the group developed the central components of what became the SAA's ethic of stewardship.

## Course Instructional Design

Tammy Stone in the *Archaeological Record* (2014:36) writes about the "shift in approach to college teaching from a teacher-centered philosophy (what do I want to cover) to a student-centered approach (what do I want them to learn and how do I ensure that they develop a deep understanding)." Teaching archaeology, then, must be more than just reciting dates and telling stories of famous discoverers of "lost civilizations"; teaching archaeology requires that course development from the outset is focused on a unified plan for providing students with reasonably identifiable learning objectives, goals, and landmarks.

There are numerous materials available to help new faculty members prepare courses, and I am not going to go further into discussion about them, but it is equally important that instructors integrate course material with their departmental curriculum. It is important that consistency is maintained across the department so that basic concepts are not only presented in classes, but that they are presented in a similar and consistent manner. Anthropological ethics, for example, can be presented within archaeology classes or cultural anthropology classes, but drawing the various bodies of ethics together in a synthetic manner will aid in student education and training. Reinforcing and expanding upon basic ideas presented within introductory or lower level classes, as a student's background and level of understanding increases due to exposure to more complex levels of interpretation and presentation, helps create new learning pathways and knowledge networks.

## Teaching Strategies

There are a variety of teaching strategies that can be used to improve student learning. Active learning involves getting students out of their chairs and involved in the class; experiential learning involves "learning by doing"; inquiry-guided learning requires students to find the answer for themselves and helps build research skills students will use throughout the rest of their careers; problem-based learning challenges students to "learn-to-learn" by using group work to seek solutions; team teaching uses two (or more) instructors to provide multiple perspectives on particular topics. All of these teaching strategies are useful and bring with them both positive and negative aspects.

We can also use different pedagogical approaches to instruction to reach students through online and distance learning opportunities. Blended classes and intensive classes allow people with full-time jobs to get instruction without having to take too much time off of work. Teaching such classes is more time-consuming and difficult, but the opportunities are endless. (See both Franklin and Marciniak, this volume, for further discussions about teaching in the distance learning environment.)

I have written elsewhere about some of the general issues involved in teaching ethnic studies classes in a university setting (Watkins 2014), but I will focus here more closely on some of the issues involved in teaching Indigenous archaeology. In the following, I will break the discussion down into four broad areas: (1) teaching Indigenous archaeology in general; (2) teaching the subject to nonarchaeologists; (3) teaching the subject in such a way that even those who have an original aversion to the topic comprehend it; and (4) teaching the overarching concept that archaeology has utility in contemporary society. While all four of these topical approaches are important, I believe the last is perhaps the most important.

## Teaching Indigenous Archaeology

Indigenous archaeology, as defined by Nicholas and Andrews (1997: 3, note 5) is "archaeology with, for, and by Indigenous peoples." It was subsequently popularized by the publication of *Indigenous Archaeology: American Indian Values and Scientific Practice* (Watkins 2000), which critically explored late–twentieth century relations between archaeologists and Native Americans, particularly in the context of reburial, repatriation, and cultural resource management. Nicholas subsequently elaborated on the definition of Indigenous archaeology as "an expression of archaeological theory and practice in which the discipline intersects with Indigenous values, knowledge, practices, ethics, and sensibilities, and through collaborative and community-originated or -directed projects, and related critical perspectives" (2008: 1660).

Teaching archaeology within a Native American Studies program carries with it challenges beyond those faced by archaeologists who teach in an archaeology or anthropology program. Questions of pedagogy in an archaeology classroom are compounded in situations where there are people who believe that archaeology is the "handmaiden of colonialism"; that archaeologists are at worst grave robbers and treasure hunters; or that *all* histories (real or imagined) are equivalent. The challenge in working in a Native American Studies environment is to accurately present the methods and theories within which archaeology operates, while giving value to non-archaeological approaches to the past.

Teaching Indigenous archaeology is more than teaching about archaeology "with, for, and by Indigenous peoples": it is about teaching alternative perspectives on the archaeological enterprise so that everyone in the classroom recognizes that alternative perspectives have *value*. In this regard, it is as much about tolerance for alternative perspectives as it is about the scientific methods. Indigenous students, especially in classes where they are the minority, need to have their varied perspectives validated by the instructor in such a way that they are not afraid to make comments that might be misinterpreted as subjective and value-laden rather than the more normal objective and supposedly value-free opinions usually expected in an academic setting.

It is important at this time to differentiate between archaeology and heritage. Archaeology is a set of techniques used by practitioners to create stories based on aspects of material culture derived from contextual relationships among artifacts. As such, archaeology relies on the tangible artifact. Heritage, however, is not as limited. Heritage is not only about the materials themselves, but it is also the intangible aspects of the artifacts—the stories, relationships, and concepts about those artifacts held by the contemporary people of the cultures whose ancestors created those materials.

Surprisingly, archaeology students who are not Indigenous can often feel uncomfortable taking an Indigenous archaeology class in a Native American Studies program setting. Even while the basics taught may be the same, the manner of presentation or the overall tenor of the class is often different than classes taught within an anthropology program. Native American Studies classes tend to approach concepts and ideas from a more critical perspective rather than a generally accepting one. For example, the "scientific method" of Western science, which is foundational to scientific archaeology, is readily accepted by non-Native students, but often roundly criticized and begrudgingly acknowledged by Indigenous students as continuing the viewpoints of the colonizer.

Occasionally, I have to cope with the notion held by some archaeology students that archaeology somehow offers "the truth" about the past and that alternative perspectives are seriously flawed if they do not follow scientific protocol or if those stories do not fit contemporary scientific information. These students seem to confuse "truth" with "scientific rigor," and believe that anything that follows a program of dispassionate objectivity is inherently better than one that allows subjectivity.

A recent discussion can illustrate this point. Canadian archaeologist Robert McGhee, writing in *American Antiquity* (2008: 581) asks, "Why are so few Native Americans engaged in archaeology?" He acknowledges the lack of educational and economic opportunity available to many Aboriginal communities, but then goes on to say, "another very significant factor is the widespread assumption that techniques developed in a rationalist scientific tradition are not appropriate to the investigation of the Aboriginal past," which somehow "allows Aboriginal individuals and groups to assume rights over their history that are not assumed by or available to non-Aboriginals."

In response to this "exceptionalism," numerous authors (Colwell-Chan-thaphonh et al. 2010; Croes 2010; Silliman 2010; and Wilcox 2010) questioned McGhee's assumptions and argued that the inclusion of tribal perspectives actually made their archaeology better in its explanatory power based on the cultural insights the tribal members had. They also argued that it is not the "rationalist scientific tradition" that tribal members oppose, but rather the belief that *only* that tradition provides explanatory information to apply to the discovery of the past (see also Sievert et al., this volume).

Another issue involved with teaching Indigenous archaeology is a personal one: as a member of the Choctaw Nation of Oklahoma, I have to balance my ethnic background with my professional one. Many American Indians believe I cannot be Indian and an archaeologist, while many archaeologists don't think I can objectively practice archaeology out of misplaced loyalties to my ethnic group. In this regard, I usually tell the story of my involvement in archaeology—about how I felt that it was at my grandmother's urging to not let the unwritten history of those who lived in the area of our homestead before we did be lost—as a means of letting the students know that we each come to the field in different ways. I also try to let Native students feel comfortable *not* wishing to come to the field. By leaving the decision totally up to them, it alleviates stress or implied pressure to become an archaeologist.

## Teaching the Subject to Nonarchaeologists

It is often difficult to teach archaeology to nonmajors because of many of the misunderstandings and misconceptions people have. We all know we don't do dinosaurs, but we now also have to compete with misconceptions generated by Spike TV's "American Digger" and the National Geographic's "Digger" about why we excavate and about the real value of artifacts we find. We must enforce the idea that artifacts without context have no scientific value—something we must also try to teach our art history colleagues.

I find it easier to teach concepts with different methods, especially when it comes to methods archaeologists use to discuss the past, particularly such things as observation and inference.

In one class, in order to teach about observation and inference, I asked students to collect data about particular car owners based on observation of the automobiles. I asked them to note particular features of the exterior of the car, as well as things they could see in the car through the car windows, and then to offer some interpretations about the car's primary user. From the material they observed, they were surprised about the amount of information they could gather. I then moved from this example to talk about how archaeologists use similar sorts of observation to provide reconstructions of past societies.

Such exercises are not irrelevant: in 2006, archaeologists from the University of Bristol in the United Kingdom "excavated" a 1991 Ford Transit van. Archaeologist Adrian Myers' (2011) report on "The Van Project," while much more detailed and "scientific" in its scope than the window observation exercise, provides another look at contemporary material culture inquiry "into small finds of the recent past" (2011: 159; see also Kryder-Reid 2019). However, by making the process fun and removing some of the "scientific verbiage," instructors can help students realize more about how archaeologists work with material remains to garner information upon which to base their interpretations of past cultures.

Why is this important? With the continuing and expanding growth of heritage projects and, indeed, the heritage industry, the general public is often exposed to the conflicts between the preservation of the past and the continuing evolution of the built environment. It is imperative that the community better understands the different benefits industry and heritage offer. Archaeology is only one discipline that can illuminate the "benefit" to the past, but in the Western hemisphere, it offers the best means of gaining information about the great length of time not within the period of time since the written record. Archaeology offers the insights into ways that people lived, flourished, and survived.

## Teaching Archaeology to Those Who Might Be Averse to It

Trying to teach archaeology to those who are averse to accepting it as having any beneficial aspects can be a challenge, especially in classrooms with descendants of those cultures that consistently have borne the brunt of the archaeological enterprise. These students usually come in with a preconceived notion of either what archaeology is in relation to Indigenous groups, or what archaeology purports to provide. Indigenous students usually are predisposed to believe that archaeologists are grave robbers (Mihesuah 1996; Riding In 1992) whose only purpose in life is to plunder graves in search of "goodies" to fill museum displays or to fulfill tenure (or other occupational) requirements. They often draw upon their readings of other scholars in this regard. For example, in 1992, Vine Deloria wrote about the perception that "only scholars have the credentials to define and explain American Indians. . . ." (1992: 595); even non-Natives (compare Custer 2005) wrote about the issue in such a way to brand archaeologists as nearly anything but objective scientists. Because of this beginning perception, it is often more difficult to address this aspect of the class without seeming to be overtly self-serving. While there is nothing wrong with being self-serving in the sense that we should be supportive of our discipline, it is important that we not be overly antagonistic about our discipline's history. There have been times in the past where notable (notorious?) members have plundered and pillaged in the name of science, but we must make it known that such instances now are the extreme minority rather than the norm.

In this regard, it helps to discuss the ethics of archaeology and its relationship not only to science but also to the many publics it purports to serve. The Society for American Archaeology's Principle #2 (Accountability) helps situate the discipline within contemporary populations. It calls on archaeologists to acknowledge public accountability and to make a commitment toward consulting with affected group(s) in order to establish working relationships that can be beneficial to all parties involved, not just the archaeologist. For a more complete discussion of this, see Watkins et al. (2000: 40–44). This discussion of ethics serves multiple purposes in that it helps all students understand that ethics are as essential to the practice of archaeology as are careful measurements and observations (see also McGill 2019).

One method I use to begin discussions of Indigenous archaeology revolves around the conflict between the concepts inherent in origin stories of North American Indigenous populations and the scientific concepts concerning the onset of human occupation in North America. I have written about this previously (Watkins 2006: 106–107), but it is important that everyone recognize that by contextualizing foundational topics within alternative cultural methods of understanding, students feel less threatened by "institutionalized truth" and more aware of alternative means of examining the same data.

For example, in teaching about the original peopling of the Western Hemisphere, I find it important to present the data about dates, geography, and theories in as unbiased a manner as possible, and then to allow discussion of any alternatives without questioning the "reality" or "validity" of the hypotheses. Next, I ask the students to offer explanations that fit those hypotheses. Ultimately, the students themselves create the models upon which they must build their arguments, without me imposing my biases (which I certainly have) upon theirs. This allows critical evaluation of the class materials without providing a model of rote acceptance of the instructor's views. In many regards, it is just as important to get students to think about alternative interpretations as it is to get students to be able to think like an "archaeologist."

## Teaching the Contemporary Relevance of Archaeology

Perhaps most difficult of all the above aspects is to teach the contemporary relevance of archaeology to anyone. As archaeologists, we can discuss the bigger picture and time depth that we can offer; we can talk about "how he who ignores the past is destined to repeat it"; about how we have to know where we've been in order to know where we're going. Still, at the end of the day, all we can do is offer our interpretations of how archaeology can help inform contemporary populations about how cultures of the past dealt with issues similar to those we face today (see also Lerner and Effland 2019).

Does this work? Occasionally, I find that some groups of students are more open to the discussion than others. I also find that some students are more disposed to being uncomfortable with discussions revolving around the past and someone's alternative interpretations of that past. I also encounter aspects of the discussion that revolve around questions of "authenticity" related to culturally determined issues such as status, gender, age, and shared cultural context—things most instructors do not think about. For example, in some of the traditional cultures within which Indigenous students were raised, "elders" (either chronologically or socially determined) are respected as knowledge bearers and therefore are sometimes seen as having "authentic" knowledge about the "past." Also, some cultures maintain separate sets of "knowledge" related to gender, such that women do not attempt to know "men's business," or vice versa. In those instances, I try to find ways of alternatively communicating the information I want them to leave with, and then go on. There are certainly some things I cannot teach them—perhaps as many they cannot learn from me—but I keep trying to find ways of reaching out to them to help them question.

I do believe an awareness of the different ways that our own culture influences—not only our communications but also the ways that our communications are accepted and interpreted—is extremely important when we are involved in trying to teach (and reach) students who are not members of the "dominant" Euro-American cultures. If we become more aware of the underlying "contexts" that influence the ways our teaching is interpreted, as well as the way our students from nondominant cultures learn, we will be better able to meet their needs as well as to be able to communicate that which we feel those students need to gain from our classes.

A student came up to me after a class where I had presented on communication styles and the differing ways that tribal people and nontribal people tend to view "consultation." She said she was momentarily curious why I spent so much time discussing how to communicate to tribal members until she realized that I was talking to the nontribal people in the class. She said that what I had been discussing was second nature to her and to her Indian classmates, because that was how they communicated with tribal elders and officials all the time. She thanked me for helping the non-Indian students understand how things can and should be done differently within historic preservation conversations, and also suggested that it would benefit non-Indian federal employees to learn how things are perceived and handled in tribal offices.

Assessing Student Learning

Finding alternative ways of assessing student learning within a college or university setting can be difficult, especially if one's classes are large. Multiple-choice and true-false exams test only particular aspects of student ability, and all too often fail to adequately measure student learning. It is imperative that students in all fields of academic study know how to communicate through the written word. I try to provide rubrics for student

Table 7.1. Grading rubric for student papers, developed and used by the author in Tribal Historic Preservation class, University of Oklahoma, Spring 2012

| Grade | Grammar | References | Clarity of thought |
|---|---|---|---|
| A | Very few grammatical mistakes. Spelling proper, few punctuation errors or mistakes. No run-on sentences or sentence fragments. Word usage proper and correct. | 7 or more references used in the paper. Reference section uses proper citation style. | Paper is logically put together with an Introduction, Body, and Conclusions. Argument well supported with outside references. Reference section consistent and well done. |
| B | Grammatical mistakes are present but not common. Spelling, punctuation, and word usage generally good, but more mistakes present. One run-on sentence or sentence fragment present. | 5–6 references used in the paper. Reference section uses proper citation style. | Paper is logically put together with and Introduction, Body, and Conclusions. Argument is supported with outside references, but references more general in nature. Reference section is consistent. |
| C | Grammatical mistakes present and more common. Problems with spelling, punctuation, and word usage more common and obvious. More than one run-on sentence or sentence fragment. | 3–4 references used in the paper. Reference section uses the proper citation style, but mistakes common. | Paper structure is less logical. One of the main parts of the paper (Introduction, Body, and Conclusions) missing or poorly developed. Argument not well supported. Reference section is minimally done. |
| D | Grammatical mistakes common. Spelling, punctuation, and word usage problematic. More than two run-on sentences or sentence fragments. | 2 references used in the paper. Reference section inconsistent, with citations missing or poorly done. | Paper poorly structured. One or more of the main parts of the paper missing. Argument missing or very poorly supported. Reference section inconsistent or poorly done. |
| F | Grammatical mistakes very common. Spelling, punctuation, and word usage poor. More than three run-on sentences or sentence fragments. | Fewer than 2 references used in the paper. Reference section inconsistent, with citations missing or poorly done. | Paper poorly structured. One or more of the main parts of the paper missing. Argument missing or very poorly supported. Reference section poorly done or missing. |

work to provide at least a minimal structure for the assignment, so that it is obvious what is expected of the student, and to remove some of the subjective aspects of grading.

Using rubrics allows students to focus on the most important components of the assignment. The rubric in Table 7.2, for example, provides what I perceive to be the most important aspects of a student presentation, divided into easily recognizable sections: Information Content, Visuals, and Personal Presentation. Each section is subdivided into subcategories, and then each subcategory is further split into declining point values based on quality or performance. By having this information at the beginning of the semester, students apply the rubric to my presentations, as well as those of their classmates, and also know where to focus their energies as they prepare their presentations.

In addition to providing rubrics for the student's paper (see Table 7.1), I try to eliminate the "all-or-nothing" idea of grading by breaking up the assignment into logical steps. I require the students to submit a formal paper topic early in the semester. About three weeks later, I require the students to provide an outline of their paper, based on their proposed topic, along with at least three references that they will use. Then I require the students to submit a "draft final" shortly after the mid-semester portion of the class. All of these steps lead to the final paper (see Bender 2019 and Messenger 2019 for similar approaches to writing assignments).

Each of these steps is graded separately. In this manner, students earn points by completing the logical steps toward a writing assignment and the process helps reduce procrastination. I require the draft final to be a nearly complete paper which I review, comment on, and return to the student for revision and resubmission, thereby giving them a taste of the academic publication process. It also makes the writing assignments more meaningful in that the student can't just turn in a paper and walk away, but has to actually see comments and address them rather than ignoring them.

I also require that students in upper level undergraduate and graduate classes create and give in-class presentations with peer evaluation. The students are required to provide copies of their presentations to the other students, and the other students evaluate the presentations based on a rubric provided. This provides two levels of learning—the student presenter gets experience creating and presenting the results of their interests, and at the same time the other students get experience evaluating the presentation against predetermined standards and guidelines. I do not offer credit points for the evaluating students. I find that reviewers are more likely to be candid if they are somewhat assured that their identity remains anonymous and that their classmates will not be able to attribute scores to specific individuals.

Table 7.2. Rubric for in-class presentation, developed and used by the author in Tribal Historic Preservation class, University of Oklahoma, Spring 2012

INFORMATION CONTENT:

| Excellent (5 points) | Good (4 points) | Fair (3 points) | Poor (1 point) |
| --- | --- | --- | --- |
| The presenter knew information presented on the topic. | The presenter seemed somewhat comfortable with the information. | The presenter seemed uncomfortable with the information. | The presenter did not seem to know the topic. |
| The information presented was based on good research/data. | The information presented was based on some research/data. | The information presented was lacking in research/data. | The information had not been researched. Research should have been more extensive. |
| All three components (introduction, summary of research topic, and a conclusion) were present. | One component—an introduction, summary of research topic, or a conclusion—was missing. | Two components—an introduction, summary of research topic, or conclusion—were missing. | It was difficult to identify what was presented. More clarification was needed. |

VISUALS:

| Excellent (5 points) | Good (4 points) | Fair (3 points) | Poor (1 point) |
| --- | --- | --- | --- |
| Slides were easy to read. They were edited. No mistakes. | Slides were a little confusing to read. A bit of editing was needed. | Slides needed reviewing for information. Edits needed. | More time should have been spent on slide content. Mistakes should have been corrected. |
| Content was clear and fit with oral presentation. | Content was somewhat clear and mostly fit with oral presentation. | Content of slides was difficult to follow and somewhat fit with oral presentation. | More time should have been spent developing the content of the slides. Errors were throughout. |
| Slides were visually appealing. | Slides were a bit busy or too dark or light. | Slides were somewhat distracting to the presentation. | An alternative background or font should have been used. |

PERSONAL PRESENTATION:

| Excellent (5 points) | Good (4 points) | Fair (3 points) | Poor (1 point) |
| --- | --- | --- | --- |
| The presenter was composed and spoke clearly. | The presenter was nervous but spoke clearly. | The presenter was nervous and mumbled or used a lot of word spacers. | The presenter needs to practice presenting prior to the event. |
| The presenter made eye contact with the audience. | The presenter made some eye contact with the audience but fidgeted a bit. | The presenter made very little eye contact with the audience and fidgeted a bit. | The presenter made very little eye contact with the audience and fidgeted constantly. |

(continued)

Table 7.2—*Continued*

| Excellent (5 points) | Good (4 points) | Fair (3 points) | Poor (1 point) |
|---|---|---|---|
| The presenter glanced at notes to make points, but did not read the presentation. | The presenter glanced at notes to make points, and did read some of the presentation. | The presenter read much of the presentation. | The presenter read the presentation. |
| The presenter was organized and stayed within the 15 minutes. | The presenter was somewhat organized but went a little long. | The presenter needs to work on organization and/or went long. | The presenter was disorganized and the presentation went long. |

## Conclusions

It is important that people involved with heritage studies programs—and those instructors who teach within programs that delve into heritage topics and issues—recognize that different sociocultural contexts will have direct influence not only on the content and/or structure of heritage studies programs or courses but also on the long-term impact that such programs will have. Those of us who straddle different cultural backgrounds have dealt with many of these issues throughout our careers, and have learned how to better approach the topics around which heritage education is based.

As an American Indian archaeologist, I do have divided loyalties, and students generally perceive shifts from "objective" presentation of data to a stance advocating for a particular position. As archaeologists, we have particular issues we push for—cultural preservation, stewardship, ethics—but it is important that we advocate for archaeology without shutting the door on the free discussion of other perspectives. The university setting is one where free range of thought should be welcome and encouraged, and where students feel comfortable offering thoughts that might not be widely held, but that nonetheless are *their* thoughts and feelings. It is not our place to shut down conversation, but we must also be aware that we can sometimes be perceived to be the antithesis of one group or another.

This then should be our challenge—to find ways necessary to provide students with the academic background to be successful communicators in the spoken and written realms, and to provide more effective ways of integrating tribal and other diverse perspectives in a field of study that has too often been dominated by white male perspectives. Different pedagogical approaches to instruction are necessary to increase student success, especially for nontraditional students involved in nontraditional ways of earning degrees. The increasing availability of online and distance learning opportunities via blended classes and short-term intensive classes opens up opportunities for people with full-time jobs to get degrees while still working, but teaching such classes requires more preparation and involvement by the instructor. However, by adapting differing approaches to instruction, we can continue to improve learning environments and degree opportunities for every student.

## References Cited

Bender, Susan J.
2019    Identity and Heritage: A Faculty Interview on the Use of Image in the Classroom. In *Pedagogy and Practice in Heritage Studies*, edited by Susan J. Bender and Phyllis Mauch Messenger, pp. 179–184. University Press of Florida, Gainesville.

Bender, Susan J., and George S. Smith
1998    SAA's Workshop on Teaching Archaeology in the 21st Century: Promoting a National Dialogue on Curricula Reform. *SAA Bulletin* 16(5): 11.

Bender, Susan J., and George S. Smith (editors)
2000    *Teaching Archaeology in the Twenty-First Century*. Society for American Archaeology, Washington, D.C.

Colwell-Chanthaphonh, Chip, T. J. Ferguson, Dorothy Lippert, Randall McGuire, George Nicholas, Joe Watkins, and Larry Zimmerman
2010    The Premise and Promise of Indigenous Archaeology. *American Antiquity* 75(2): 228–238.

Croes, Dale R.
2010    Courage and Thoughtful Scholarship = Indigenous Archaeology Partnerships. *American Antiquity* 75(2): 211–216.

Custer, Jay F.
2005    Ethics and the Hyperreality of the Archaeological Thought World. *North American Archaeologist* 26(1): 3–27.

Davis, Hester, Jeffrey H. Altschul, Judith Bense, Elizabeth M. Brumfiel, Shereen Lerner, James J. Miller, Vincas P. Steponaitis, and Joe Watkins
1999    Teaching Archaeology in the 21st Century: Thoughts on Undergraduate Education. *SAA Bulletin* 17(1): 18–20.

Deloria, Vine, Jr.
1992    Indians, Archaeologists, and the Future. *American Antiquity* 57(4): 595–598.

Felder, Richard M.

1996    Matters of Style. *American Society for Engineering Education Prism* 6(4): 18–23.

Harr, Jean, Gretchen Hall, Paul Schoepp, and David H. Smith

2012    How Teachers Teach to Students with Different Learning Styles. *The Clearing House* 75(3): 142–145.

Kryder-Reid, Elizabeth

2019    Do the Homeless Have Heritage? Archaeology and the Pedagogy of Discomfort. In *Pedagogy and Practice in Heritage Studies*, edited by Susan J. Bender and Phyllis Mauch Messenger, pp. 129–147. University Press of Florida, Gainesville.

Lerner, Shereen, and Richard Effland

2019    Connecting the Dots: Teaching Archaeology and Social Relevance. In *Pedagogy and Practice in Heritage Studies*, edited by Susan J. Bender and Phyllis Mauch Messenger, pp. 185–197. University Press of Florida, Gainesville.

Lynott, Mark J., David G. Anderson, Glen H. Doran, Ricardo J. Elia, Maria Franklin, K. Anne Pyburn, Joseph Schuldenrein, and Dean R. Snow

1999    Teaching Archaeology in the 21st Century: Thoughts on Graduate Education. *SAA Bulletin* 17(1): 21–22.

McGhee, Robert

2008    Aboriginalism and the Problems of Indigenous Archaeology. *American Antiquity* 73(4): 579–597.

McGill, Alicia Ebbitt

2019    Assessing Student Learning in Heritage Studies: What Does It Mean for Students to "Understand" Archaeological Ethics? In *Pedagogy and Practice in Heritage Studies*, edited by Susan J. Bender and Phyllis Mauch Messenger, pp. 50–71. University Press of Florida, Gainesville.

Messenger, Lewis C., Jr.

2019    Experiencing Antiquity in the First Person through Archaeological Fiction: The Pedagogical Opportunities of BACAB CAAS. In *Pedagogy and Practice in Heritage Studies*, edited by Susan J. Bender and Phyllis Mauch Messenger, pp. 165–178. University Press of Florida, Gainesville.

Mihesuah, Devon A.

1996    American Indians, Anthropologists, Pothunters, and Repatriation: Ethical, Religious, and Political Differences. *American Indian Quarterly* 20(2): 229–237.

Myers, Adrian T.

2011    Contemporary Archaeology in Transit: The Artifacts of a 1991 Van. *International Journal of Historical Archaeology* 15: 138–161.

Nicholas, George P.

2008    Native Peoples and Archaeology. In *Encyclopedia of Archaeology*, edited by Deborah M. Pearsall, pp. 1660–1669. Academic Press, New York.

Nicholas, George P., and Thomas D. Andrews

1997    Indigenous Archaeology in the Postmodern World. In *At a Crossroads: Archaeologists and First Peoples in Canada*, edited by George P. Nicholas and Thomas D. Andrews, pp. 1–18. Archaeology Press, Simon Fraser University, Burnaby, British Columbia.

Pewewardy, Cornel

2002    Learning Styles of American Indian/Alaska Native Students: A Review of the Literature and Implications for Practice. *Journal of American Indian Education* 41(3): 1–81.

Price, Melanie, Michael Kallam, and John Love

2009    The Learning Styles of Native American Students and Implications for Classroom Practice. *Proceedings of the Native American Studies Conference*, pp. 36–45. Southeastern Oklahoma State University. Durant, Oklahoma. Available online at http://www.se.edu/nas/files/2013/03/NAS-2009-Proceedings-M-Price.pdf.

Pyburn, K. Anne, and George S. Smith

2015    The MATRIX Project (Making Archaeology Teaching Relevant in the XXIst Century): An Approach to the Efficient Sharing of Professional Knowledge and Skills with a Large Audience. In *Sharing Archaeology: Academe, Practice, and the Public*, edited by Peter G. Stone and Zhao Hui, pp. 132–140. Routledge Press, New York.

Riding In, James

1992    Without Ethics and Morality: A Historical Overview of Imperial Archaeology and American Indians. *Arizona Law Journal* 24(1): 11–34.

Riener, Cedar, and Daniel Willingham

2010    The Myth of Learning Styles. *Change: The Magazine of Higher Learning* 42(5): 32–35.

Silliman, Stephen

2010    The Value and Diversity of Indigenous Archaeology: A Response to McGhee. *American Antiquity* 75(2): 216–220.

Stone, Tammy

2014    Integrating the Concept of Diverse Interest Groups into Undergraduate Curriculum in Archaeology. *SAA Archaeological Record* 14(1): 36–39.

Watkins, Joe

2000    *Indigenous Archaeology: American Indian Values and Scientific Practice*. Alta-Mira Press, Walnut Creek, California.

2006    Communicating Archaeology: Words to the Wise. *Journal of Social Archaeology* 6(1): 100–118.

2014    Teaching Indigenous Classes in Non-Indigenous Classrooms. In *Exploring Race in Predominately White Classrooms: Scholars of Color Reflect*, edited by George Yancy and Maria del Guadalupe Davidson, pp. 203–214. Routledge Press, New York.

Watkins, Joe, Lynne Goldstein, Karen Vitelli, and Leigh Jenkins

2000    Accountability: Responsibilities of Archaeologists to Other Interest Groups. In *Ethics in American Archaeology*, 2nd rev. ed., edited by Mark Lynott and Alison Wylie, pp. 40–44. Society for American Archaeology, Washington, D.C.

Weiant, Clarence W.

1952    An Inductive Approach in the Teaching of Archaeology. *American Antiquity* 17(3): 251–253.

Wilcox, Michael

2010　Saving Indigenous Peoples from Ourselves: Separate but Equal Archaeology is Not Scientific Archaeology. *American Antiquity* 75(2): 221–227.

Wylie, Alison

2005　The Promise and Perils of an Ethic of Stewardship. In *Embedding Ethics*, edited by Lynn Meskell and Peter Pels, pp. 47–68. Berg, Oxford.

# 8

## Challenging the Silo Mentality

Creating a Heritage Studies and Public History Program at the University
of Minnesota and the Minnesota Historical Society

KATHERINE HAYES, GREG DONOFRIO, PATRICIA EMERSON,
TIM HOOGLAND, PHYLLIS MAUCH MESSENGER,
KEVIN P. MURPHY, PATRICK NUNNALLY, CHRIS TAYLOR,
AND ANDUIN WILHIDE

In August 2017, the University of Minnesota launched a new interdisciplinary graduate program in Heritage Studies and Public History (HSPH) in partnership with the Minnesota Historical Society (Heritage Studies and Public History 2017). The program addresses the critical need for diversity and inclusion among scholar/practitioners in the interdisciplinary field of heritage studies, whether they work in museums, agencies, or other private or public sector settings. This chapter describes how the program came into being and what the students and institutional partners hope it will provide.

In spring 2011, the Institute for Advanced Study (IAS) at the University of Minnesota (UMN) awarded funding to an interdisciplinary group called the "Teaching Heritage Collaborative." This cluster of faculty and staff formed a working group to explore how to create curriculum around heritage studies that would not only draw upon the expertise of multiple disciplines, but would also demonstrate the advantages of an interdisciplinary approach to community-engaged heritage research and management. As a group, we had been introduced to one another in 2009–10 through the aptly named "Locating Heritage Collaborative." The core group of conveners represented archaeology, historic preservation in architecture, landscape architecture, and public history, with participation from faculty in museum studies, forestry and wildlife, American studies, American Indian studies, and African and African American studies, as well as colleagues in museums and community organizations in the Twin Cities area.

The Teaching Heritage Collaborative sought to address these core questions: How can we prepare and train professionals who hold the interdisciplinary concept of heritage as central to their approach? How do we (and future professionals) understand the role of *engagement* in our practice with community partners, multiple public audiences, other institutions, and other disciplines? How do we adapt our disciplines and fields of study to be more representative of a shifting demographic to represent multiple narratives and attract more diverse practitioners?

We wrestled with the varied ways we defined "heritage," recognizing that it is a term that encompasses many ideas about uses of the past in the present. It refers to the protection, preservation, or education about objects and subjects of study across a wide range of disciplines, and with varying approaches to engagement with multiple audiences. Until relatively recently, topics as diverse as landscapes, histories, folk art, archaeological remains, archives, architecture and the built environment, the natural environment, languages, and traditional cultural practices were studied and protected primarily by specialized practitioners and communities (compare Schofield 2014). Scholars in those fields now recognize the significant elision of concepts previously approached as distinct realms, like culture and nature, social memory and history, past and present. As our fields are increasingly subsumed under the broader concept of heritage (Logan and Smith 2010; see also Chilton, this volume), diverse practitioners recognize many commonalities of concern across their disciplines. For example, all heritage professionals must deal with questions of how to protect, preserve, and represent the value of heritage resources (recognizing that even the concept of "resources" is problematic) to (and with) stakeholders and wider publics, especially in light of contested/conflicting values and issues of social justice (see Harrison 2013; Smith 2006; King, Watkins, this volume). The interdisciplinary conversations among our colleagues and with visiting scholars in the years since the Teaching Heritage Collaborative was established have opened new opportunities for addressing those concerns. We have drawn on other definitions of heritage, as well, for example that used by the University of Massachusetts–Amherst's Center for Heritage & Society: "Heritage is the full range of our inherited traditions, monuments, objects, and culture" (2011). Little and Shackel frame cultural heritage as "whatever matters to people today that proves some connection between past and present" (2014: 39).

The University of Minnesota, a Tier I research university and public land-grant institution chartered in 1851, is a place with exciting potential to bring together multiple perspectives in heritage studies teaching. The flagship Twin Cities campus is located in a rapidly diversifying urban area with a multitude of heritage resources. The nationally recognized Minnesota Historical Society (MNHS), headquartered in St. Paul, offers unique opportunities for students to connect with its museums, historic sites, outreach programs, and many institutional and community partners. In addition to MNHS, other cultural and heritage organizations are located throughout the Twin Cities, and there are some 600 museums throughout the state. Minnesota is home to seven Anishinaabe (Ojibwe) and four Dakota reservations, as well as significant immigrant communities, including northern and eastern Europeans who arrived in the nineteenth and early twentieth centuries, and Hmong, Mexican, and Somali immigrants (among others) in more recent years.

From this vantage point, the Teaching Heritage Collaborative began to take stock of where we were with regard to teaching heritage studies at the University of Minnesota. We identified several programs with similar goals. They included an M.S. degree program in architecture with a concentration in heritage conservation and preservation (located in the College of Design [CDes]); an M.A. in cultural heritage management (anthropology) with a focus on archaeology (located in the College of Liberal Arts [CLA]); a museum studies graduate minor (administered by CDes); and the Tourism Center with its related class on heritage tourism and visitor behavior analysis (located in the College of Food, Agricultural and Natural Resources Sciences [CFANS]). While no formal program in public history existed, there was significant interest from both faculty and students.

Students from multiple disciplines expressed interest in learning about heritage issues and career opportunities in related fields. A critical step in building these opportunities was revitalizing the relationship between the university and public history organizations. The University of Minnesota and the Minnesota Historical Society had benefited from a close relationship until the 1960s. It was university scholars who had produced the definitive works on state history. As the focus of the academy shifted away from state and local history in the 1970s and 1980s, however, the two institutions drifted apart. The rise of the Public History movement created new ways of thinking about the relationship of scholarship to public audiences while museums challenged themselves to broaden their narratives and interpretive models (Pitman et al. 1992). In archaeology and historic preservation, the development of heritage protection laws created new public roles that, in Minnesota, were filled first by academics, but were later taken over by practitioners from other agencies. In these fields, scholars and practitioners became estranged from one another, despite the fact that our students very often moved from one domain to the other.

In each of our disciplines, we had been engaging in an ad hoc assembly of student internships and learning opportunities, by reaching out to the network of Twin Cities agencies, organizations, and community groups working with heritage issues. These experiences are invaluable to our students, yet we each were approaching them from our own disciplinary perspectives. We recognized that this has placed unnecessary restrictions on the opportunities students may find, and may not best prepare students for the cross-disciplinary realities of professional practice. This indexes not only a lack of shared concepts and goals to teach to our students, but also reflects a disconnect from what community heritage organizations wish for in the graduates that we send to them. Thus, while the university and the Twin Cities are ideal venues for teaching and training future heritage professionals, we needed a concerted effort, initiated by the work of the Teaching Heritage Collaborative, to envision a coherent curricular structure, and to assess the benefits such a curriculum would provide by coordinating its content with community partners (see also Messenger 2019).

An Overview of the Perspectives Being Brought Together

Those of us who met with regularity under the Teaching Heritage Collaborative umbrella shared an interest in heritage as we understood it. We soon found, however, that our specific approaches converged and diverged in ways that were rather important to understand, in part as a way to recognize the different language we use to talk about heritage and the work we do that is related to heritage. Our individual and/or disciplinary perspectives and goals in the group, as well as the status of existing programs prior to establishment of the HSPH program, are described below.

## Archaeology

Archaeology is represented at UMN by a small number of faculty and researchers in anthropology; PhD graduate students; and an enthusiastic group of undergraduates, mainly majoring in anthropology, classics and Near Eastern studies, art history, history, and geography (all in CLA), who take our courses. Rather than continuing to steer students into the traditional career tracks of academic research versus cultural resource management, we wish to broaden all their options into the cultural heritage sector, with work connected to development, management, interpretation, and preservation issues related to the world's archaeological and historical sites, including engagement with descendant and associated communities. This field of practice requires archaeologists to become applied anthropologists (Pyburn and Wilk 1995; Shackel and Chambers 2004), working closely with developers and tourism offices; with nongovernmental agencies; and with historians, sociologists, interpreters, preservation and planning professionals, museum staff, art historians, and writers (Bender and Smith 2000; Carman 2000; du Cros and Lee 2007). We aim to build more explicit ties to these other departments in our curriculum, as well as connect with community partners.

Not only does heritage encompass multiple kinds of professional positions for archaeologists, it de-centers archaeology itself. There has been a growing recognition among professionals in the field, and reinforced through legislation, especially the Native American Graves Protection and Repatriation Act, or NAGPRA (see Jameson 2008; Messenger and Smith 2010; Soderland and Lilley 2015; Sievert et al., this volume), that archaeologists are but one group of specialists who have an interest in the study, interpretation, and disposition of the past. There is increasing awareness that professionals working in this arena need a broader set of skills and a greater understanding of such issues as globalization, economics, politics, and tourism (see Pyburn and Smith 2015; MacDonald, this volume). In addition, grappling with the ongoing legacy of settler colonialism, and even religious and political movements, has changed the nature of work throughout the world (see du Cros and Lee 2007; Fairclough et al. 2008; Scham 2019). Archaeologists and heritage managers recognize the need to consult and collaborate with, not only descendant communities, but also collectors, museum curators, developers, tourism professionals, and politicians, as part of a larger and more complex cultural heritage sector (see Clark, Marciniak, and Watkins, this volume; Elia et al. 2019).

Our approach to educating future heritage professionals in this program walks a fine line. While we do wish for our students to be successful in their job search on completing the degree, we do not want their program to be entirely instrumentalist (Hamilakis 2004), not least by reproducing divisions between cultural resource management (CRM) or agency archaeologists and academics, instilling a narrow focus on archaeological practice, or by thinking solely in terms of the "marketability" of students as employees (Aitchison 2004; see also Shackel, this volume). Thus, our desire to engage in an interdisciplinary heritage curriculum is also a means to encourage critical thinking about the state of the field, and to imagine the jobs that do not currently exist, but that we hope for in the future.

### Historic Preservation

Since 2008, the School of Architecture, situated within CDes, has offered an M.S. with a concentration in heritage conservation and preservation. Its faculty consists of a half dozen adjunct and tenured or tenure-track professors who teach classes that are the requirements or core components of the curriculum, such as an introduction to historic preservation, architectural history, documentation of historic buildings and landscapes, historic building conservation, world heritage, and preservation economics. While these classes draw both upper-level undergraduates and graduate students from a broad range of majors across the university, the pedagogical objectives of the program are primarily oriented toward students enrolled in the heritage conservation and preservation degree program. These students tend to have two distinct backgrounds. Roughly half are studying for a Master of Architecture and seek a "concurrent degree" in heritage as a specialized addendum to their training in architectural design. The other half come to the program having completed undergraduate degrees in subjects other than architecture; most have liberal arts backgrounds in anthropology, history, and art history.

Professional, university-based historic preservation education programs established in the late 1960s and later have been housed within older departments of architecture, landscape architecture, planning, and especially architectural history. Regardless of departmental affiliation, preservation education has always been construed as broadly interdisciplinary professional training combining coursework in the history, analysis, and documentation of architecture, and to a lesser extent landscape, as well as policy, law, and economics (Tomlan 1994; see also National Council for Preservation Education 2012). It has also focused somewhat narrowly on preserving "the physical reality of buildings, structures, objects, and places," the "artifactual context of our environment" (Stipe 2003: 452), rather than contemporary communities. This is perhaps because the skills and knowledge it prioritizes seem to correspond to our perceptions of job opportunities currently available to our graduates. These include government positions administering federal, state, and local preservation laws, jobs in the nonprofit and education sectors, and private work in architectural design and the conservation of architectural materials (Visser 2009).

Several more recent heritage concepts or approaches rooted in public history and anthropology suggest a need for preservationists to reconsider the meanings and uses of historic places for communities in the present. Cultural resource specialists are, in general, increasingly encouraged to go beyond merely consulting the public about matters of historical significance and potential impacts to historic resources. Greater attention to community engagement will be necessary to identify, understand, document, and, indeed, protect a fuller range of sites and practices that have cultural values associated with nature, religion, and subsistence, to name only a few (King 1998; Morgan et al. 2006; Getty Conservation Institute, Los Angeles 2004). In a similar vein, some suggest that public history will enable us to move "beyond preservation," so that historic sites become relevant and stabilizing forces for communities (Hurley 2010). Assessing a broader range of heritage values deemed important by diverse constituencies will require methodologies that preservationists are not now generally being taught, including ethnographic and community planning approaches to observation, interviews, and mapping (Mason 2002). Thus the influence of our pedagogical design on the education of future generations of preservation professionals is particularly meaningful in light of current debates among preservation professionals.

## Landscapes

Although there is a graduate degree program in landscape architecture (in CDes), it does not explicitly focus on heritage issues. With regard to the preservation of cultural landscapes, the practice itself is relatively new, so a literature of pedagogy has yet to emerge fully. The National Park Service brought the preservation of landscapes fully into the National Register–based historic preservation program in the early 1990s (Alanen and Melnick 2000). Since then, while the number of historic landscape reports has proliferated, the scholarly exploration of theoretical, methodological, and ethical issues to arise from the practice has lagged. To date, the programmatic questions of cultural landscape preservation are largely matters of incorporating the concerns for landscapes into existing CRM frameworks; much remains to be done, including developing appropriate pedagogical responses.

The project of developing an interdisciplinary graduate program has brought exposure and greater familiarity with heritage-based disciplines other than those concentrating on material culture or built form (for example, architecture). It has been particularly instructive to understand the broader dynamic of the "heritage concept" as disciplines such as archaeology, public history, and some of the newer scholarship in architectural history and preservation have developed. "Heritage" as a cultural dynamic offers important avenues for unpacking the very complex set of imperatives that have created the cultural landscape, and that will in the best instances guide its preservation. That dynamic will continue to inform the teaching of heritage landscape preservation in important ways that have yet to unfold.

## Public History

Public history can encompass a wide array of people, productions, and activities that involve doing history in the public realm with multiple audiences. Public history takes place in historical societies, in academia, in museums, in documentaries, in living history sites, and in how people experience the landscapes of places. It includes two key components: creating more inclusive historical narratives that represent a wide array of experiences, and engaging publics in shaping historical consciousness (see Elliot 2007; Horton and Horton 2006; Porter et al. 1986; Stanton 2006; Walkowitz and Knauer 2009). The academic field of public history in the United States emerged in the 1970s and 1980s from the New Social History movement (Tyrell 2005).

Public history at the University of Minnesota has been sustained by a small group of dedicated faculty, staff, and students who seek to engage individuals and communities in the varied processes of history making and making history matter. We take to heart the goal of sharing authority in historical research, documentation, and storytelling, based on ideas first set forth by Michael Frisch (1990). University faculty and students have engaged in coursework, conferences, and exhibitions through two national projects, the Guantánamo Public Memory Project (2013, 2014) and the Humanities Action Lab (2015). Both of these projects allowed students and community members to address contemporary social justice issues, including human rights and incarceration, in complex, interdisciplinary ways that modeled critical thinking and analysis. Both projects included exhibits and projects that involved MNHS staff and sites.

There are also many opportunities for undergraduate and graduate students to get involved with community partners in various avenues of doing history. For example, the university and the historical society co-sponsor National History Day as a means of building applied learning experiences for middle and high school students. The Minnesota program has also pioneered a mentorship program for undergraduates that builds connections between the campus and History Day classrooms. Each year thirty undergraduate mentors are selected for a paid service-learning program that requires 100 hours of support to their assigned school. Graduate students assigned to History Day support the mentors, as well as coordinate a library field trip program that brings thousands of high school students onto campus to conduct research at university libraries. Students in interdisciplinary undergraduate and graduate courses on public history discuss issues in the field and then focus on neighborhoods in the Twin Cities and coordinate public history projects with community partners.

The world of digital media has opened up a number of possibilities for creating community-based digital archives, as well as finding new avenues for digital storytelling and digital history. The university's Immigration History Research Center provides public history opportunities on campus, including encouraging recent immigrant and refugee students to work with graduate students and faculty on creating digital archives—for example, the

"Minnesota 2.0" Digital Facebook Archive and the "Sheeko: Somali Youth Oral History" project (Immigration History Research Center 2009, 2011). Another resource and opportunity for digital publishing about heritage is *Open Rivers: Rethinking Water, Place & Community*, an online journal published jointly by IAS and University Libraries. Issue Seven, published in summer 2017, was a thematic issue on "Heritage, Open Space & Water" (see Nunnally et al. 2017).

For students, creating their own public history program has involved participating in classes in other departments where aspects of public history are addressed (geography, historic preservation, American studies, cultural studies) and taking directed study courses with individual professors to address topics related to their interests. With a cultural landscape where disciplines operate in a silo mentality, it can be challenging for students to find interdisciplinary, supportive, and sustainable networks with others interested in public history. It can be difficult to find classes that provide the kinds of professional training needed in public history such as oral history, museum exhibit design, or video and web production. Moreover, public history initiatives are most successful when trusting relationships with community partners can be developed through sustained effort.

### Minnesota Historical Society

MNHS is a broadly encompassing historical organization, although the public knows it best through its History Center museum in St. Paul and twenty-five additional historic sites and museums located throughout Minnesota. It also supports the administration of the Minnesota History Day partnership and other educational outreach programs, state archives and archaeological collections, a library with digital and paper collections, and publications. The organization also manages and distributes the Minnesota Historical and Cultural Heritage Grants Program, part of the Arts and Cultural Heritage Fund of the state created by a constitutional amendment voted on by the citizens of the state in 2008. MNHS shares broad strategic priorities of diversity and community engagement with the university, exemplifying the grounds for interinstitutional collaboration. For example, a 2014 MNHS strategic planning report (Minnesota Historical Society 2013) specifically notes that, "as historical and cultural life becomes more integrated in human rights agendas, larger and smaller museums are reaching out to under-represented population groups in their own communities, especially racial and ethnic communities, immigrants, LGBT communities, people with disabilities and women." Additionally, the Minnesota State Historic Preservation Office (SHPO) has established clear goals to research and document the history of "properties associated with underrepresented groups" throughout the state, frequently in partnership with MNHS (Minnesota Historical Society, State Historic Preservation Office 2012).[1]

MNHS coordinates a Museum Fellows program in partnership with UMN, which models some of the ways that higher education can be brought together with community and diversity priorities in heritage studies. The program examines core principles related to increasing inclusion in museums. Class readings outline the perceived power and authority assigned to museums and the challenges that museums face in becoming more inclusive organizations. Visiting museum professionals and community members provide insight into how theory meets practice in a real-world setting. A paid summer internship provides an opportunity for students to become part of the institutional fabric of MNHS, working across the institution or on team projects related to the institutional strategic priority for diversity and inclusion. The catalyzing experience of the program is a museum-study trip to Washington, D.C. Students visit many of the iconic museums in the D.C. area and meet museum professionals including educators, curators, collections managers, and museum directors (see Figure 8.1). This experience provides an opportunity for students to see that even the most prestigious museums in our country are facing the same core issues related to staff diversity, inclusive narratives, community engagement, and public perception as discussed in the course and experienced at MNHS through the internship. This program emphasizes the importance of experiential learning and cohort building, professional network development for the Museum Fellows, and exposure to a breadth of heritage-related work rather than that of just a single department. While it is not an exclusive program, organizers place an emphasis on recruiting diverse students as a way to introduce Fellows to various careers in the museums field to address the lack of diversity on museum staffs.

Figure 8.1. The Museum Fellows from the University of Minnesota toured museums in Washington, D.C., and met with Lonnie Bunch, founding director of the National Museum of African American History and Culture. Photograph by Chris Taylor, courtesy of the Minnesota Historical Society.

## Bringing the Stakeholders to the Table

In 2011–12, the Teaching Heritage Collaborative began the process of identifying common interests and priorities in heritage/public history curricula through a series of stakeholder meetings. These were comprised of two major groups, university-affiliated faculty, students, and researchers, and nonuniversity heritage professionals and organization representatives. After meeting with stakeholders from both within and outside of the university, and conducting a broad survey of heritage-related graduate programs in the United States, we identified a set of goals and themes common across all of our programs. Supporting increased diversity and inclusiveness in the field is a top priority, both in terms of the content of our work, and in terms of the community of professional practitioners. There is broad support for creating cohorts of students from disparate disciplines as we acknowledge that these cohorts will help to change the nature of the field into an inherently interdisciplinary practice. We also prioritize including coursework that takes place outside of the classroom and university setting and that engages with professional organizations and communities through experiential learning.

Perhaps more difficult than bringing academic disciplines together, however, we recognize the significant challenges of aligning the university curricular framework with nonacademic settings for the students' experiential learning. These challenges include the fiscal constraints of the university which, as a land-grant university, recognizes the value of community and interinstitutional partnerships, but which thus far has not been able to commit substantial resources to support community-engaged scholarship, for example, by fully incorporating it into tenure requirements, recognizing it as service work, or supporting teaching across colleges or institutions. Nevertheless, we see promising changes that have helped pave the way for approval of the HSPH program.

With these goals and challenges in mind, in summer 2013 we initiated a partnership between the university and the historical society in order to model and test our curricular priorities. Supported by an Arts and Cultural Heritage Fund grant, the partnership supported collaboration on several projects that would create learning opportunities for students *and* generate new heritage interpretive programs. From these models, we hoped eventually to create durable curriculum structures linking the two institutions. These projects included the Guantánamo Public Memory Project (a consortium of universities working on issues of contemporary significance through public history projects), the Bohemian Flats public archaeology project (focused on the site of a historic immigrant neighborhood; see Figure 8.2), and Historic Fort Snelling interpretive programs (a reconstructed 1820s military fort with interpretive potential spanning more than 120 years; see Figure 8.3). Each project drew upon the sites or resources of both institutions, giving students experience in digital humanities, exhibit preparation, community engagement, and work with collections of all sorts, in courses on public history, historical archaeology, and archival research methods. At this stage of the partnership, neither institution was structured to allow true co-instruction, so cooperation between faculty and staff included sharing research materials, providing guest presentations, and supervising students from classes in MNHS internships.

The partnership and the projects readily identified the myriad prospects and pitfalls in collaborative teaching. On the "prospects" side, there are a multitude of projects under MNHS's purview that have been identified as

Figure 8.2. Research on Bohemian Flats resulted in publications, an online database, and a public exhibit (*Remembering the Bohemian Flats: One Place, Many Voices*) displayed in the lobby of Mill City Museum, not far from the site of the original settlement on the banks of the Mississippi River. Visitors included descendants of families who had lived there. Photograph courtesy of the Minnesota Historical Society.

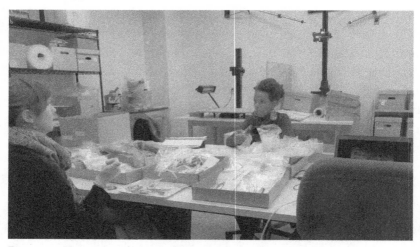

Figure 8.3. University of Minnesota students participated in collaborative research at historic sites as part of the MNHS/UMN Heritage Partnership. Graduate research assistant Kelly Wolf (*left*) and undergraduate Meron Tebeje (*right*) are shown inventorying artifacts excavated from the Wood Barracks at Historic Ft. Snelling. Photograph by Nancy Buck Hoffman, courtesy of the Minnesota Historical Society.

possibilities for student experience, and these projects are necessarily inter-disciplinary. For example, exhibits may include components from collections, archives, and oral history; and the audiences at MNHS sites are of all ages and backgrounds, requiring broad communications skills. Providing the example of how university students can be brought into these projects has generated broad interest in continued collaborations. On the "pitfalls" side, we found that a surprisingly difficult issue was scheduling. Universities operate on an academic calendar, and while historical organizations do have school children as a significant audience, they are bound to other kinds of seasons as well. On the one hand, exhibit cycles, grant cycles, tourist seasons, and other considerations mean that MNHS does not necessarily have projects that fit neatly into semesters. On the other hand, university departments may not be terribly flexible either when planning curriculum; we have found that some exciting project possibilities could not be incorporated into a schedule of classes defined as much as three years in advance to facilitate how students map their major coursework. Imagine, on top of this, coordinating a semester-bound course with community partners whose schedules are different and who may not be able to coordinate with hypothetical students in some future semester's class. One obvious way around these issues is to plan for coordinated and even co-instructed courses absent specific content, for which communities might then apply to be a focus. Such models do exist (see Center for Urban and Regional Affairs 2015), but as noted earlier, these interinstitutional curricular structures for the most part did not yet exist for heritage studies (compare both MacDonald and Shackel, this volume).

Perhaps most challenging, yet essential to the partnership's efforts, is how best to recruit underrepresented minority and American Indian students to these program opportunities. Many heritage fields are skewed toward students who have the means to engage in unpaid internships for experience, without which employment is far less likely (see also King, this volume). If we are to take seriously the charge to diversify the field, we need to provide funding to students who are underrepresented precisely because their communities are economically disadvantaged.

## What Structures Do We Have in Place?

In partnership with MNHS, the University of Minnesota has now launched an interdisciplinary program of graduate study in heritage studies and public history, offering a terminal master's degree and a doctoral minor program (Heritage Studies and Public History 2017), with its first cohort in fall 2017. Students take courses taught by university faculty, MNHS staff of various departments (with adjunct status), or team-taught by both. Master's students also carry out two paid in-semester internships and a paid summer professional fellowship at MNHS or one of our partnering heritage organizations. All students take two required seminars: one on core concepts and ethics (HSPH 8001, Who Owns the Past), and one on issues of diversity, power, and privilege in heritage work (HSPH 8003, Race and Indigeneity in Heritage Representation). Master's students are additionally required to take a survey of professional practice (taught by MNHS staff in exhibits, collections, historic sites, education, and management) and a capstone course taught as a workshop with team-designed, community-engaged projects. Students also have track-specific courses and internships relevant to archaeology, historic preservation, and public history (other tracks may be added as the program develops). Placing beginning students in cohorts, regardless of track, instills a sense of common mission, and provides opportunities for students to develop interdisciplinary perspectives. They will finish the program by presenting their capstone degree projects in the final semester with their cohort, faculty and staff, and any of their community partners. The internship and fellowship opportunities provide students with a range of professional experiences and a portfolio, which enhances their resumés beyond their course transcripts. We have already begun to partner with smaller community organizations and other museums, in addition to MNHS, placing students with them for internships paid through the program.

Bringing this program into being has not been easy; there were many structural problems to be resolved since the program is shared by, not only the University and MNHS, but also two colleges (and multiple departments) within the university. Memoranda of agreement between colleges and institutions had to be created and approved by chairs, deans, lawyers, and governing boards. Budgets with instructional and facilities costs and tuition revenues had to be developed, including how those costs and revenues would be shared and what the impact would be on individual departments. An HSPH curriculum committee was appointed, with representation from both colleges and MNHS. The committee is responsible for integrating its calendar of key deadlines and decisions (admissions, course listings, appointment of faculty, and so on) with that of CDes, which is handling the first three-year administrative cycle. Museum staff who wish to be lead instructors in the program must submit their credentials to the graduate school in order to be added to the university's roster of graduate faculty. While many existing courses can fulfill requirements in each student's individualized program, the four core courses had to be created for the program and their syllabi approved by several committees from each college before the program could be presented to the Board of Regents for final approval. Perhaps most critical, commitments of student funding by the university have been slow to arrive, although we are actively pursuing external grants and foundation funds for this purpose.[2]

We believe the development of an interdisciplinary scholar-practitioner program is worth the effort that has been expended to date; we see it as the ideal way to achieve the goal of graduating employable candidates for the various fields engaged in heritage work. Combining the expertise of both institutions creates the core strength of the program, as we seek to increase engagement with diverse communities and to create more interdisciplinary opportunities for students. Students will benefit from a deep grounding in academic theory and practice, while also building experience to increase their employment opportunities upon completion of the program. The theory should inform students' level of engagement and critical understanding of the experiential opportunities, while the experiential opportunities create a deeper understanding and application of the theory. The result will be a cohort of graduates who not only have both the knowledge and skills to have a choice of career options, but who will also begin to change the fields themselves by refusing to accept the division between scholarly and practicing careers, and by bringing greater capacity to equity and inclusion goals. With the emphasis on breaking down dominant structures of power and authority and making heritage studies and practice more accessible to all, we expect that this program will increase diversity and bring a broader perspective to both academia and the practice of heritage studies outside of the academy.

Some issues also remain within the intellectual project itself. Will the method and theory of heritage studies as its own discipline (not a combination of archaeology, preservation, public history, and natural resources) follow automatically from creating HSPH cohorts? Our ongoing association as a collaborative continues to wrestle with development of common goals and concepts. Perhaps in part this is because we tend to be project-oriented, or, if you like, management-oriented in our collaboration, needing specific context to explore in order to understand one another. This understanding has led us to design our core concepts course as a series of case studies that may be addressed from our diverse perspectives, as a way of evoking commonalities (and differences) through dialogue. Also, while we readily agree on an inclusive epistemology—which comes with the understanding that heritage values are locally constructed—we also understand that we need not share the same toolkit of methods. This argues that we cannot entirely leave behind our own home disciplines when it comes to teaching that toolkit. We have noted in our review of heritage studies graduate programs that very few have overcome this hurdle, and very often the "interdisciplinary" program is dominated by one or two departments, and does not fully engage in team teaching. We continue to discuss these issues with our colleagues at other institutions and benefit from their experiences (see also both MacDonald and Shackel, this volume; Pluckhahn 2019).

If we are to move toward a truly interdisciplinary collaboration and curriculum, we must step back to the drawing board of theory and method. Method, in this case, would not consist of how to excavate a site or complete documentation of a structure or use archives. For us, method should consist of a number of components, including: how to communicate with various stakeholders about the importance of the past; how to navigate between competing or conflicting claims; how to accommodate multiple epistemologies; how to understand and apply approaches to sustainability, conservation, and preservation; and how to measure the real effects of heritage preservation projects on communities (see Chilton and Mason 2010; for discussions of critical heritage studies, see both Chilton and Zimmerman, this volume). We also need to better formulate theoretical approaches: why do we remember, or forget, the past (Connerton 1989, 2009; Harrison 2007)? What do we mean by "public" or global heritage (Messenger and Smith 2010)? How does knowledge of the past circulate? How is that knowledge made meaningful, or how is it abused? What would a decolonized heritage studies look like? Where are the multiple sites of these processes:

archives, sites, neighborhoods, museums, but also websites and other digital media, classrooms, community or family settings? All of these issues and approaches are ones that can, and should, begin outside of specific disciplines, if we are to break the gravity of "resource"-centered approaches. As we prepare students for the rapidly shifting transdisciplinary field of heritage studies, we ourselves must come to some shared understanding of what that is.

## Acknowledgments

The authors wish to acknowledge support from the University of Minnesota (CDes, CLA, Graduate School, IAS) and the Minnesota Historical Society, which has enabled the HSPH Program to come to fruition. We also acknowledge these sources of grant and program funding: the Minnesota Historical and Cultural Heritage Grants Program, part of the Arts and Cultural Heritage Fund of the state created by a constitutional amendment voted on by the citizens of the state in 2008; and the Institute for Advanced Study funding for research and creative collaboratives.

## Notes

1. Until early 2018, the Minnesota SHPO was administratively housed within the Historical Society, but has now been shifted to the state Department of Administration.

2. In March 2018 the Andrew W. Mellon Foundation awarded a two-year $350,000 grant to the University of Minnesota for the HSPH program in support of "Diversifying the Heritage Profession through Immersive Interdisciplinary Graduate Training."

## References Cited

Aitchison, Kenneth
2004    Supply, Demand, and a Failure of Understanding: Addressing the Culture Clash between Archaeologists' Expectations for Training and Employment in "Academia" versus "Practice." *World Archaeology* 36(2): 203–219.
Alanen, Arnold R., and Robert Z. Melnick (editors)
2000    *Preserving Cultural Landscapes in America.* Center Books on Contemporary Landscape Design, Johns Hopkins University Press, Baltimore.
Bender, Susan J., and George S. Smith (editors)
2000    *Teaching Archaeology in the 21st Century.* Society for American Archaeology, Washington, D.C.
Carman, John
2000    "Theorising a Realm of Practice": Introducing Archaeological Heritage Management as a Research Field. *International Journal of Heritage Studies* 6(4): 303–308.

Center for Urban and Regional Affairs

2015    Center for Urban and Regional Affairs Resilient Communities Project. Electronic document, http://www.cura.umn.edu/RCP. Accessed March 1, 2017.

Chilton, Elizabeth S., and Randall Mason

2010    NSF White Paper: A Call for a Social Science of the Past. SBE 2020: Future Research in the Social, Behavioral, and Economic Sciences. Electronic document, http://www.nsf.gov/sbe/sbe_2020/2020_pdfs/Chilton_Elizabeth_297.pdf. Accessed March 17, 2012.

Connerton, Paul

1989    *How Societies Remember*. Cambridge University Press, Cambridge.

2009    *How Modernity Forgets*. Cambridge University Press, Cambridge.

du Cros, Hilary, and Y. F. Lee (editors)

2007    *Cultural Heritage Management in China: Preserving the Cities of the Pearl River Delta*. Routledge, New York.

Elia, Ricardo J., Amalia Pérez-Juez, and Meredith Anderson

2019    Teaching Heritage in the Field: An Example from Menorca, Spain. In *Pedagogy and Practice in Heritage Studies*, edited by Susan J. Bender and Phyllis Mauch Messenger, pp. 94–111. University Press of Florida, Gainesville.

Elliot, Michael

2007    *Custerology: The Enduring Legacy of the Indian Wars and George Armstrong Custer*. University of Chicago Press, Chicago, Illinois.

Fairclough, Graham, Rodney Harrison, John Jameson, Jr., and John Schofield (editors)

2008    *The Heritage Reader*. Routledge, New York.

Frisch, Michael

1990    *A Shared Authority: Essays on the Craft and Meaning of Oral and Public History*. SUNY Press, New York.

Getty Conservation Institute, Los Angeles

2004    Fixing Historic Preservation: A Constructive Critique of "Significance." *Places* 16(1): 64–71.

Guantánamo Public Memory Project

2013    Guantánamo Public Memory Project. Electronic document, http://gitmomemory.org/. Accessed February 15, 2016.

2014    Guantánamo Public Memory Project Exhibition. Electronic document, http://ias.umn.edu/gtmo-in-msp/. Accessed February 16, 2016.

Hamilakis, Yannis

2004    Archaeology and the Politics of Pedagogy. *World Archaeology* 36(2): 287–309.

Harrison, Rodney

2013    *Heritage: Critical Approaches*. Routledge, New York.

Harrison, Simon

2007    Forgetful and Memorious Landscapes. *Social Anthropology* 12(2): 135–151.

Heritage Studies and Public History

2017    Masters in Heritage Studies and Public History. Electronic document, http://hsph.design.umn.edu/about.html. Accessed March 1, 2017.

Horton, James, and Lois Horton (editors)

2006    *Slavery and Public History: The Tough Stuff of Memory.* University of North Carolina Press, Chapel Hill.

Humanities Action Lab

2015    States of Incarceration: A National Dialogue of Local Histories. Electronic document, http://humanitiesactionlab.org/. Accessed February 16, 2016.

Hurley, Andrew

2010    *Beyond Preservation: Using Public History to Revitalize Inner Cities.* Temple University Press, Philadelphia, Pennsylvania.

Immigration History Research Center

2009    Minnesota 2.0 Project Collection (Digital Archive). Electronic document, http://ihrc.umn.edu/research/vitrage/all/ma/ihrc3908.html. Accessed April 2, 2012.

2011    Sheeko: Somali Youth Oral History Collection. Electronic document, http://ihrc.umn.edu/research/vitrage/all/sa/ihrc3926.html. Accessed March 30, 2012.

Jameson, John H., Jr.

2008    Cultural Heritage Management in the United States: Past, Present, and Future. In *The Heritage Reader*, edited by Graham Fairclough, Rodney Harrison, John H. Jameson, Jr., and John Schofield, pp. 42–61. Routledge, New York.

King, Thomas F.

1998    How the Archeologists Stole Culture: A Gap in American Environmental Impact Assessment Practice and How to Fill It. *Environmental Impact Assessment Review* 18: 117–133.

Little, Barbara J., and Paul A. Shackel

2014    *Archaeology, Heritage, and Civic Engagement: Working Toward the Public Good.* Left Coast Press, Walnut Creek, California.

Logan, William S., and Laurajane Smith

2010    Series General Co-Editors' Foreword. In *Heritage and Globalisation* (Key Issues in Cultural Heritage series), edited by Sophia Labadi and Colin Long, pp. xi–xii. Routledge, London.

Mason, Randall

2002    Assessing Values in Conservation Planning: Methodological Issues and Choices. In *Assessing the Values of Cultural Heritage*, edited by Marta de la Torre, pp. 5–30. Research Report. Getty Conservation Institute, Los Angeles. Electronic document, http://www.getty.edu/conservation/publications_resources/pdf_publications/pdf/assessing.pdf. Accessed February 14, 2016.

Messenger, Phyllis Mauch

2019    Archaeologists and the Pedagogy of Heritage: Preparing Graduate Students for Tomorrow's Interdisciplinary, Engaged Work in Heritage. In *Public Engagement and Education: Developing and Fostering Stewardship for and Archaeological Future*, edited by Katherine M. Erdman, pp. 137–156. Berghahn Books, New York.

Messenger, Phyllis Mauch, and George S. Smith (editors)

2010    *Cultural Heritage Management: A Global Perspective.* University Press of Florida, Gainesville.

Minnesota Historical Society

2013    The Future of History Matters: 20-Year Vision and Five-Year Strategic Plan for History in Minnesota and the Minnesota Historical Society, by Franke Wilson Consulting and Access Philanthropy for the Minnesota Historical Society. Electronic document, http://legacy.mnhs.org/sites/legacy.mnhs.org/files/pdfs/Legacy_Strategic_Report_2014_MNHS_Memo.pdf. Accessed May 20, 2014.

Minnesota Historical Society, State Historic Preservation Office

2012    A New Season: Preservation Plan for Minnesota's Historic Properties, 2012–2017. Electronic document, http://www.mnhs.org/shpo/planning/docs_pdfs/preservationplan_2012-2017.pdf. Accessed May 20, 2014.

Morgan, David, Nancy Morgan, and Brenda Barrett

2006    Finding a Place for the Commonplace: Hurricane Katrina, Communities, and Preservation Law. *American Anthropologist* 108(4): 706–718.

National Council for Preservation Education (NCPE)

2012    The National Council for Preservation Education Standards for Historic Preservation Degree Granting Graduate and Undergraduate Programs with Protocols for Evaluating NCPE Associate Membership. Electronic document, http://www.ncpe.us/ncpestds.html. Accessed March 18, 2012.

Nunnally, Patrick, Phyllis Mauch Messenger, and Laurie Moberg (editors)

2017    Heritage, Open Space & Water. *Open Rivers: Rethinking Water, Place & Community*, no. 7. http://editions.lib.umn.edu/openrivers/issue/issue-seven-summer-2017/. Accessed October 1, 2017.

Pitman, Bonnie, James Affolter, Gail Anderson, and Nina Archabal

1992    *Excellence and Equity: Education and the Public Dimension of Museums*. American Association of Museums, Washington, D.C.

Pluckhahn, Thomas J.

2019    The Challenges of Curriculum Change and the Pedagogy of Public Archaeology and CRM at the University of South Florida. In *Pedagogy and Practice in Heritage Studies*, edited by Susan J. Bender and Phyllis Mauch Messenger, pp. 72–93. University Press of Florida, Gainesville.

Porter, Susan Benson, Stephen Brier, and Roy Rosenzweig

1986    *Presenting the Past: Essays on History and the Public*. Temple University Press, Philadelphia.

Pyburn, K. Anne, and George S. Smith

2015    The MATRIX Project (Making Archaeology Teaching Relevant in the XXIst Century): An Approach to the Efficient Sharing of Professional Knowledge and Skills with a Large Audience. In *Sharing Archaeology: Academe, Practice, and the Public*, edited by Peter G. Stone and Zhao Hui, pp. 132–140. Routledge, New York.

Pyburn, K. Anne, and Richard Wilk

1995    Responsible Archaeology Is Applied Anthropology. In *Ethics in American Archaeology: Challenges for the 1990s*, edited by Mark Lynott and Alison Wylie, pp. 71–76. Society for American Archaeology, Washington, D.C.

Scham, Sandra

2019    Educating Students about the Modern Realities of Exploring the Ancient Middle East. In *Pedagogy and Practice in Heritage Studies*, edited by Susan J. Bender and Phyllis Mauch Messenger, pp. 112–128. University Press of Florida, Gainesville.

Schofield, John (editor)

2014    *Who Needs Experts? Counter-mapping Cultural Heritage.* Ashgate, Surrey, UK.

Shackel, Paul A., and E. J. Chambers (editors)

2004    *Places in Mind: Public Archaeology as Applied Anthropology.* Routledge, New York.

Smith, Laurajane

2006    *Uses of Heritage.* Routledge, New York.

Soderland, Hilary, and Ian Lilley

2015    The Fusion of Law and Ethics in Cultural Heritage Management: The 21st Century Confronts Archaeology. *Journal of Field Archaeology* 40(5): 508–522.

Stanton, Cathy

2006    *The Lowell Experiment: Public History in a Postindustrial City.* University of Massachusetts Press, Amherst.

Stipe, Robert E.

2003    Where Do We Go from Here? In *A Richer Heritage: Historic Preservation in the Twenty-First Century,* edited by Robert E. Stipe, pp. 451–494. University of North Carolina Press, Chapel Hill.

Tomlan, Michael

1994    Preservation Education: Alongside Architecture in Academia. *Journal of Architectural Education* 47(4): 187–196.

Tyrell, Ian

2005    *Historians in Public: The Practice of American History 1890–1970.* University of Chicago Press, Chicago.

University of Massachusetts Amherst

2011    Center for Heritage & Society. Electronic document, http://www.umass.edu/chs/about/whatisheritage.html. Accessed January 26, 2016.

Visser, Thomas D.

2009    The Status of Professional Career Openings in Historic Preservation in the United States. *Preservation Education and Research* 2: 73–84.

Walkowitz, Daniel J., and Lisa Maya Knauer (editors)

2009    *Contested Histories in Public Space: Memory, Race and Nation.* Duke University Press, Durham, North Carolina.

# TEN PRINCIPLES OF VALUES-BASED HERITAGE PRACTICE

KATE CLARK

Over the past few decades, heritage practice has evolved from being a strongly "expert-driven" discipline to one that embraces diverse voices, skills, and approaches. In that time, I have been lucky to work with many different people who care about their own heritage and that of others; this is what they have taught me about our work.

## 1. A Heritage Asset Can Be Anything at All (So Long as It Is Worth Keeping)

A heritage asset can be anything at all. At a personal level, it might be photographs in an album. At a national level, it might be our great buildings. It includes individual heritage assets, such as historic ships, items in museums, or works of art. It can also include landscapes, urban places, or the countryside. Natural heritage assets include species and habitats. Heritage can also include intangible assets, such as language, culture, faith, tradition, or knowledge.

Some heritage assets are formally "protected" as monuments, historic buildings or species, held in museums, or open to the public as heritage attractions or parks. But heritage goes well beyond these assets. The wider historic or cultural environment around us, for example, may not be protected, but aspects are often important and worth keeping. Equally, assets of local significance may be important but not protected. Things that matter to you are part of your own heritage.

## 2. What Makes a Heritage Asset Worth Keeping Is Its Value

What distinguishes a heritage asset from anything else is that we value it enough to want to keep it for the future, often beyond its original use. You break a cup, so you can no longer drink out of it. If it can't be used again, you throw it away unless it has value to you. It is that value that justifies keeping it. We value things in many different ways. They may be useful or have financial value. Things can also be valued because of their meaning, because they are beautiful, because they tell a story, or because they are associated with important events or people. They can excite emotional responses, including awe, fear, contentment, or peace. Places and things shape us and our identity.

Our stories are indelibly written in them, to be interpreted by us, and by future generations.

### 3. Heritage Practice Is Both a Technical and a Social Discipline

Heritage practice involves all of the different activities needed to hand heritage on to future generations, from physical care—conservation, repair, and maintenance—through to other activities that help sustain heritage such as finding new uses, involving people, planning and decision making, engagement, or interpretation. It therefore embraces both technical and social skills. But above all, heritage practitioners are facilitators, not dictators—they are there to help people care for what matters to them.

### 4. No Single Community or Discipline Has a Monopoly on Heritage Practice

Heritage practitioners come from many different backgrounds. In addition to those who hold traditional cultural knowledge, or who are passionate about local places or things, there are many others. They include anthropologists, architects and surveyors, curators, planners, archivists, ecologists, landscape architects, archaeologists, and conservators. There are people who know about restoring historic vehicles—locomotives, airplanes, and farm machinery, or particular materials or periods of time. Others have skills in oral history, language, and digital preservation.

Managing heritage also requires skills in marketing, retail, project management, interpretation, events management, or community engagement.

Heritage practitioners can be found in private practice or businesses, in government and the public sector, and in communities. Some are professionals; others, volunteers.

Many organizations deal with heritage. Some, such as museums or heritage attractions, might see heritage as their primary focus. There are many others, from businesses and public bodies to private individuals, who care for heritage assets, but it is not their core purpose.

### 5. Heritage Practice Is Not about Preserving Heritage Values, but Preserving What Is Valued

The ultimate aim of heritage practice is to hand on things to future generations. But the whole reason for preserving something is its value to people. Value informs decisions about what and how to preserve things. Therefore, understanding why something is important is critical to finding a future
for it.

Values-based heritage practice starts by understanding what is there and why it matters, and uses that to find a future for it. Values-based practice is a "bottom-up" process. It is very different from a "top-down" visionary process that seeks to impose solutions on places, communities, or things.

### 6. Heritage Values Are Complex, Contested, and Varied

People value things in many different ways, and the way that they do so is not static. Perceptions of value are shaped by cultural context and can change with time and with knowledge. Political, economic, social, technical, and other developments affect the way we see value.

This is what makes heritage difficult, contested, and often politically charged. Managing heritage almost always involves dealing with conflicting values of some sort. Heritage has the power to divide, as well as to bring people together, and to be manipulated and abused. Understanding and being aware of that potential is critical.

### 7. Looking after Heritage Can Bring Wider Benefits for Others

Handing on what matters to future generations involves activities that bring benefits in their own right. There are environmental benefits to reusing buildings, objects, and historic materials. There are economic benefits to local economies in the craft skills of repair, maintenance, and conservation. There are social benefits for people in acts of remembrance, in learning and in understanding the heritage of others. There are benefits for communities in coming together to celebrate stories and events. Caring for one kind of heritage can bring benefits for another. Heritage practitioners have a role in recognizing, delivering, articulating, and communicating those benefits.

## 8. How We Look after Heritage Matters

Heritage practitioners are in a privileged role, often in the space between the communities who value things and the institutions and political and policy mechanisms that can potentially enable those things to be preserved. Their role is to understand and represent the value of the asset in its widest sense. That brings ethical responsibilities to the communities they represent, as well as responsibilities for transparency, trustworthiness, accountability, and for providing a service to the public. This is particularly important where practitioners and communities come from different cultural contexts.

## 9. Caring for Cultural Heritage Is Part of the Wider Process of Acknowledging Public Good

Heritage assets that have a wider value to the community can be seen as part of the wider public or community "commons." The role of the practitioner is to help protect that which is of value to the public. Where heritage assets are formally protected, the justification for doing so lies in that wider public interest or community commons. In a democratic society, elected officials are ultimately accountable for legislation and policy relating to protecting heritage assets, and heritage practitioners play a critical and responsible role in advising them.

But where heritage is not formally protected, practitioners also have a role in discovering the stories that connect people to places and things, particularly where those stories have been neglected, and, in doing so, helping people to fall in love with and cherish their culture and heritage

## 10. Ultimately, Heritage Practice Can Deliver Public Value in Three Ways

Heritage practitioners add value: (1) by helping people to preserve that which is of significance or meaning to a wider community; (2) by doing so in a way that creates wider public benefits and helps make the case for the benefits of looking after heritage; and (3) by providing a service to the public, and acting responsibly, ethically, and transparently in doing so. Taken together, those three habits make up values-based practice.

# 9

# Public Issues Anthropology as a Framework for Teaching Archaeology at the University of Waterloo

ROBERT I. MACDONALD

For humans, heritage is the nexus that connects the past with the future. A key component in the construction of identity—both individual and cultural—heritage is constantly being created and interpreted from information about the past. Archaeological anthropologists have traditionally focused on what the archaeological record can tell us about the people who originally created it and how we can use this knowledge to contribute to our social science. Far less attention has been paid to how this information may affect living descendants of those ancient cultures. Increasingly, however, we find ourselves confronted by Indigenous and other descendant communities that view the archaeological record as an important part of their cultural heritage and not the exclusive domain of science. This chapter explores how the developing field of public interest/issues anthropology is being used at the University of Waterloo as a framework for teaching an expanding variety of professionals how to approach archaeology and heritage in ways that are holistic, transdisciplinary, respectful, and socially engaged.

Consistently ranked as one of the top universities in Canada, the University of Waterloo is perhaps best known for its strengths in engineering, computer science, and physics. Within its orbit have developed institutions such as Blackberry, the Perimeter Institute for Theoretical Physics, the Institute for Quantum Computing, and the Waterloo Institute for Nanotechnology. A world leader in cooperative education and experiential learning, the University of Waterloo also offers a wide range of programs across its faculties of Arts, Applied Health Sciences, Environment, Mathematics, and Science. Within the Faculty of Arts, archaeology has been a vital component of the Anthropology Department since the late 1970s, and it remains a recognizable area of strength today. Although a modest department, with a full-time core faculty of around seven, it still manages to offer both bachelor's and master's degrees. This is achieved in large measure by optimizing capacity under a public anthropology theme, which not only facilitates and encourages cooperation among faculty and students spanning the subdisciplines of anthropology, but explicitly demands it (University of Waterloo, Dept. of Anthropology 2012a: 3, 2012b: 1–2).

## Public Issues Anthropology

Public anthropology (Borofsky 2011; Hedican 2016), also known as public interest anthropology (Sanday and Jannowitz 2004), has been described by the topical review editors of the *American Anthropologist* as not a field of anthropology per se, but rather a form of anthropological expression that seeks to connect our work with those outside our discipline for whom our work is of particular relevance and interest (Griffith et al. 2013: 125). Although it has gained increasing prominence over the last decade or so—as evidenced by the 2008 creation of the standing Committee on Practicing, Applied and Public Interest Anthropology by the American Anthropological Association (Bennett and Fiske 2008), and the 2010 addition of a Public Anthropology Review section in the *American Anthropologist*—it stems from a recurring quest for relevance in the contemporary world that can be traced back to the pioneering work of Franz Boas (Checker et al. 2010: 5; Sanday 2003; Sanday and Jannowitz 2004: 64–65). As protean as anthropology itself, public anthropology has values explicitly focused on social justice, racial harmony, equality, human rights and well-being, and to the provision of anthropological analyses to multiple publics (Adams 2005: 434; see McGuire 2008 for a specifically archaeological approach). It strives to ground theory, research, and knowledge production in the interest of solving social issues, thereby keeping knowledge generation and theory development engaged in social action (Sanday and Jannowitz 2004: 65). As public anthropology advocate Robert Borofsky notes, it also differs from traditional applied anthropology in its emphasis on public accountability and its concern with understanding the hegemonic structures that frame and restrict solutions to problems as a way of more effectively addressing these problems (Borofsky 2011; see also Vine 2011).

At the University of Waterloo, public anthropology has been embraced with the addition of the term "issues," which underscores a desire to focus on matters not only of public interest, but of public concern (University of Waterloo, Department of Anthropology 2012a: 2). This seeks to add clarity to the program title from the viewpoint of prospective students who may not already be familiar with this aspect of anthropology. Since 2007, the graduate program in public issues anthropology—one of only six formal programs in public anthropology in North America (Borofsky 2011)—has built on a three-decade tradition of holistic anthropology committed to the four main subfields of archaeological, biological, cultural, and linguistic anthropology. The stated goal is to instill in students "an anthropological sensibility that builds knowledge and skills for life and work beyond the University" (University of Waterloo, Department of Anthropology 2012a: 1). In addition to addressing the aspirations of the anthropology department faculty, this program supports the University of Waterloo's objective to "maximize its academic and societal relevance by . . . introducing new academic programs in response to long-term societal needs and by providing service to society through cultural enrichment and knowledge transfer" (University of Waterloo 2006: 3). Students in the public issues anthropology M.A. program are taught to identify the relevance of anthropological findings and approaches for addressing current topics of public discourse.

The required coursework is designed to incorporate and be relevant for all of the traditional subdisciplines of anthropology. For example, the principle graduate seminar employs a modular structure organized under the direction of a designated instructor. Each faculty member, including adjunct faculty, has an opportunity to lead the seminar and bring forward for discussion themes and case studies from their own work that illustrate aspects of public issues anthropology. Together, students and faculty explore the challenges and benefits of critically examining topics that often cross-cut the traditional subdisciplines of anthropology. While the thesis research a student ultimately pursues in the program may focus on a topic specific to just one of the traditional anthropology subdisciplines, a public issues anthropology approach is required. The success of this graduate program has informed the renewal of the undergraduate curriculum with a view to integrating it more fully with the public issues anthropology theme (University of Waterloo, Department of Anthropology 2012a: 2–3).

## Cultural Resource Management

For a growing number of archaeological anthropologists employed in the field of cultural resource management (CRM), programs like the public issues anthropology program at the University of Waterloo are seen as critical to the continuing relevance and development of archaeology. CRM employs more archaeologists worldwide than any other branch of the discipline: an estimated 14,000 practitioners in the United States alone conduct nearly $1 billion dollars–worth of business per year (Doelle and Altschul 2009). As such, it is the branch of archaeology that interacts most closely with the rest of the world, in arenas as diverse as politics, identity and heritage, medicine, traditional ecological knowledge, environment and climate change, tourism and economic development, and the media (Carman 2000). Training of future practitioners in this field must therefore look far beyond the traditional scope of archaeological anthropology.

At the University of Waterloo, it is intended that the archaeology stream, grounded in public issues anthropology, will not only train students for key roles in the CRM industry but will also position them to articulate with the expanding international field of transdisciplinary studies. Like public anthropology, this is an area of endeavor that recognizes the fact that many complex contemporary issues, such as global warming or ethnic strife, cannot be solved by one or even a few points of view. Built around the concepts of transformative praxis, constructive problem solving, and real-world engagement, it seeks collaboration across academic disciplines and beyond academia in solving problems and addressing global issues (see also Hayes et al., this volume; Scham 2019). In an age of increasing specialization, such trends are reminiscent of the values of four-field anthropology that were instilled in many of us as undergraduates, and although those four fields now have many subfields of their own, we are now seeing a return to the broader perspectives and common sense of purpose that were inherent in that holistic approach (see also Sabloff 2011).

## Heritage

A related development is the growing interest of archaeological anthropologists in the subject of heritage, in particular the field of critical heritage studies (Harrison 2013; Smith 2004; see also Chilton, this volume).

Archaeological anthropologists have traditionally focused on what the archaeological record can tell us about the people who originally created it and how we can use this knowledge to contribute to our social science. We have reconstructed past lifeways, compiled these into narratives of culture history, and teased out insights regarding the processes of cultural evolution. As social scientists, we have shared this knowledge among ourselves, through the established modes of academic communication, and with the public at large, through an increasingly varied array of media. Yet, while we are certainly not ignorant of the potential social and political implications of scientific knowledge, we have paid much less attention to how the knowledge we create and share regarding the past may affect living descendants of the ancient cultures we study and the larger society in which these descendants live. Yet increasingly, particularly where Indigenous peoples are involved, we find ourselves confronted by descendant communities that view the archaeological record as an important part of their cultural heritage and not the exclusive domain of professional archaeologists. As anthropologists, this presents us with both a challenge and an opportunity to gain insights into the uniquely human values of cultural heritage, while at the same time playing an active role in the creation of that heritage. This creates an ethical imperative to approach the subject from a public issues anthropology perspective, that is to say, a perspective that is not academically detached from the project, but engaged in a manner that is ethical, well-balanced, and socially responsible (see, for example, the IPinCH project 2015; see also Clark, King, and Shackel, this volume).

For humans, heritage is both the nexus that connects the past with the future and a key component in the construction of identity—both individual and cultural. Heritage is constantly being created and interpreted from information about the past (Smith 2000). Kathleen Adams (2005: 436) argues that, in the heritage realm, public interest anthropology goes beyond simply giving voice to minorities and mapping out competing regimes of power; it should also actively advocate for and contribute to the promotion of equality, social justice, and conflict resolution. In light of these definitions, it is clear that, although perhaps not labeled as such, public issues anthropology has actually been developing in the context of Canadian archaeology for well over a decade.

## Indigenous Archaeology

In their 1996 *American Antiquity* article, Jane Kelley and Ron Williamson mapped out the position of archaeology within anthropology as this relationship has developed in Canada. In so doing, they identified a core interest in Indigenous ethnography that had been slowly vacated by sociocultural anthropologists over the latter part of the twentieth century. At the same time, they saw archaeologists moving into this "vacant core," as they called it, as they increasingly worked with—and for—First Nations on issues of cultural heritage. While perhaps initially prompted by the development of so-called "ethnoarchaeology," even by 1996 archaeologists were already starting to appreciate the value of emic perspectives and the political propriety of incorporating multiple voices, as they engaged in collaborative projects to document and manage archaeological resources, collect traditional ecological knowledge, and integrate this information into the sometimes rapidly evolving reality of First Nations society (see also Sievert et al. and Watkins, this volume; McGill 2019). Kelley and Williamson (1996: 17) concluded that the rise of heritage planning and management, both for and by First Nations, would lead to continued growth in applied anthropology, perhaps now better defined as public anthropology.

In the same year that the article by Kelley and Williamson was published, Bruce Trigger added a concluding chapter to the second edition of his landmark book, *A History of Archaeological Thought* (1996), entitled "The Relevance of Archaeology," in which he articulated some of the fundamental linkages between archaeology and anthropology. He attributed the strong tradition of middle-range and high-level theory building in archaeology to this long-standing relationship and argued for its continuation and ongoing improvement. The result of this collaboration, in his view, has been the development of a social science with a theoretical foundation robust enough to deal with modern social and political challenges, such as relativism, subjectivity, nationalism, colonialism, and gender bias (Trigger 1996: 529–548). In other words, in archaeological anthropology, we have a discipline uniquely qualified to address certain public issues, especially those for which long historical perspectives are relevant.

Building on this strong foundation, Indigenous archaeology has developed worldwide almost everywhere that descendant populations of Indigenous people have come to appreciate the significance of archaeological and other heritage information and resources in the politics of identity (for example, Bruchac et al. 2010; Colwell-Chanthaphonh 2012; Murray 2011; Nicholas 2008; Peck et al. 2003; Phillips and Allen 2010). While the concept of Indigenous archaeology may still be in flux, it arguably incorporates Eldon Yellowhorn's (2006) notion of internalist archaeology, wherein Indigenous people recognize and seek to understand a secular antiquity. It also incorporates the ideal of developing heritage professionals within descendant populations, as articulated by Indigenous archaeologists such as Joe Watkins (2000, 2005, and this volume) and Sonya Atalay (2006, 2012), and embraces the complex discourse that will be required as we attempt to tease apart the social, political, ideological, and epistemological issues that currently separate Indigenous peoples from dominant cultures (see also Ferris 2009; Ferris et al. 2014). Facilitating such a discourse by providing insights and vocabulary seems to be precisely the sort of arena where public issues anthropology can make a contribution. Since failure to consider or adequately address the heritage concerns of First Nations has touched off larger social conflicts in well-known cases such as the Oka crisis in Canada (Williamson 2010: 36) and the Standing Rock crisis in the United States (Colwell 2016), the stakes will be high.

## Case Study in Public Issues Anthropology: Learning about Archaeology, Contested Heritage, and Identity Politics at the University of Waterloo

Many undergraduate students pursuing a career in archaeological anthropology at the University of Waterloo get their first exposure to archaeological fieldwork through Ontario-based field schools or through summer employment in the provincial cultural resource management industry. For over a decade, best practices when dealing with Indigenous archaeological sites have included engagement with First Nations in order to address concerns they may have with respect to the work. This has come about in part as a result of several court decisions, which have upheld treaty and Indigenous rights with respect to archaeological heritage (for example, Birchall 2007). Since 2011, such engagement has been stipulated as a requirement of archaeological licensing by the provincial government, although the specifics of such engagement have not been defined (Ontario Ministry of Tourism, Culture and Sport 2011a, 2011b). To date, the most popular form of engagement has been the addition of trained First Nations liaisons, or monitors, to archaeological field crews. Students are thus engaging with representatives of descendant communities on a daily basis when working on Indigenous archaeological sites in Ontario. Providing these students with at least some basic contextual information and understanding prior to this engagement is essential, especially in situations where contested heritage might arise.

Contested heritage occurs in two main forms in Ontario. The older form is the long-standing polemic, between Indigenous peoples and the mostly non-Indigenous archaeological establishment, which involves the critique that traditional archaeology reflects an ongoing colonial master narrative (for example, Ferris 2009). Beyond the mandatory engagement requirements for archaeology now in place, this issue is being addressed through collaborative projects. Recently, faculty and students from the University of Waterloo joined a panel of Indigenous advisors and museum staff in a project to design the First Nations gallery for the new Waterloo Region Museum. It is noteworthy that this particular gallery was in part the result of public consultation across the Regional Municipality of Waterloo, which called for the presentation of regional Indigenous culture history. The result was an exhibit that presented the precontact archaeological culture history, the culture history of the European contact period, and the modern cultural expression of the First Nations in a first-person voice that underscored one of their primary messages: not only do they have a broad and deep history in the area but they are still active and engaged members of society in the Waterloo Region. One of the Waterloo students who participated in this project produced an honors thesis that looked at how the presentation of First Nations culture history in museums has evolved over the last twenty-five years (Taylor 2011).

More recently, a second form of contested heritage has arisen, involving factions of Indigenous people contesting one another's archaeological heritage. This has developed as a result of dislocations, primarily during the seventeenth- and eighteenth-century period of European contact, which involved a sequence of tenure by ancestral Wendat (Huron), Haudenosaunee (Iroquois), and Anishinaabeg (Algonquian) populations. Archaeological sites have thus become commodities in the ongoing quest for power and redress of colonial injustices. Competing claims are exemplified by one particular site that archaeologists had identified as a fifteenth-century ancestral Wendat settlement on the basis of its geographical location within the

Wendat homeland, the typical Late Woodland period artifact assemblage, and the typical longhouse settlement patterns. The same site was deemed to be Haudenosaunee (that is, people of the longhouse) by a representative of the Six Nations of the Grand River (Iroquois) community by virtue of the presence of longhouses, while a representative of a local Anishinaabeg community asserted that they weren't longhouses at all, but rather Anishinaabeg Midewewin medicine lodges (see Williamson and MacDonald 2015). Students and staff working on the project had to be thoroughly briefed to help mitigate what became a fairly tense dispute over who had cultural or ethnic "authority" over the site.

Ironically, while ethnicity is notoriously difficult to identify in the archaeological record, it does suggest that the ebb and flow of community membership and identity were no less dynamic in the past than they were historically or now. This, together with mtDNA evidence, which demonstrates gene flow across language groups in central North America for at least 3,000 years (Pfeiffer et al. 2014), underscores the futility of attempting to trace ethnic identity very far into the archaeological past. The complex sociopolitics of heritage and identity are increasingly being articulated by Indigenous and non-Indigenous writers alike, both in the academic literature (for example, Battiste and Henderson 2000; Palmater 2011) and in the popular press (King 2012). In his best-selling book, *A Fair Country: Telling Truths About Canada*, pre-eminent Canadian essayist John Ralston Saul (2008) presents a compelling argument that Canada is essentially a Métis nation, shaped as much by Indigenous values as it is by imported European ones in a thoroughly integrated whole that is now impossible to disentangle.

Staying abreast of this discourse is an ongoing challenge for archaeological anthropologists striving to keep their discipline relevant and their students appropriately informed. This is an environment where disputes frequently evoke very passionate responses by the people involved, and these can appear threatening to the uninitiated or unprepared, especially student field workers. While a solid grounding in the underlying factors driving the contested heritage and identity politics is not a shield from difficult encounters, it goes a long way toward mitigating the natural emotional response and promoting a more appropriate, well-reasoned one.

Senior undergraduates and graduate students pursuing thesis research in the public issues anthropology program at the University of Waterloo are often already experienced in First Nations engagement and related themes. Research projects completed to date include topics such as the following: stewardship of archaeological sites threatened by climate change and more direct cultural activities; repatriation of human remains to First Nations; environmental archaeology as long-term human ecology; discourses on decolonization and Indigenous revolution in modern North America; collaborative archaeology and Indigenous perspectives on archaeological topics and research questions; the appropriate long-term curation of material culture as a legacy of archaeological investigations; situating a recent European immigrant community within the spectrum of settler-Indigenous relations; and critiques of museum presentations of archaeological materials and First Nations culture. The recent addition of an Ontario-based archaeological anthropologist to the faculty promises to sustain and expand this project into the future.

## Conclusion

As Trigger (1996: 544–545) pointed out, in archaeological anthropology we have a discipline uniquely qualified to address certain public issues, especially those for which long historical perspectives are relevant. Dealing with heritage is one such issue and a particularly complex one where the heritage of Indigenous people is involved. The coming generations of archaeological anthropologists will need to know much more than how to find out what happened in the past. They will need to know the implications of such information in the social and political context of the present and how best to work with descendant populations, various other publics, social scientists, and policy makers, to ensure that such information is put to the best possible use. At the University of Waterloo, public issues anthropology provides a framework for teaching archaeology and heritage resource management that will enable students to pursue a broad range of careers that are holistic, transdisciplinary, respectful, and socially engaged.

## References Cited

Adams, Kathleen M.
2005    Public Interest Anthropology in Heritage Sites: Writing Culture and Righting Wrongs, *International Journal of Heritage Studies* 11(5): 433–439.

Atalay, Sonya

2012    *Community-Based Archaeology: Research with, by, and for Indigenous and Local Communities.* University of California Press, Oakland.

Atalay, Sonya (editor)

2006    Special Issue: Decolonizing Archaeology. *American Indian Quarterly* 30(3).

Battiste, Marie, and James (Sa'ke'j) Youngblood Henderson

2000    *Protecting Indigenous Knowledge and Heritage: A Global Challenge.* Purich, Saskatoon, Saskatchewan.

Bennett, Linda, and Shirley Fiske

2008    New Committee on Practicing, Applied and Public Interest Anthropology. *Anthropology News* April: 24.

Birchall, Chuck

2007    Hiawatha et al. v. Minister of the Environment, Ontario Realty Corp. and Council of Huron-Wendat Nation, *Ecobulletin*, CBA national environmental, energy and resources law section newsletter. Electronic document, http://www.cba.org/cba/newsletters/pdf/ENV-Hiawatha.pdf. Accessed March 15, 2015.

Borofsky, Rob

2011    Defining Public Anthropology: A Personal Perspective (2007). Electronic document, http://www.publicanthropology.org/public-anthropology/. Accessed March 15, 2015.

Bruchac, Margaret, Siobhan Hart, and H. Martin Wobst (editors)

2010    *Indigenous Archaeologies: A Reader on Decolonization.* Left Coast Press, Walnut Creek, California.

Carman, John

2000    "Theorising a Realm of Practice": Introducing Archaeological Heritage Management as a Research Field. *International Journal of Heritage Studies* 6(4): 303–308.

Checker, Melissa, David Vine, and Alaka Wali (editors)

2010    From the Public Anthropology Review Editors: A Sea Change in Anthropology? Public Anthropology Reviews. *American Anthropologist* 112(1): 5–6.

Colwell-Chanthaphonh, Chip

2012    Archaeology and Indigenous Collaboration. In *Archaeological Theory Today*, 2nd ed., edited by Ian Hodder, pp. 267–291. Polity, Cambridge.

2016    How the Archaeological Review behind the Dakota Access Pipeline Went Wrong. Electronic document, http://theconversation.com/how-the-archaeological-review-behind-the-dakota-access-pipeline-went-wrong-67815. Accessed February 14, 2017.

Doelle, William H., and Jeffrey H. Altschul

2009    Preparing for Work in the Billion-Dollar CRM Industry. *Anthropology News* April: 27.

Ferris, Neal

2009    *The Archaeology of Native-Lived Colonialism: Challenging History in the Great Lakes.* University of Arizona Press, Tucson.

Ferris, Neal, Rodney Harrison, and Michael V. Wilcox (editors)

2014    *Rethinking Colonial Pasts through Archaeology.* Oxford University Press, Oxford.

Griffith, David, Shao-hua Liu, Michael Paolisso, and Angela Stuesse (editors)

2013    From the Incoming Public Anthropology Review Editors: Enduring Whims and Public Anthropology. *American Anthropologist* 115(1): 125–131.

Harrison, Rodney

2013    *Heritage: Critical Approaches.* Routledge, New York.

Hedican, Edward J.

2016    Public Anthropology: Engaging Social Issues in the Modern World. University of Toronto Press, Toronto, Ontario.

Intellectual Property Issues in Cultural Heritage (IPinCH)

2015    IPinCH, Intellectual Property Issues in Cultural Heritage: Theory, Practice, Policy, Ethics. Simon Fraser University, Burnaby, British Columbia. Electronic document, http://www.sfu.ca/ipinch/. Accessed March 16, 2015.

Kelley, Jane H., and Ronald F. Williamson

1996    The Positioning of Archaeology within Anthropology: A Canadian Historical Perspective. *American Antiquity* 61(1): 5–20.

King, Thomas

2012    *The Inconvenient Indian: A Curious Account of Native People in North America.* Doubleday Canada, Toronto, Ontario.

McGill, Alicia Ebbitt

2019    Assessing Student Learning in Heritage Studies: What Does It Mean for Students to "Understand" Archaeological Ethics? In *Pedagogy and Practice in Heritage Studies,* edited by Susan J. Bender and Phyllis Mauch Messenger, pp. 50–71. University Press of Florida: Gainesville.

McGuire, Randall

2008    *Archaeology as Political Action.* University of California Press, Berkeley.

Murray, Tim

2011    Archaeologists and Indigenous People: A Maturing Relationship? *Annual Review of Anthropology* 40: 363–378.

Nicholas, George P.

2008    Native Peoples and Archaeology. In *Encyclopedia of Archaeology,* vol. 3, edited by Deborah M. Pearsall, pp. 1660–1669. Academic Press, New York.

Ontario Ministry of Tourism, Culture and Sport

2011a   Standards and Guidelines for Consultant Archaeologists. Queen's Printer for Ontario, Toronto.

2011b   Engaging Aboriginal Communities in Archaeology: A Draft Technical Bulletin for Consultant Archaeologists in Ontario. Queen's Printer for Ontario, Toronto.

Palmater, Pamela D.

2011    *Beyond Blood: Rethinking Indigenous Identity.* Purich, Saskatoon, Saskatchewan.

Peck, Trevor, Evelyn Siegfried, and Gerald Oetelaar (editors)

2003    *Indigenous Peoples and Archaeology.* University of Calgary Press, Calgary, Alberta.

Pfeiffer, Susan, Ronald F. Williamson, Judith C. Sealy, David G. Smith, and Meradeth H. Snow

2014    Stable Dietary Isotopes and mtDNA from Woodland Period Southern Ontario

People: Results from a Tooth Sampling Protocol. *Journal of Archaeological Science* 42: 334–345.

Phillips, Caroline, and Harry Allen (editors)

2010    *Bridging the Divide: Indigenous Communities and Archaeology into the 21st Century*. Left Coast Press, Walnut Creek, California.

Sabloff, Jeremy A.

2011    Where Have You Gone, Margaret Mead? Anthropology and Public Intellectuals. *American Anthropologist* 113(3): 408–416.

Sanday, Peggy Reeves

2003    Public Interest Anthropology: A Model for Engaged Social Science. Paper prepared for SAR Workshop, Chicago, Illinois. Electronic document, http://www.sas.upenn.edu/~psanday/SARdiscussion paper.65.html. Accessed March 15, 2015.

Sanday, Peggy Reeves, and Karl Jannowitz

2004    Public Interest Anthropology: A Boasian Service-Learning Initiative. *Michigan Journal of Community Service Learning* (Summer): 64–75.

Saul, John Ralston

2008    *A Fair Country: Telling Truths about Canada*. Penguin Canada, Toronto, Ontario.

Scham, Sandra

2019    Educating Students about the Modern Realities of Exploring the Ancient Middle East. In *Pedagogy and Practice in Heritage Studies*, edited by Susan J. Bender and Phyllis Mauch Messenger, pp. 112–128. University Press of Florida, Gainesville.

Smith, Laurajane

2000    "Doing Archaeology": Cultural Heritage Management and Its Role in Identifying the Link between Archaeological Practice and Theory. *International Journal of Heritage Studies* 6(4): 309–316.

2004    *Archaeological Theory and the Politics of Cultural Heritage*. Routledge, New York.

Taylor, Evan

2011    Whose Spirit Sings? Twenty-Five Years of Transformation in First Nations Museum Representation. Unpublished B.A. honors thesis submitted to the Department of Anthropology, University of Waterloo, Waterloo, Ontario.

Trigger, Bruce G.

1996    *A History of Archaeological Thought*. 2nd ed. Cambridge University Press, Cambridge.

University of Waterloo

2006    Pursuing Global Excellence: Seizing Opportunities for Canada—University of Waterloo (UW) Sixth Decade Plan (2007–2017). Electronic document, https://uwaterloo.ca/strategic-plan/sixth-decade-plan. Accessed March 15, 2015.

University of Waterloo, Department of Anthropology

2012a    Department of Anthropology: Self-Study for the Academic Review of the Undergraduate Program in Anthropology, vol. 1. Report prepared by the Department of Anthropology, Faculty of Arts, University of Waterloo, Waterloo, Ontario.

2012b   *MA in Public Issues Anthropology Graduate Handbook 2012–2013*. Department of Anthropology, Faculty of Arts, University of Waterloo, Waterloo, Ontario.

Vine, David

2011   "Public Anthropology" in Its Second Decade: Robert Borofsky's Center for a Public Anthropology. *American Anthropologist* 113(2): 336–349.

Watkins, Joe

2000   *Indigenous Archaeology: American Indian Values and Scientific Practice*. Alta-Mira Press, Walnut Creek, California.

2005   Through Wary Eyes: Indigenous Perspectives on Archaeology. *Annual Review of Anthropology* 34: 429–449.

Williamson, Ronald F.

2010   Planning for Ontario's Past: Accomplishments and Continuing Challenges. *Revista de Arqueologia Americana* 28: 7–45.

Williamson, Ronald F., and Robert I. MacDonald

2015   Echoes of the Iroquois Wars: Contested Heritage and Identity in the Ancestral Homeland of the Huron-Wendat. In *Identity and Heritage: Contemporary Challenges in a Globalized World*, edited by Peter F. Biehl, Douglas C. Comer, Christopher Prescott, and Hilary A. Soderland, pp. 97–106. Springer, New York.

Yellowhorn, Eldon

2006   The Awakening of Internalist Archaeology in the Aboriginal World. In *The Archaeology of Bruce Trigger: Theoretical Empiricism*, edited by Ronald F. Williamson and Michael S. Bisson, pp. 194–209. McGill-Queen's University Press, Montreal.

# 10

## Making Heritage Happen

### The University of Denver Amache Field School

BONNIE J. CLARK

A Different Kind of Field School

Since 2008, the University of Denver (DU) has held biennial field schools focused on Amache, a site where over 10,000 Americans of Japanese ancestry unwillingly spent much of World War II. It is not an easy history, but five seasons of enthusiastic crews, joined by hundreds of site visitors, suggest it is one that can reach a broad population. To illustrate some of what makes the project so successful, one could start with a close look at the crew portrait (see Figure 10.1) taken near the end of the 2012 season. It illustrates some of the social networks and varied heritage engagements through which the crews come together.

First, the photo was taken not at Amache itself, where crews of students, interns, and volunteers do archaeology. Rather it was taken outside the Amache Preservation Society museum in nearby Granada, Colorado. The museum is where the crews spent most of their afternoons, processing new collections, learning to do archival research, and creating new exhibits. Second, this photograph also shows our intergenerational and diverse crew.

Flanking either end of the front row are our two high school interns. On the left is Abby. At the time, she lived in Granada and was a member of the Amache Preservation Society, the caretakers of the museum. It is a group comprised largely of Granada High School students led by her father, a social studies teacher at the school. On the right is Kelli, whose grandfather was born at Amache. She served as our 2012 descendant community high school intern. Along with a dozen other members of his family, her grand-

Figure 10.1. 2012 University of Denver (DU) Amache crew at the Amache Museum. Photograph by staff of the DU Amache Project, courtesy of the project.

father, Eugene, had visited the previous field school. That year my students found his birth announcement in the camp newspapers archived at the museum. Eugene encouraged Kelli to join the 2012 field school. He also made a return visit that year and is the source of the levity captured in this photo. He cracked a joke just before this picture was snapped.

Just behind Abby is Bill. A retired M.D., Bill was pursuing an associate's degree in archaeology at his local community college. He first found out about the project when he came to the DU campus to see an exhibit of the Amache archaeology collection. He arrived at the opening with copies of his report cards from the Amache elementary school. They are among the items my students added to the collections of the museum in the summer of 2012. Standing behind Bill is his son Michael. In my conversations with Michael, it was clear he came largely in support of his father, but by day two of their volunteer stint, Michael was hooked. Finally, next to Bill is Kirsten, who was unaware members of her family were interned until she came across a photograph of both sets of her grandparents labeled "Amache Concentration Camp." She contacted me after finding the DU Amache project website and spent two weeks with us in 2012, and one in 2014. That latter year, she was joined by her mother for a few days of work and to meet other Amache internees at our community open house.

Of course, the field school wouldn't happen without the undergraduate students, who came from across the country. Because I need to reserve space for my community volunteers and high school interns, placement in the field school is quite competitive. Each of these students fought for a spot in this nontraditional field school where training in archaeological field techniques was balanced by museum studies and a crash course in collaborative research. The undergrads are joined by graduate students, two of whom served as archaeology crew chiefs and one as the museum crew chief. In every field school, at least one of those crew chiefs has also been pursing thesis research connected to the site.

Getting all these different stakeholders to the table is no mean feat. To understand the structure of this field school involves returning to our pre-field groundwork. Amache is a site where there are in essence two communities of ownership, the local community, which legally owns it, and the Japanese American community, who have a moral ownership. Interviews confirm what is implied by the yearly pilgrimage to Amache; for many it is a sacred site (Hanes 2012). Without the blessing of the Japanese American community, any research there would have been morally reprehensible. Yet to frame it that way, to refer to "the Japanese American community" as if that single entity exists, is to create a fiction; there is no one such community. Embarking on this project meant working with a multitude of Japanese American individuals and groups, especially former Amache internees and their families, who are spread across many states.

Equally important was connection with more local community organizations, especially the Amache Preservation Society, or APS. Before our project started, the APS was doing wonderful community outreach using their museum collections, but they had no system in place for managing them. The creation of a comprehensive collections management system was identified in a preliminary development plan as one of the most pressing issues faced by site managers (Ellis 2004). My goals were originally more focused on the tangible history present on-site. However, it became clear that any archaeological work at Amache would need to be accomplished in tandem with work in the museum. I was lucky in my institutional location, because the University of Denver Anthropology Department has a specialization in museum and heritage studies. Equally fortunate was the fact that John Hopper, who leads the APS, was happy to help us come up with a work plan that would meet both his goals for the museum and those suggested for collections management.

In 2008, three years after the legwork for this project started, the first field season was finally on its way (Clark et al. 2008). The pattern of intergenerational community involvement was set that year. We brought in as volunteers local Granada High School students who were members of the APS. That first year the involvement of the APS students was limited by their needs to hold summer jobs or work on the family farm. In subsequent years we have avoided that conflict by paying the APS students as interns. That those first local high schoolers were able to work alongside someone their age who had family who had been interned in the camp was mostly a stroke of good luck. During my prefield research and community consultation in Los Angeles, I met Gary, a former Amache internee and retired professional photographer. I was introduced to Gary during a visit to the Japanese American National Museum, where he works as a volunteer. After I told him about our upcoming fieldwork plans, he asked to join us at Amache. Although community consultation and oral histories were always a planned part of the research (Clark et al. 2008), incorporating former internees as volunteers had not been. Quite frankly, it really hadn't occurred to me that any of them would want to join us in the field. From the earliest consultation on, it became clear that among the most difficult memories of camp were those surrounding environmental conditions. Amacheans speak passionately about the hot, dry summers and the punishing, sandy wind that characterizes the High Plains setting of the site. One woman I spoke to recently about what she remembered of camp said simply, "the wind." Add in that not a one of them is younger than 70 and you can imagine my surprise at Gary's request. Not only was he interested in coming out to learn archaeology and serve (during the two weeks he was there) as the site photographer, he wanted to bring along his grandson. Of course, I was thrilled at the prospect.

Institutionalizing this bit of good luck was greatly aided by the fact that the Amache Historical Society, a Los Angeles–based group with whom I consulted prior to going into the field, invited me and my graduate students to attend their 2009 reunion held in Las Vegas, Nevada. There we were able to meet hundreds of former internees and to spread the word about our project. That was the first time we distributed our newsletter, which is now sent yearly to hundreds of people. The reunion organizers also graciously allowed us to facilitate group conversations germane to our research. It was during those conversations that I met Carlene, who as a former biology teacher was fascinated by one element of our research design, the study of Amache's gardens (Clark 2017). She asked to join us for the 2010 field research. Later, another former internee, Anita, got on board. She found out about the project through her relatives in California's central valley. I spent over a week there in the lead-up to our second field season, once again doing community consultation, handing out newsletters, and actively recruiting for the high school intern position set aside for the descendant of an internee.

This discussion about how we have connected to community might seem like a foray into minutia. But social network theory tells us that to build a robust network takes many interactions. Although archaeologists have embraced network theory for its applications to the analysis of past communities (for example, Mills et al. 2013), we have done little to apply it to our current practice. Yet each time my students talk about their research in the community, every answer to an emailed query about the project answered by a staff member, each conversation I might have with a former internee, these all knit the web of the project more tightly together. These interactions are sometimes centered on what we find doing archaeology, but also about what we don't, or we can't find. And in asking and answering questions, we don't just trade information, we forge ties. For those of us who do (or want to do) this kind of heritage work, it is critical to be explicit that these acts are not just community service or "outreach." An ongoing conversation is what makes our pedagogy engaged and our research robust. Alison Wylie posits that collaborative archaeology is epistemologically sound because it opens up our discipline to a range of ideas (2015). People with a different outlook, especially those not inculcated by years of archaeological training, provide tools for new ways of thinking about artifacts, sites, even the nature of the past itself. Thus collaborators can be thought of as bringing to the table different "cognitive and epistemic resources," that is tools for knowing the world (Wylie 2015: 206).

## Creating Communities of Memory

Shanks and McGuire suggest that archaeology is a form of commemoration, a creation of memory rooted in present-day concerns (Shanks and McGuire 1996). At Amache those concerns are richly imagined and embodied by a multigenerational, multiethnic community of memory. Something that is clear in student field journals and the course evaluations is that working side by side with community stakeholders greatly enriches the field school learning experience. The very make-up of the field school means students confront head-on some of the thornier questions of a body of scholarship of which most of them are unaware: critical heritage studies. This burgeoning interdisciplinary field (Winter 2015; see also both Chilton and Zimmerman, this volume) is comprised of thinkers who ask such difficult questions as who owns the past, who can speak for it, and does it matter today. When my students survey the barracks block where one of their crew members lived as a child, they do not need to hear a lecture about how this history still matters, how it impacts the present day. They hear it in the stories told of life in the camp, or of family who still won't talk about their unjust incarceration. At the museum they do not need to be reminded to consider multivocality because they are working with community members throughout the process. That engagement takes multiple forms, including conducting donor interviews for recently acquired collections, discussing the import of a site photograph, or working together to create an exhibit or museum handout.

Toward the end of the field school, we hold an evening seminar on collaborative archaeology. By then the community volunteers, interns, and students have enough familiarity with each other and the community engagement goals of the project that they can talk with candor and authority. We explore some of the more difficult issues that arise when you work on a site of civil injustice, such as those regarding the freighted nature of terminology. We must always discuss the linguistic choices made both in the museum and in our person-to-person interactions. For example, if members of the DU Amache field school call this a concentration camp—now the preferred term for many national Japanese American groups—do we push out other stakeholders like the children of former camp employees? Do we risk alienating the local residents who live with this site in their backyard? As valuable as the seminar conversations are, they are merely an extension of dialogue that begins much more informally and earlier on. It often happens as former internees or descendants discuss their motivations for participation in the field school with their crewmates. Indeed, although I structure activities to address collaboration explicitly, in reality the varied people who participate in the field school have done most of the heavy lifting of engaged pedagogy for me (see also Kryder-Reid 2019).

Perhaps one of the biggest questions in critical heritage studies is the very nature of heritage itself (Harrison 2010; Chilton, this volume). Is it the tangible remains of the past that we, collectively or individually, have inherited? Is it a set of traditions? Is it collective memories? Laurajane Smith (2006) contends that heritage is a process, a series of acts in the present that refer to the past. These often have a tangible component, and are in fact often strongest with a physical referent, but places or things do not in themselves constitute heritage. Rather they are, for example, the location where memories are searched, shared, or recaptured. On-site, the heritage process can take the form of group conversations about what happened here, or, in the context of archaeological research, what *could* have happened here.

At Amache this often unfolds recursively. An object or feature is found and we puzzle over its function. Then a community member might remember a story Auntie So-and-So once told. "Could that be important?" Or perhaps there was a picture in a family scrapbook that could shed light. And suddenly what happens in the field moves back into the community, as individual and shared memories are probed, sometimes for the first time. Especially at sites with a shadowed past, physical evidence grants "material authority to the construction of identities" (Smith 2006: 50). In the decades immediately following World War II, many internees or their children faced disbelief when they discussed the camp experience. For them the physical evidence of the site becomes not just a touchstone for, but an affirmation of, that history and their role in it.

So how do we best teach our students about heritage as a process? A generation of field school training in archaeological processes tells us the answer: by involving them in it (see also King, this volume). As suggested above, much of this can be accomplished by thoughtful recruitment of community members as crew, site visitors, or collaborators. But it should also be formalized in the pedagogy, whether it is through student-led research like oral history, through co-created interpretation, or through pairing students and volunteers for the mundane tasks of fieldwork. Reflection on their roles,

Figure 10.2. Community members and archaeologists interact during the summer 2016 University of Denver Amache Field School open house. Standing in front of a recently reconstructed barrack, former internees share where they lived at Amache. Photograph courtesy of Nancy Ukai.

whether as sounding board or collaborator, helps students understand their experience as part of our expanding discipline. It also helps them understand that the preservation of heritage must go far beyond concern for sites and objects alone.

## Curating Heritage

One of the reasons I was so pleased to be part of this volume (and the SAA session that preceded it) was the emphasis on how archaeologists were preparing their students to be part of the larger world of heritage work. Although elements of the heritage industry might make some of us uncomfortable, it is not going away. Heritage tourism in particular is eyed by private and public entities alike as a way to infuse funds into struggling communities while at the same time preserving historic resources. Heritage museums, restored historic structures, identified travel corridors, and online guides are just some of the products of this growing industry. Although we are right to be wary of uncritically embracing heritage tourism, we ignore it at our peril. That is especially true because archaeologists have a specific type of expertise to provide, one that is often welcomed by other practitioners and source communities (Shackel and Chambers 2004).

Clearly, if we want our students to be effective heritage professionals, they need field training that goes beyond sampling methods and straight sidewalls. Experience in giving site tours, talking to the media, and producing data for the Web are common expansions of the archaeology field school into this realm. Yet I would side with engaged practitioners like Joyce (2003) and Hantman (2004), who call for embracing the site museum. Museums are critical locations of public archaeology and our research lives longer there than almost anywhere else. They are also valuable community resources, often helping turn archaeological sites into sustainable heritage sites (see also Elia et al. 2019).

Incorporating the other end of archaeology—the museum where our objects end up—was very much a practical and ethical necessity for the Amache project. There was an expectation by the town of Granada, who owns the site, that what we recovered would eventually end up in the Amache Preservation Society (APS) museum. Developing the curriculum of the field school to help the APS organize their collections and set up collections management meant staff and crew would meet a previously identified need. It also meant that through our efforts future collections would be protected. My staff and I go to great pains to ensure that students understand their museum efforts as an ethical obligation related to archeological practice (Lynott and Wylie 2000).

Five field seasons of the DU Amache project suggest that incorporating the museum into archaeological training is not just ethically sound, it is also good pedagogy that provides valuable training in real-world heritage skills. The DU Amache project consistently draws in students primarily interested in museum studies. Even those who are more interested in archaeological training find that spending their afternoon engaging with complete objects and historic documents enriches their appreciation and understanding of the materials on site. We train students in object management and collections research and in turn they often find an unexpected affinity for these practices. Each student also works with staff, especially the graduate student serving as the museum crew chief, to design an applied museum project. Their work has culminated in updated exhibits, online reference materi-

Figure 10.3. University of Denver Amache Field School open house activity designed by a DU field school student. She is engaging here with two sisters whose mother worked at camp as a teacher. Photograph by staff of the DU Amache Project, courtesy of the project.

als, resources for the APS students, and public programming. In 2014, for example, a student created an activity for our open houses where visitors painted Japanese characters onto stones from the local Arkansas River (see Figure 10.3). This popular activity benefited from the student's Japanese language skills while incorporating cultural and archaeological background. Although it is challenging to pull off such projects in the short time frame of a field school, especially professional-looking exhibits, the museum projects are something in which the students take considerable pride.

Our efforts in the museum are also very productive in building ties with the local community. The mayor of Granada visited the museum several times throughout our first field school. In casual conversations with area residents, we realized that many of them had never been inside the APS museum before. Thus, we decided to hold an open house at the museum and promoted it locally. Given that the town of Granada has a population of about 400, the more than 20 people who joined us that first summer represented a not insignificant slice of the population. The connections established that summer, and the visible contribution to their community through museum improvements, have served as a strong foundation for our growing relationship to the town as a whole. Each summer since then, we have opened up the museum to the surrounding community throughout the field school, and especially at the open house. Not only do visits by local residents highlight the significance of the area's history, it gives them a chance to meet those whose family members had been in the camp. As their seemingly disparate stories intertwine (for example, in memories of the popular local soda fountain that operated during the war), it becomes clear that the camp is not just Japanese American history, but is in fact a shared heritage.

At the 2008 American Anthropological Association meetings, Alison Wylie delivered the keynote speech to the Archaeology Division. In her address, Wylie made a bold proclamation: that archaeology done in collaboration with concerned communities is the new New Archaeology (Wylie 2008). Similar to the New Archaeology of the 1960s, collaborative work challenges practitioners to rethink method and theory, research priorities and timelines, and the "taken-for-granteds" of epistemology like what is considered evidence. Field schools should be leading the way by training students in this engaged archaeology of the future (see also King, this volume; Elia et al. 2019). In this stance I share the opinion of proponents of Indigenous field schools, like those in the Silliman (2008) volume, *Collaborating at the Trowel's Edge*. The field school, especially one that strives to include multigenerational crews from different source communities, can frame a robust heritage practice. It encourages opportunities for the past to be embodied, recalled, and sometimes even challenged. It can also instigate deep engagement across differences of age and ancestry, both in the moments we script, and the many in between. The outcome is new communities of memory, people who share a connection to a past through what they created together in the present.

## Acknowledgments

This chapter is dedicated to Dr. William (Bill) Sueoka and all of the Amacheans who have been part of our DU Amache field schools. Their participation had made this project a life-changing experience. Support for volunteer and intern participation in the DU field school has been provided by the University of Denver, Center for Community Engagement and Service Learning. The field school as a whole has been generously funded for many years by both History Colorado's State Historical Fund and the Japanese American Association of Colorado. A hearty thank-you to all of our volunteers and funders for their support.

## References Cited

Clark, Bonnie J.

2017    Cultivating Community: The Archaeology of Japanese American Confinement at Amache. In *Legacies of Space and Intangible Heritage: Archaeology, Ethnohistory, and the Politics of Cultural Continuity in the Americas*, edited by F. Armstrong-Fumero and J. H. Gutierrez, pp. 79–96. University Press of Colorado, Boulder.

Clark, Bonnie J., April Kamp-Whittaker, and Dana Ogo Shew

2008    *The Tangible History of Amache: Archaeology Research Design and Methodology for Field Investigations, Summer 2008*. University of Denver, Department of Anthropology.

Elia, Ricardo J., Amalia Pérez-Juez, and Meredith Anderson

2019    Teaching Heritage in the Field: An Example from Menorca, Spain. In *Pedagogy and Practice in Heritage Studies*, edited by Susan J. Bender and Phyllis Mauch Messenger, pp. 94–111. University Press of Florida, Gainesville.

Ellis, Sheri Murray

2004    *Camp Amache, Prowers County, Colorado: Site Management, Preservation, and Interpretive Plan*. SWCA Environmental Consultants, Salt Lake City, Utah.

Hanes, Erin M.

2012    Opening Pandora's Box: A Traditional Cultural Property Evaluation of the Amache World War II Japanese Internment Camp, Granada, Colorado. Master's thesis, Department of Anthropology, Sonoma State University, Rohnert Park, California.

Hantman, Jeffrey L.

2004    Monacan Meditation: Regional and Individual Archaeologies in the Contemporary Politics of Indian Heritage. In *Places in Mind: Public Archaeology as Applied Anthropology*, edited by Paul A. Shackel and Erve J. Chambers, pp. 19–34. Routledge, New York.

Harrison, Rodney

2010    What is Heritage? In *Understanding the Politics of Heritage*, edited by Rodney Harrison, pp. 5–42. Manchester University Press, Manchester, UK.

Joyce, Rosemary

2003    Working in Museums as an Archaeological Anthropologist. In *Archaeology is Anthropology*, edited by Susan D. Gillespie and Deborah L. Nichols, pp. 99–109. Archeological Papers of the American Anthropological Association, no. 13.

Kryder-Reid, Elizabeth

2019    Do the Homeless Have Heritage? Archaeology and the Pedagogy of Discomfort. In *Pedagogy and Practice in Heritage Studies*, edited by Susan J. Bender and Phyllis Mauch Messenger, pp. 129–147. University Press of Florida, Gainesville.

Lynott, Mark J., and Alison Wylie (editors)

2000    *Ethics in American Archaeology,* 2nd rev. ed. Society for American Archaeology, Washington, D.C.

Mills, Barbara J., Jeffery J. Clark, Matthew A. Peeples, W. R. Haas, Jr., John M. Roberts, Jr., J. Brett Hill, Deborah L. Huntley, Lewis Borck, Ronald L. Breiger, Aaron Clauset, and M. Steven Shackley

2013    Transformation of Social Networks in the Late Pre-Hispanic US Southwest. *Proceedings of the National Academy of Science* (PNAS) 110(15): 5785–5790.

Shackel, Paul A., and Erve J. Chambers (editors)

2004    *Places in Mind: Public Archaeology as Applied Anthropology*. Routledge, New York.

Shanks, Michael, and Randall H. McGuire

1996    The Craft of Archaeology. *American Antiquity* 61(1): 75–88.

Silliman, Stephen W. (editor)

2008    *Collaborating at the Trowel's Edge: Teaching and Learning in Indigenous Archaeology*. University of Arizona Press, Tucson.

Smith, Laurajane

2006    *Uses of Heritage*. Routledge, London.

Winter, Tim

2015    President's Welcome—Association of Critical Heritage Studies. Electronic document, http://www.criticalheritagestudies.org/presidents-welcome/. Accessed July 28, 2016.

Wylie, Alison

2008    Legacies of Collaboration: Transformative Criticism in Archaeology: The Archaeology Division Distinguished Lecture. American Anthropological Association annual meetings, San Francisco, California.

2015    A Plurality of Pluralisms: Collaborative Practice in Archaeology. In *Objectivity in Science: New Perspectives from Science and Technology Studies*, edited by Flavia Padovani, Alan Richardson, and Jonathan Y. Tsou, pp: 189–210. Springer International, Basel, Switzerland.

# 11

# Rising, Falling, Assembling

## Pedagogy in British Archaeology

HANNAH COBB AND KARINA CROUCHER

This chapter critically outlines the development of pedagogy in archaeology in British Higher Education. In this context, heritage, following Smith's (2006) definition of it as the cultural relevance and use of the past in the present, is largely taught under the umbrella of archaeology at the undergraduate level. Greater specialization takes place at master's and doctoral levels, but in this chapter archaeology and heritage can be taken as largely interchangeable when understanding how these subjects are taught.

Before we can examine the specifics of archaeological pedagogy, however, it is important to understand the fundamental bifurcation that characterizes British Higher Education (HE) more generally: that is the deeply entrenched divide between teaching and research. While many have highlighted that this is a false division (see Cobb and Croucher 2014 for more detail), the structures of the HE system have developed in such a manner as to cleave research from teaching at the fundamental levels of intellectual and financial value. This is realized through the monitoring of research in the Research Excellence Framework (REF, formerly the Research Assessment Exercise, or RAE) and teaching in the Teaching Excellence Framework (TEF). The RAE/REF is an exercise that has taken place every five years since 1986; it ranks research outputs according to their perceived academic value and, more recently, through an added social impact measure. The TEF has since been introduced (in 2014), and grades institutions (gold, silver, or bronze) according to their teaching standards (and more specifically, their monitoring of their teaching). Clearly, there are significant differences in the two streams of measurement: one is based upon expert evaluation of research publications and the other on metrics from student satisfaction surveys and graduate earnings. These differences demonstrate an imbalance in which teaching is fundamentally undervalued, compared to the "great god research" (Fagan 2000: 125). The only thing that these two strands of measurement have in common is their link to funding. A high REF score enables an institution to gain more government funding, and a high TEF score enables it to charge higher tuition fees. This situation highlights not only the division of teaching and research, and the undervaluation of pedagogy, but also the neoliberal agenda currently influencing higher education, a topic that will be discussed later.

## The Rise and Fall of Pedagogy in British Archaeology

The scene we set above of the current situation in UK Higher Education provides an important context for understanding the relationship between pedagogy and the discipline of archaeology, for ultimately the division between research and teaching underwrites the fortunes of archaeological pedagogy in Britain. Thus the rise of archaeological pedagogy corresponds with a period before these measures were introduced, although it was also shaped by a convergence of additional factors. The counter modern theoretical critiques of the 1980s and 1990s, combined with external developments such as critical pedagogy (for example, Freire 2000; Kincheloe 2008; Malott and Porfilio 2011; see also Zimmerman, this volume), played an important part in developing a disciplinary self-consciousness about pedagogy. Equally, the exponential increase in the 1990s in both student numbers and the growth of the archaeological profession itself were motivating factors, as was the introduction of benchmarking in British Higher Education as part of the broader pan-European Bologna Process (which sought to standardize higher education across Europe). This led to the first major workshop on teaching and learning in UK archaeology held in Lampeter in 2000 and its subsequent publication as an edited volume a year later (Rainbird and Hamilakis 2001). Pedagogic research was also supported by the government-funded quasi autonomous nongovernmental organization (QUANGO), the Learning and Teaching Support Network (LTSN), and its successor, the Higher Education Academy (HEA), from the late 1990s onward. The HEA operated from a central office (in York, UK) with twenty-six dedicated Subject Centres, including the Subject Centre for History, Classics and Archaeology (with its base in Glasgow, and separate offices for the three disciplinary strands). The impact of the HEA, in particular, with its subject-specific pedagogic research funding and support, led to a notable proliferation in research into archaeological pedagogy in the first decade of the twenty-first century. This research was not marginalized from non-pedagogic subjects. Rather, it had a mainstream and international presence, including conference sessions at the World Archaeology Congress (Dublin, Ireland, 2008) and Inter-Congress (Kingston, Jamaica, 2007), the European Association of Archaeologists Conferences (Krakow, Poland, 2005; and Zadar, Croatia, 2007), and the Council for British Archaeology's annual conference (2005). There was also a plenary session dedicated to the subject at the Theoretical Archaeology Group's conference in Glasgow in 2004 and many other conferences and publications. These included a special edition of *World Archaeology* (Dowson 2004), edited volumes (Rainbird and Hamilakis 2001; Hamilakis and Rainbird 2004; Henson et al. 2004), Teaching and Learning Guides (Aitchison and Giles 2006; Dowson 2005; Grant and Giles 2005; Kilbride 2005; Croucher and Romer 2007; Phillips and Gilchrist 2005; Hicks et al. 2009), a dedicated Annual HEA Conference on Teaching and Learning in Archaeology (established in 2003, running annually until 2009), Web resources (for example, an Archaeology Image Bank; Archaeology Alive; the HEA website as a repository for events, publications, and resources), and a variety of initiatives supported by HEA Teaching Development Grants (for example, Stevens 2005; Finlay 2005; Welham 2005; Wilkinson 2007). Together, these created a momentum that eventually led to the establishment, in 2007, of a peer-reviewed journal dedicated to the topic (named *RAE: Research in Archaeological Education*), with an editorial board of established, world-leading researchers in archaeology.

The *RAE* Journal provided a rigorous, peer-reviewed, and "REF-able"[1] avenue for pedagogic research in archaeology. However, its success led to a paradox. In encouraging a dedicated avenue for publication, researchers in this field gained a centralized forum for output, and so the incentive to publish elsewhere diminished. Further, the *RAE* Journal had been made possible through the support of the HEA's History, Classics and Archaeology Subject Centre, but funding changes and shifting organizational priorities of the HEA resulted in declined resources for the journal's publication after just two editions (Sinclair et al. 2007; Croucher and Cobb 2008); the third edition (edited by Sinclair) remains in press (as of 2018). The inception of the journal demonstrated an appetite for producing high-quality pedagogic research outputs. Yet by 2010, the rise of archaeological pedagogy in the United Kingdom was over; funding cuts and the subsequent restructuring and diminishment of the HEA have seen the momentum for and funding of pedagogical research significantly diminished, while the inception of the TEF has fundamentally changed the way in which teaching is measured (that is, by its end users, rather than in peer-reviewed innovation and research). Since the demise of the journal, and the HEA Subject Centre for Archaeology, Classics and History, while there is an appetite for research and publication on archaeological pedagogy (for example, Cobb and Croucher 2012, 2014, 2016; Everill and Nicholls 2011; Everill et al. 2015; Mytum 2012; Cobb et al. 2012), it remains marginalized in REF terms, with no experts on pedagogic research on any of the RAE and REF archaeology panels to date.

Training vs. Pedagogy?

It is perhaps unfair to paint a picture of the rise and then complete fall of archaeology pedagogy, however. In the vacuum left by the demise of the HEA, the one area of continued vibrant debate relating to teaching practice in British archaeology pertains to the question of training. This is a consequence of the rise of developer-led archaeology and the cultural resource management (CRM) industry since the 1990s, and its ultimate reliance on graduates. Indeed Aitchison and Rocks-Macqueen (2013: 12) demonstrate that UK archaeology is now a graduate industry; all those working in the subject under the age of 40 hold a minimum of an undergraduate degree in archaeology, and nearly half hold a master's-level postgraduate qualification. The tension that logically follows from this picture is over who should train future archaeologists, the university or the employer? Aitchison (2004) and Flatman (2015) review these arguments in detail, but they can be summarized as the CRM industry highlighting that the time-pressured conditions of developer-led work means that they need those at entry level in the sector to be already well-trained, fully formed field archaeologists. In contrast, academics argue that archaeological degrees are not simply taken by future archaeologists. Archaeology degrees provide a wide range of transferable skills (Croucher et al. 2008) and therefore lend themselves well to any liberal arts career path. Therefore it should not be incumbent upon a degree to provide pure vocational training, but rather to facilitate a

broad enough coverage of subjects to enrich student inquiry, develop transferable and specific skills, and support the future employability of all those
who take the degree, whatever career they will follow. Ultimately Aitchison
(2004), Flatman (2015), and all those who have reviewed this debate (for
example, Henson 2011), conclude that the answer is not so simple that one
or the other should have sole responsibility for training. Flatman argues, for
instance, that we should rise above the commercial vs. academic question
of who should provide training (Flatman 2015). Instead, he argues, we may
overcome this by standardizing (and archiving) our teaching, embracing
online methods as a route to learning, to foster greater collaboration between HE and CRM for training, and to accept and "[s]tart thinking about
what a totally free market educational sector would look like. Accept the
fact that this free market model may be inevitable" (Flatman 2015: 154; and
see Marciniak, this volume).

The "who should provide training" debate has existed since the 1990s
and will remain pertinent for as long as graduates are the main employees in the UK commercial sector. And rightly so; a profession that does not
scrutinize, challenge, and strive to develop its training methods would be
problematic. What we argue as important here, however, is that the debate
about training has come to dominate debates about pedagogy in the second
decade of the twenty-first century. Indeed, often the terms "pedagogy" and
"training" are presented as interchangeable (compare Flatman 2015), when
in fact pedagogy is about the processes and practices of teaching and learning and thus training could be argued to be just *one part* of pedagogy (see
also Zimmerman, this volume). We argue, then, that we do ourselves a disservice if training becomes the central focus of the debate about pedagogy
in British archaeology. More than this, we play into the hands of the neoliberal agenda that shapes both HE and the CRM sector. This is because training implies an instrumentalist, banking model of teaching which reduces
teaching (and thus pedagogy) to economic terms, to its contribution to the
labor market by producing commoditized knowledge or workers as commodities (Olssen and Peters 2005). Hamilakis cites the work of sociologist
Bernstein to eloquently argue that:

a view of education as training in utilitarian technical competences,
[is] a view that ruptures the link between knowledge and the self, denigrating the ability to make ethical judgements and develop a wider

vision about the world. It is a definition of knowledge as a commodity to be sold and exchanged, rather than as a life-transforming, experiential process; it is the final product now, rather than the process itself that is being valorized. (Hamilakis 2004: 289)

Thus, if we reduce discussions about the processes of teaching and learning in archaeology to be simply about training, we negate the need to understand those processes because a focus on training is a focus on economic output, not the intellectual process that produces such output. Thus the "who is responsible for training" debate does two things: it undermines pedagogic processes in and of themselves, connecting pedagogic success not with learning but with a financial/labor market output, but crucially it also shifts the focus from pedagogy altogether because it is so output-oriented. It is no surprise, then, that Flatman (2015) has noted that there has been little recent development in British archaeological pedagogy; that the last major volume on pedagogy (as opposed to training) was produced in 2004 (Dowson 2004); and that Hamilakis' 2004 stinging critique of the impacts of neoliberalism on archaeological pedagogy falls on deaf ears, when the debate is so distractingly oriented on exactly the issue that undermines pedagogic enquiry—training, and whose responsibility it is.

Re-energizing Archaeological Pedagogy

How should we revitalize pedagogy in archaeology then? Higher Education, as with much of Western society, is now framed within and emerges from neoliberalism. Neoliberalism can be broadly defined as an economic and political model that prioritizes free market capitalism, but where state power is a central factor in imposing financial market imperatives (Hill and Kumar 2009; Saad-Filho and Johnston 2005a, 2005b), and where "the pattern of power is established on contract, which in turn is premised upon a need for compliance, monitoring, and accountability organized in a management line and established through a purchase contract based upon measurable outputs" (Olssen and Peters 2005: 325). The REF and TEF that dominate British HE are obvious examples of the latter.

Because higher education is so fundamentally part of this system, the focus on training seems naturalized as a primary concern of archaeological pedagogy. Thus, to resist the hierarchical, monitoring, economically focused framework of neoliberalism in our pedagogic practice, we argue, we need to reformulate our approach to pedagogy in a holistic manner. To do so, we draw upon assemblage theory and associated relational theories, exploring the assemblages of HE and the possibilities that arise from them.

Assemblage theory as conceived by Deleuze and Guattari (1987 [1980]), and further developed by DeLanda (2006), explores how people and things are intermeshed and interconnected, and equally affective. In this way, assemblage theory provides scope to examine how entities come into being not in isolated ways but as components of a broader whole, and that assemblages have the potential to be more than the sum of their parts (DeLanda 2006). Other archaeologists have utilized these approaches to examine different elements of the past (for example, Alberti et al. 2013; Watts 2013; Conneller 2011; Crellin 2017; Fowler 2017; Hamilakis and Jones 2017, Harris 2017, Lucas 2017, Robinson 2017, and other articles within the 2017 special edition of *Cambridge Archaeological Journal* on Assemblage Theory; Jervis 2016); this approach has also been applied very successfully to examine the archaeological record and the practice of understanding this in the present (Lucas 2012; Cobb and Croucher 2014). In turn, we have argued that this approach is valuable in transforming pedagogic research because it allows us to move beyond traditional "banking" models of teaching and learning and instead consider and develop the different ways teaching and learning occur. Crucially for archaeology and heritage, an assemblage approach allows us to pick apart how the material dimensions of our learning environments can be both constitutive of, or constraining within, the processes and practices of teaching and learning. The critical pedagogy critique of the traditional banking, instrumentalist model of learning, for instance, discusses the lecturer standing before the students, banking knowledge with the passive student body. But consider the lecture theater or seminar room setting: the benches, seats, table, the setup of the room angled toward the lecturer at front, and the whiteboard, blackboard, or projector screen. It is not people alone who enable a banking model of teaching to occur, it is also the very materials of the lecture theater itself that do so. This is no new observation, but for archaeology it provides an important insight applicable to the other learning contexts we regularly use. The training excavation, for example, can provide equally hierarchical and banking material circumstances for learning. Imagine, for example, a research excavation, where students are being trained: an open trench with students troweling away the contexts.

As different parts of the trench are identified as important, simply the way that supervisors react and the material conditions they create reinforce a banking experience. Let us imagine, in the trench, that a linear stone-built feature emerges and the project director decides that this is the most crucial piece of archaeology on the site. Immediately students are moved off the feature. Only the director will excavate this now. Instead, the students trowel away the soil around this linear stone feature. The materiality of the site is as affective in the students' learning experience as the person teaching them how to be an archaeologist. Thus, as buckets, hands, and trowels together remove the soil contexts, so the stone feature becomes increasingly prominent on the site, directing the way people move around the trench, where buckets can sit and wheelbarrows can run. In turn, this is emphasized by the project director as they perch atop the stone feature, troweling, brushing, and photographing it, finding artifacts, noticing and recording different contexts, while the students move bucket after bucket of soil from around its base. In this way, power dynamics emerge. Student identity, director identity, and those of the supervisors who mediate between, are all brought into being in the assemblage of the trench. And when the director decides to plan the linear stone feature and they stretch their tape across the trench, the tape bisects the contexts surrounding the feature—the tape itself divides and affects. And so does the director, as they step on recently troweled soil, standing over the rest of students in the trench on the vantage point of the stone feature, with their planning board; the physicality of the many parts of the assemblage is as divisive as the lecture theater, reproducing a banking mode of teaching and learning and hierarchies of knowledge, territorializing what (parts of the archaeology) and who (which archaeologists) are important and what and who are marginalized.

We argue, however, that recognizing the assemblages of teaching and learning, and particularly the equally affective role of material things in the processes of teaching and learning, allow us to radically challenge linear, banking models, and recenter and re-examine how students are and can be active in the learning process. The materiality of the learning experience not only creates and reinforces hierarchies of teacher and student, but also has the potential to reinforce divisions along the lines of gender, sexuality, ethnicity, and disability (Cobb and Croucher 2016). An awareness of this allows us to challenge the very conditions that reinforce inequalities. The field and the lecture theater, for instance, are two sides of the same coin;

they are part of a broader assemblage of "being at university" for each student, which encompasses all their different learning environments. Thus, the power relations and learning experiences in one learning environment may so forcefully reinforce those at another. But these assemblages allow us to subvert normative practices, too. Crucially, an assemblage approach reframes students as themselves part of wider assemblages with the power to affect teaching and learning (for more detail, see Cobb and Croucher 2014, 2016, 2018). When we acknowledge the multiple assemblages of which each student is part, we can challenge homogenizing views and recenter and empower the student. At the heart of this is recognizing that multiple assemblages exist at different scales. For instance, considering the material components of the assemblage of the lecture theater, we can take the example of the mobile telephone in the pocket and hand of almost every student, or the laptop or tablet that many students will have with them. Perhaps not all students in a lecture theater, but a likely high proportion, will be using these devices during the lecture, to connect to other assemblages that extend elsewhere, outside of the lecture theater, and using Facebook, Twitter, Instagram, Snapchat, and other social media, detracting from the lecture that the students are meant to be following. In many ways, the materiality of the lecture theater is complicit in allowing students to drift from the assemblage of the lecture theater—the wireless network to which they connect, the bench that they may "subtly" hide their phone behind, the focus of all other eyes on the front to allow them to look elsewhere, and the handout of lecture notes distributed by the lecturer also allow, even encourage, their attention to wander. But what if these devices become recentered as tools that render students active? Interactive polling methods, for instance, such as Turning Technology's Responseware, do exactly this, as we have described elsewhere (Cobb and Croucher 2016). In the field, too, understanding the way students, materials, and the assemblages of learning emerge allows us to create empowering, student-centered learning experiences that themselves have the power to act far beyond the context of the student's own learning context. It is in field or lab work, which itself is active research, that it is most explicit that the learning assemblages of which students (and lecturers) are a part of, extend beyond the immediate learning assemblages. Here, what emerges from the assemblage of students, soil, trench, and supervisors forms part of the creation of the broader assemblages of heritage, at local, national, and international scales (for example, see Cobb and Croucher

2014 for the instance of a student drawing a reconstruction of Viking Boat Burial which then went "viral").

Ultimately, considering the different learning environments as assemblages enables the rethinking of the mechanisms of learning. Critically, this includes the material components of the different assemblages. The assemblages are not discrete entities, but rather aspects of each permeate each other and are present in the multiple assemblages that create the whole of the education system, as well as the lives of students and lecturers in their own assemblages beyond the classroom, field, or other learning assemblage. Such an approach empowers lecturers and students in recognizing the interconnected nature of teaching, learning, research, excavation, and other archaeological endeavors. This encourages a change on the ground in valuing teaching, students, and in recognizing the assemblages that emerge in what we do as archaeologists. Further, this also has implications for the diversity of our discipline, exposing both how nonnormative students can be excluded from learning environments, and how this can be challenged (see specific examples in Cobb and Croucher 2016; Croucher et al. 2014).

Conclusion

We write this chapter at a time of considerable flux in both Higher Education and in the archaeological profession in the United Kingdom. For the latter, the spector of Brexit (the political and economic withdrawal of Britain from the European Union) looks set to reduce the archaeological workforce, stymie opportunities for research funding (Gardner and Harrison 2017), and change the character of developer-funded (CRM) archaeology, with the potential removal of the polluter-pays and precautionary principles (Lennox 2017). Meanwhile politics is also shaping HE; here responsibility for the standards, quality, and funding of Higher Education are moving from the nongovernmental Higher Education Funding Council for England (HEFCE) to the newly created government department, the Office for Students (OfS). Given these huge structural changes, archaeological pedagogy will undoubtedly respond and change again in the future. It is perhaps wrong, then, to characterize archaeological pedagogy in Britain as a story of rise and fall; as we have outlined, in the decade following the wane of the HEA's subject-specific support for archaeology, questions of training remain a key concern, and our own advocacy for an assemblage approach to pedagogy has also been substantive. Momentum for pedagogic research may not reflect that which existed a decade ago, but a rumbling resistance to the undervaluation of pedagogy is still making itself heard. The trick now, we suggest, is to make that rumble a roar once more. Now, more than ever, when the bifurcation of teaching and research that structures British higher education is so dominant and the neoliberal agenda so all-encompassing in our academic and professional (CRM) practice, and, as further changes gather like storm clouds on the horizon, taking an assemblage approach to pedagogy offers an opportunity to re-establish that momentum. It is only by recognizing the holistic nature of archaeology and heritage that we have the means to subvert and dispute the ways that teaching and research are segregated within the challenging times that demarcate archaeology and heritage in Britain today.

## Note

1. High-quality submissions, or 3- and 4-star–rated publications.

## References Cited

Aitchison, Kenneth
2004    Supply, Demand and a Failure of Understanding: Addressing the Culture Clash between Archaeologists' Expectations for Training and Employment in "Academia" Versus "Practice." *World Archaeology* 36(2): 219–230.
Aitchison, Kenneth, and Melanie Giles
2006    Employability and Curriculum Design. *Guides for Teaching and Learning in Archaeology*, no. 4. Higher Education Academy, Subject Centre for History, Classics and Archaeology, Liverpool, UK. Electronic document, https://www.heacademy.ac.uk/system/files/number4_teaching_and_learning_guide_employability.pdf. Accessed June 15, 2018.
Aitchison, Kenneth, and Douglas Rocks-Macqueen
2013    Archaeology Labour Market Intelligence: Profiling the Profession 2011–2012. Landward Archaeology, London.
Alberti, Benjamin, Andrew Meirion Jones, and Joshua Pollard (editors)
2013    *Archaeology after Interpretation: Returning Materials to Archaeological Theory.* Left Coast Press, Walnut Creek, California.
Cobb, Hannah, and Karina Croucher
2012    Field Schools, Transferable Skills and Enhancing Employability. In *Global Perspectives on Archaeological Field Schools: Constructions of Knowledge and Experience*, edited by Harold Mytum, pp. 25–40. Springer, London.
2014    Assembling Archaeological Pedagogy: A Theoretical Framework for Valuing

Pedagogy in Archaeological Interpretation. *Archaeological Dialogues* 21(2): 197–216.

2016 Personal, Political, Pedagogic: Challenging the Binary Bind in Archaeological Teaching, Learning and Fieldwork. *Journal of Archaeological Method and Theory* 23(3): 949–969.

2018 *Archaeology: A Relational Approach to Teaching, Practice and Research.* Oxford University Press, Oxford, UK.

Cobb, Hannah, Oliver J. T. Harris, Cara Jones, and Philip Richardson (editors)

2012 *Reconsidering Archaeological Fieldwork: Exploring On-Site Relationships between Theory and Practice.* Springer, London.

Conneller, Chantal

2011 *An Archaeology of Materials.* Routledge, London.

Crellin, Rachel J.

2017 Changing Assemblages: Tracing Vibrant Matter in Burial Assemblages. *Cambridge Archaeological Journal* 27(1): 111–125.

Croucher, Karina, and Hannah Cobb (editors)

2008 Prehistoric Pedagogies: Approaches to Teaching European Prehistoric Archaeology. *Special Collection in Research in Archaeological Education*, 2.

Croucher, Karina, Hannah Cobb, and Ange Brennan

2008 *Investigating the Role of Fieldwork in Teaching and Learning Archaeology.* Carnegie, Lancaster, UK.

Croucher, Karina, Hannah Cobb, and Eleanor Conlin Casella

2014 Feminist Pedagogy: Implications and Practice. In *Género y Arqueología en Mesoamérica: Homenaje a Rosemary A. Joyce*, edited by María J. Rodríguez-Shadow and Susan Kellogg, pp. 121–136. Centro de Estudios de Antropología de la Mujer, Lomas de Plateros, México, D.F.

Croucher, Karina, and Wendelin Romer

2007 Inclusivity and Curriculum Design. *Guides for Teaching and Learning in Archaeology*, no. 6. Higher Education Academy, Subject Centre for History, Classics and Archaeology, Liverpool, UK. Electronic document, https://www.heacademy.ac.uk/system/files/number6_teaching_and_learning_guide_inclusivity.pdf. Accessed March 15, 2018.

DeLanda, M.

2006 *A New Philosophy of Society: Assemblage Theory and Social Complexity.* Bloomsbury, London.

Deleuze, G., and F. Guattari

1987 [1980] *A Thousand Plateaus: Capitalism and Schizophrenia.* Translated by B. Massumi. University of Minnesota Press, Minneapolis.

Dowson, T.

2005 Teamwork and Archaeology: Developing Teambuilding Skills in Archaeology Students. *Guides to Teaching and Learning in Archaeology*, no. 4. Higher Education Academy Subject Centre for History, Classics and Archaeology, Manchester, UK.

Dowson, Thomas A. (editor)

2004 Archaeological Pedagogies. *World Archaeology* 36(2).

Everill, P., N. Finneran, and J. Flatman

2015    Training and Teaching in the Historic Environment. *Historic Environment: Policy & Practice* 6(2): 93–97.

Everill, Paul, and Rachel Nicholls

2011    *Archaeological Fieldwork Training: Provision and Assessment in Higher Education.* Submitted to University of Winchester/Higher Education Academy, Winchester, UK.

Fagan, Brian M.

2000    Strategies for Change in Teaching and Learning. In *Teaching Archaeology in the Twenty-First Century*, edited by Susan J. Bender and George S. Smith, pp. 125–132. Society for American Archaeology, Washington, D.C.

Finlay, Nyree

2005    *Practical Work Portfolios and Field Experience: An Evaluation of Modes of Assessment for Archaeological Skills.* Higher Education Academy, Subject Centre for History, Classics and Archaeology, Liverpool, UK.

Flatman, J.

2015    "A Slight Degree of Tension": Training the Archaeologists of the Future. *Historic Environment: Policy & Practice* 6(2): 142–155.

Fowler, Chris

2017    Relational Typologies, Assemblage Theory and Early Bronze Age Burials. *Cambridge Archaeological Journal* 27(1): 95–109.

Freire, Paulo

2000    *Pedagogy of the Oppressed* (30th anniversary ed.). Continuum, New York.

Gardner, Andrew, and Rodney Harrison

2017    Brexit, Archaeology and Heritage: Reflections and Agendas. *Papers from the Institute of Archaeology* 27(1): Art. 24.

Grant, Cathy, and Melanie Giles

2005    Moving Image Resources for Archaeology Teaching, Learning and Research. *Guides to Teaching and Learning in Archaeology*, no. 2. Higher Education Academy, Subject Centre for History, Classics and Archaeology, Manchester, UK. Electronic document, https://www.heacademy.ac.uk/knowledge-hub/number-2-guides-teaching-and-learning-archaeology. Accessed March 15, 2018.

Hamilakis, Yannis

2004    Archaeology and the Politics of Pedagogy. *World Archaeology* 36(2): 287–309.

Hamilakis, Yannis, and Andrew Meirion Jones

2017    Archaeology and Assemblage. *Cambridge Archaeological Journal* 27(1): 77–84.

Hamilakis, Yannis, and Paul Rainbird

2004    Archaeology in Higher Education. In *Education and the Historic Environment*, edited by Don Henson, Peter Stone, and Mike Corbishley, pp. 47–54. Routledge, London.

Harris, Oliver J. T.

2017    Assemblages and Scale in Archaeology. *Cambridge Archaeological Journal* 27(1): 127–139.

Henson, Don

2011    Education is a Central Issue for All Archaeologists. *British Archaeology* 119: 64–65.

Henson, Don, Peter Stone, and Mike Corbishley (editors)

2004    *Education and the Historic Environment.* Routledge/English Heritage, London.

Hicks, Dan, Gustav Milne, John Shepherd, and Robin Skeates

2009    Excavating the Archived: Archive Archaeology and the Higher Education Sector. *Guidelines for Teaching and Learning*, No 7. Museum of London Archaeology.

Hill, Dave, and Ravi Kumar (editors)

2009    *Global Neoliberalism and Education and Its Consequences.* Routledge, London.

Jervis, Ben

2016    Assemblage Theory and Town Foundation in Medieval England. *Cambridge Archaeological Journal* 26(3): 381–395.

Kilbride, William

2005    Data into Information into Knowledge: Online Resources into Teaching and Learning for Archaeology. *Guides for Teaching and Learning in Archaeology*, no. 1. Higher Education Academy, Subject Centre for History, Classics and Archaeology, Manchester, UK. https://www.heacademy.ac.uk/system/files/number1_teaching_and_learning_guide_data_into_information.pdf. Accessed March 15, 2018.

Kincheloe, J. L.

2008    *Knowledge and Critical Pedagogy: An Introduction.* Springer, London.

Lennox, Rob

2017    CIfA Statement on EU Withdrawal Bill Environmental Amendments. Chartered Institute for Archaeologists (CIfA), Reading, UK. Electronic document, http://www.archaeologists.net/news/cifa-statement-eu-withdrawal-bill-environmental-amendments-1511468536. Accessed March 15, 2018.

Lucas, Gavin

2012    *Understanding the Archaeological Record.* Cambridge University Press, Cambridge.

2017    Variations on a Theme: Assemblage Archaeology. *Cambridge Archaeological Journal* 27(1): 187–190.

Malott, Curry Stephenson, and Brad J. Porfilio (editors)

2011    *Critical Pedagogy in the Twenty-First Century: A New Generation of Scholars.* Information Age, Charlotte, North Carolina.

Mytum, Harold (editor)

2012    *Global Perspectives on Archaeological Field Schools: Constructions of Knowledge and Experience.* Springer, London.

Olssen, Mark, and Michael A. Peters

2005    Neoliberalism, Higher Education and the Knowledge Economy: From the Free Market to Knowledge Capitalism. *Journal of Education Policy* 20(3): 313–345.

Phillips, Tim, and Roberta Gilchrist

2005    *Inclusive, Accessible, Archaeology. Phase 1: Disability and Archaeological Fieldwork.* University of Reading and Bournemouth University, UK.

Rainbird, Paul, and Yannis Hamilakis (editors)

2001    *Interrogating Pedagogies: Archaeology in Higher Education.* Archaeopress, Oxford.

Robinson, David

2017    Assemblage Theory and the Capacity to Value: An Archaeological Approach from Cache Cave, California, USA. *Cambridge Archaeological Journal* 27(1): 155–168.

Saad-Filho, Alfredo, and Deborah Johnston

2005a   Introduction. In *Neoliberalism: A Critical Reader,* edited by Alfredo Saad-Filho, and Deborah Johnston, pp. 1–6. Pluto Press, London.

Saad-Filho, Alfredo, and Deborah Johnston (editors)

2005b   *Neoliberalism: A Critical Reader.* Pluto Press, London.

Sinclair, Anthony, Karina Croucher, and Thomas A. Dowson

2007    *Research in Archaeological Education,* vol. 1 [journal no longer available online].

Smith, Laurajane

2006    *Uses of Heritage.* Routledge, London.

Stevens, Fay

2005    *Reflective Pedagogies: Promoting Reflexive Practice in Archaeological Fieldtrips.* Higher Education Academy, Subject Centre for History, Classics and Archaeology, Liverpool, UK.

Watts, Christopher M. (editor)

2013    *Relational Archaeologies: Humans, Animals, Things.* Routledge, New York.

Welham, Kate

2005    *Enhancing Learning and Teaching of Key Archaeological Field Skills.* Higher Education Academy, Subject Centre for History, Classics and Archaeology, Liverpool, UK.

Wilkinson, K.

2007    *Communicating the Excavation Experience: Production of a Training Film and Handbook.* Higher Education Academy, Subject Centre for History, Classics and Archaeology, Liverpool, UK. Electronic document, http://www.heacademy. ac.uk/hca/projects/detail/round    6_communicating_the_excavation_experience. Accessed March 15, 2018.

# 12

## Archaeological Heritage in Europe in the Distance Learning Environment

ARKADIUSZ MARCINIAK

Recent decades in Europe have introduced dynamic changes in the field of protection and management of archaeological resources. The upsurge in infrastructure development, urban expansion, and intensive agriculture has brought about the large-scale destruction of numerous archaeological sites and landscapes. Of similar magnitude was the internationalization and standardization of archaeological heritage management as manifested by the adoption of the Valetta Convention (1992) and the European Landscape Convention (2000) and their implementation in national legal regulations.[1] Archaeological heritage management has become an important element of sustainable development and has been integrated into planning. The public has been recognized as a stakeholder in the decision-making process of heritage management (see Chilton, MacDonald, and Shackel, this volume), and its role as a consumer of the products of archaeological activity has become increasingly apparent. A rapid increase of development funding projects has brought new concerns for professional standards and accountability to archaeology (for example, Schlanger and Aitchison 2010; Willems 1998, 2008).

These dynamic changes have increased the demand for properly trained professionals, in particular, archaeological heritage officers at different levels of local and federal administration, who can promptly and accurately react to the ongoing challenges. This is especially challenging considering the different scholarly and professional traditions across Europe and the number of practicing professionals who were trained long before these changes occurred. As the definition of an archaeologist varies significantly across Europe, from one extreme where there is no legal definition, as in Greece, to the other where it is defined in terms of what the person does, as in Britain, there are highly diverse requirements for entry and progression in the profession (see also Cobb and Croucher, this volume). This is further strengthened by lack of need to maintain Continuing Professional Development as a requirement for practicing as archaeologists and heritage professionals (John Collis, personal communication 2009).

In order to meet the challenges of the dynamically changing panorama of practicing archaeology, a professional vocational system is needed to adequately react to the emerging challenges by equipping the end users with the newest knowledge and competencies. This requires an implementation of efficient and flexible training tools, which should be easily accessible to them. These requirements are met by dynamically developing e-learning solutions as efficient tools supporting the didactic process (see also Collison et al. 2000; Horton and Horton 2003; Politis 2008). A major advantage of this mode of content delivery is the ease of meeting expectations of various dispersed groups, at all possible scales with limited time and logistical constraints, by offering a wide range of training that can take place at any time and in any place.

This chapter provides a short overview of an innovative and recently developed vocational training system in the domain of archaeological heritage. This innovative training system is composed of two elements: (1) a database of e-learning resources in archaeological heritage in the form of the E-Archaeology Heritage Content Repository, and (2) a methodology of the distance learning course production and training modalities in the distance learning environment, along with the Heritage Educational Portal, which is in the form of a MOOC (Massive Open Online Course). These developments will be discussed in the theoretical framework that made the emergence of this system possible, as well as in reference to existing forms of distance learning and its current applications in archaeology and archaeological heritage.

## Distance Learning Solutions in Archaeology and Archaeological Heritage

E-learning is a form of distance education in which the development of skills and knowledge is realized through the use of modern electronic technologies. This is a broad category referring to any type of learning environment that is computer-enhanced and supported by multiple computer and online multimedia technologies. The process of learning is independent in time and place, and the trainer and trainee are bridged through the use of these technologies. The content of e-learning courses is communicated using different media, including text, voice, and sound. The efficiency of training directly depends not only on the quality of training materials, but also on their interesting and stimulating form. E-learning solutions in archaeology have been implemented for more than two decades (for example, Politis 2008).

E-learning education is of a universal character and can be used by and directed to a wide audience. It is particularly suitable for working professionals who lack time for participating in traditional training and/or are working in remote geographical territories, as well as for others who may be disabled, unemployed, and the like. Selection of methods for e-learning course delivery in the Internet environment can easily be directed by the explicitly defined character and expectations of the target group. Efficiency of any methodology can only be measured and evaluated by its application to the preparation of training materials and its further testing in training.

Different forms of distance learning are dynamically growing in different public institutions as well as at schools, colleges, and academic institutions across many disciplines (see also Franklin, this volume). E-learning is supported by multiple computer and online multimedia technologies. The following broad types of e-learning are distinguished depending upon the methods of didactic material acquisition: (1) computer-based training (CBT), (2) videoconferences, (3) mobile learning (M-learning), and (4) Web-based training (WBT).

The first two solutions are relatively simple. CBT refers to the production and distribution of didactic material on CD-ROMs and other portable devices. Videoconferences make it possible for people in different locations to see and hear each other at the same time. It requires software allowing audio and video streaming to be coded and decoded (Carliner 2002; Horton 2012). Mobile learning has different meanings. In the most general terms, it refers to learning with different mobile devices, including notebooks, pads, MP3 players, or mobile phones. A large body of applications comprise M-learning methods. These include the use of mobile devices to teach the general public about the archaeological and historical environment, as well as for undergraduate and postgraduate teaching and learning in archaeology.

Geographic Information Systems (GIS), Global Positioning Systems (GPS), and mobile technologies are set to deliver information and audiovisual resources of heritage outside museums or heritage sites, making it possible for their individualized exploration. Similar results are achieved by the use of podcasts that can take on a number of forms, including audio-only, enhanced audio (that is, sound with still images), or video. Used to support learning and teaching in different aspects of archaeology, they consist of recordings of lectures (audio-only), audio-only podcasts for use on fieldtrips, enhanced-audio skills podcasts, and Interactive QuickTime Virtual Reality (QTVR) and audio soundtrack. The availability of user-friendly software packages and hardware make the production of such digital resources increasingly easier.

The WBT is a sophisticated approach to distance learning in which training is delivered by the Internet or intranet. The WBT course is explicitly designed to be placed on the Internet and provided by the Learning Management System/Learning Content Management System (LMS/LCMS) multiuser environment. The LMS/LCMS makes it possible to create, store, manage, and deliver digital learning content. It is usually written in an XML-based (Extensible Markup Language) framework, known as SCORM (Shareable Content Object Reference Model)—a standard making it possible to share learning objects among different learning management systems. The SCORM standard has a global applicability and allows an e-learning course to launch on multiple platforms for distance education (for example, Blackboard, Moodle, Dokeos, Olat, Edumatic). Implementing a course in SCORM guarantees its convenient maintenance, modifications, and extensions.

The recently developed innovative vocational training system in the domain of archaeological heritage is an example of a new pedagogical strategy aimed at building Intelligent Tutoring Systems (ITS) immersed in e-learning content repositories. This strategy is made of two intertwined but internally separate elements, namely, the didactic content and method of conducting teaching. This approach is designed to conduct personalized learning in response to identified needs of trainees by means of an e-learning course that is given a definite structure by the trainer. The ITS system makes it possible to incorporate new content components that meet the pre-set criteria, such as subject, level of difficulty, and level of interactivity based upon materials stored in the repository. Sample pedagogical patterns used in the process of personalizing learning include incorporating content retrieved from the repository into a learning pathway realized by the trainee so that any identified deficiencies may be overcome (Similar Content Strategy Pattern), or supplementing the learning pathway with content from the repository that complements the topics under discussion with a case study illustrating the given topic (Case Study Inclusion Strategy Pattern). From a technical standpoint, the adopted solution is based on Sequencing and Navigation (SN) mechanisms of the SCORM 2004 specification, making it possible to search the repository for content that meets predefined criteria, in particular the content that best satisfies the previously identified needs of the dedicated group of trainers. In this approach pedagogical patterns are built as ready-made templates coded in SN language. They facilitate an easy and straightforward customized e-learning course employing a predefined educational strategy addressing needs and expectation of the end users by using didactic resources available in the content repository (see J. Marciniak 2014).

Integrated Vocational Training System of Archaeological Heritage in the Distance Learning Environment

An innovative integrated vocational training system of archaeological heritage has been developed in the past decade. It is made of two major elements along with accompanying methodologies: (1) the E-Archaeology Heritage Content Repository—a kind of interactive database for uploading, storing, and producing training materials in the domain of archaeological heritage and associated fields, and (2) the Heritage Educational Portal (HEP), which is currently the largest MOOC in the domain of heritage studies. It has been developed in three consecutive educational projects financed by different programs of the European Union and coordinated by the author. The consortium was made by partners from nine European countries, including Germany, Italy, Latvia, the Netherlands, Poland, Portugal, Spain, Sweden, and the United Kingdom, and representing all segments of the archaeological heritage sector supported by representatives from the natural heritage profession.

## The Didactic Content—E-Archaeology Heritage Content Repository

The E-Archaeology Heritage Content Repository is the database of e-learning resources in archaeological heritage.[2] It is hosted at Adam Mickiewicz University in Poznań, Poland. It contains didactic materials covering a wide range of issues in the domain of archaeological heritage (see details below). The materials are available for use in the form of smaller entities relevant to teaching according to the nomenclature of the Universal Curricular Taxonomy System (UCTS). They have the form of learning objects, which are then grouped in the logically arranged larger units of material, such as modules and curricula (see also McGill 2019; Moe 2019). Until very recently, they were built in DHTML (dynamic HTML) or flash technology, both of which were recognized by major Web browsers. They are now constructed using HTML5 Java script to facilitate the use of didactic materials on mobile devices. It needs to be reiterated that the availability of didactic materials in a SCORM system provides a technical means for launching the e-learning course on multiple platforms for distance education.

Repository properties are defined as words from the domain of archaeological heritage protection and management. They have been used to describe major didactic entities in the form of learning objects, modules, and curricula stored in the E-Archaeology Heritage Content Repository. They originate from the ontology constructed as WordNet-based ontology (J. Marciniak 2011). It refers to a system of the semantic similarity of concepts and words originating from WordNet, which has the form of a thesaurus grouping together words based on their meaning (for example, Fellbaum 2012). The current ontology consists of approximately 1,650 words ascribed to about 150 categories. The use of WordNet-based ontology made it possible to ascribe a semantic field to any given word in the Content Repository.

The learning object (LO) is the smallest didactic element. It refers to a coherent piece of knowledge or relevant case study. Altogether, in the current version of Content Repository there are about 8,500 LOs in German, English, Italian, Latvian, Polish, Portuguese, and Spanish. The availability of e-learning content in the form of learning objects makes it possible to (1) sort out existing resources in a flexible way, (2) describe them in a systematic manner, and (3) construct an infinite number of e-learning training curricula. In particular, it makes it possible to collate a coherent set of LOs in an infinite way to meet the requirements of ever-changing training goals for a wide range of target groups.

A module is defined as a coherent set of didactic materials covering complex but coherently related issues. It is composed of a number of learning units that are internally integrated and cover different aspects of the training curriculum. Altogether, there are currently 240 modules in the E-Archaeology Heritage Content Repository in all languages mentioned above.

A curriculum is a set of well-designed didactic materials tailored to the needs of different trainee groups. From the technical viewpoints, a curriculum is composed of a number of modules. The content of these curricula is constructed in such a way as to meet the needs and expectations of each such group, as well as their competencies and different training intensities. Altogether, there are currently nineteen curricula in the E-Archaeology Heritage Content Repository. They are directed to a wide range of end users with different degrees of competence. Their number is rapidly growing as the trainings are executed.

One of the major functionalities of the Repository is the advanced search engine of the available didactic materials. It is facilitated by tagging of all content based on the WordNet-based ontology in addition to the standard SCORM metadata (see details below). A semantic search using tags makes searching the repository significantly easier and much more efficient. The other functionalities comprise browsing and filtering, downloading content as SCORM packages, and supplying it with a new content.

The didactic materials from the E-Archaeology Heritage Content Repository cover a broad range of issues of archaeological heritage. They are available in the form of modules with accompanying case studies (see Table 12.1). All of them are available in English, Polish, and Spanish, and different sets of modules are available in German, Latvian, Italian, and Portuguese (for example, Kok et al. 2012; A. Marciniak 2009, 2012).

The module "Theorizing cultural heritage" reflects and critically assesses the concept of cultural heritage, both its tangible form and its intangible representations. It addresses a number of relevant issues of contemporary cultural heritage including relations with the public, its role in sustainable development, relationship with the recent and contemporary past, authenticity, as well as tourism and entertainment. The following module, "Mentalities and perspectives in archaeological heritage management," aims to discuss different perspectives in the practice of archaeological heritage

Table 12.1. Twenty-three didactic materials available in the E-Archaeology Heritage Content Repository

| |
|---|
| Theorizing cultural heritage |
| Mentalities and perspectives in archaeological heritage management |
| Concepts of understanding—spatial valorisation of archaeological heritage resources |
| Aerial survey in archaeological protection and management systems |
| Geographic Information System as a method of management of spatial data |
| Geophysical prospection in archaeological protection and management systems |
| Images of the past |
| Cultural biography of landscape |
| International conventions and legal frameworks |
| Sustainable development in the archaeological heritage sector |
| Management cycle and information systems in the archaeological heritage sector |
| Commercial archaeology |
| A single voice? Archaeological heritage, information boards, and public dialogue |
| Methods of engagement, publicity, and media relationships |
| Public outreach—museums, schools, services |
| Introduction to archaeology for construction engineers |
| Introduction to construction engineering for archaeologists |
| Archaeology and politics |
| Public archaeology |
| Urban archaeology |
| Perspectives on looting, illicit antiquities trade, art, and heritage |
| Problematic heritage |
| Maritime archaeology |

*Source*: Courtesy of the author.

management in relation to landscape and planning. It stresses the increasing significance of different public constituencies whose needs and expectations ought to be identified, addressed, and met in practice. The module "Concepts of understanding—spatial valorisation of archaeological heritage resources" provides an overview of the impact of different archaeological paradigms on the recognition and valorization of archaeological resources, as well as strategies of protection and management of archaeological heritage.

Three modules discuss methods of recognizing and recording archaeological resources, as well as managing and analyzing spatial data for the needs of archaeological heritage protection and management. The module "Aerial survey in archaeological protection and management systems" offers a systematic overview of aerial prospection in the practice of heritage management. The module "Geophysical prospection in archaeological protection and management systems" aims to provide an overview of the techniques of geophysical survey and presents major instruments and their use. A module called "Geographic Information System as a method of management of spatial data" is aimed at providing a brief discussion of GIS in the context of its use in archaeological heritage management practice, as well as presenting a background and solid introduction to major applications and types of information for which a GIS is well suited.

The module "Images of the past" discusses how images of the past are created and valorized by incorporating elements of archaeological heritage. It presents the role of these images in creating and maintaining local and regional identities. The module "Cultural biography of landscape" discusses the metaphor of the cultural biography of landscape and its use as a tool for sustainable development. The module "International conventions and legal frameworks" is a systematic overview of international conventions and charters in the domain of conservation and preservation of cultural heritage prepared by world (for example, UNESCO or ICOMOS) and European (mainly Council of Europe) bodies over the past fifty years (see also Chilton, this volume).

The module "Sustainable development in the archaeological heritage sector" discusses how the concept of sustainability can be translated into the cultural field. It further presents how cultural diversity was recognized as being under threat due to the pressure of globalization and global economy. The module "Management cycle and information systems in the archaeological heritage sector" offers an overview of a range of practical issues directly connected with management of archaeological heritage, such as registration, documentation, archiving, evaluation, protection/conservation, interpretation, synthesis, and communication (presentation and maintenance). The module "Commercial archaeology" discusses the relationship between commercial archaeology and archaeological heritage management.

The next module, "A single voice? Archaeological heritage, information boards and public dialogue," discusses a range of issues related to the presentation of archaeological heritage and communication with the general public. This is exemplified by a role of information boards at monuments and sites as a dominant method of communication with the general public. The module "Public outreach—museums, schools, services" presents the importance of multimedia technologies and the Internet for the way archaeology is communicated to the public. The module "Methods and engagement, publicity and media relationships" discusses the importance of communication with the public, methods of engagement, publicity, and media relationships.[3]

The module "Archaeology and politics" provides an overview of how archaeology has been strictly tied to the political context and embedded in the political discourses of the time (see also MacDonald, this volume). The module "Public archaeology" provides an overview of the developments that triggered the engagement with the public in various parts of the world. It further presents major facets of community-based archaeology (see Clark, this volume). The module "Perspectives on looting, illicit antiquities trade, art and heritage" provides an overview of issues related to looting and illicit trade of antiques and art objects. The module "Problematic heritage" addresses the constructive nature of cultural and archaeological heritage. It presents mechanisms of turning past objects into heritage assets by including some of them while excluding others. It further discusses the process of materialization and construction of collective memory and presents the characteristic features of fearsome and neglected cultural heritage. The module "Urban archaeology" presents an interdisciplinary character of archaeology and management of historic towns with complicated stratigraphy. It explores the legal and organizational framework of urban archaeology, its history, and its different facets. Another module, "Maritime archaeology," provides an overview of maritime archaeology by discussing types of maritime culture heritage, major archaeological maritime techniques, and different means of its monitoring, protecting, and managing.[4]

Two additional modules were produced to facilitate cooperation between archaeologists and civil engineers. The module "Introduction to archaeology for construction engineers" provides an overview of archaeology and archaeological practice for constructional engineers by systematically presenting major elements of the archaeological process. In the same way, the module "Introduction to construction engineering for archaeologists" provides an introduction to the engineering projects, their major components, and the basic principles of project management and control.[5]

Eight modules aim to address the most important issues in integrated cultural and natural heritage.[6] The first module, "Europe's cultural landscapes: opportunities and threats," provides an introduction to Europe's cultural landscapes as the basis for understanding the importance of crossing disciplinary boundaries to safeguard natural and cultural heritage. It is argued that both cultural and natural heritage are integrated elements of the landscape that can be considered to be under threat. The following module, "Heritage strategies: what, why, where, how, by whom and for whom?," presents the development of different heritage strategies, including the historical reasoning behind their implementation, the social framework in which they have been developed, the different mechanisms involved, and the long-term objectives of this development. It further discusses the social value of the cultural and natural heritage in the construction of new social and national identities. The next module, "Nature conservation for cultural heritage experts," is designed for cultural heritage workers who need or want to learn more about nature conservation. Beyond providing general background knowledge, it informs heritage managers of ways in which nature conservation can have an impact upon or affect cultural heritage. The module "Cultural heritage management for nature heritage" aims to introduce the concept of cultural heritage, its different areas of expertise, and the different strategies in its management (public and private sectors). It further presents the European framework for the protection and safeguarding of cultural heritage, highlighting the main European conventions and regulations with the aim of introducing key legislation, policy documents, and international charters.

The following module, "Traverse the disciplines of ecology and archaeology: the new horizon," goes into basic strategies for crossovers between natural and cultural heritage trying to overcome this divide. It considers the development within the field of archaeology and ecology in relation to public discourse, presents the general knowledge base for landscape management and knowledge transfer for the wider public, and discusses means of presenting the landscape as it pertains to public engagement. The module "Integrating heritage in land use planning" deals with the integration of natural and cultural heritage in land-use planning, which pertains to aspects of landscape, societal values, and governance. Practices of ecology and archaeology within land-use planning are presented in general terms identifying areas of tension. The module "Ownership and benefits" discusses recent shifts in understanding the role of heritage that has become linked to human rights; this context brings heritage to societal values, such as justice and well-being. In both natural and cultural heritage sectors, there is a general increase in the public influence deciding on what is to be considered heritage and how that heritage may be used. The final module, "Participatory practices," addresses four key components of natural and cultural heritage: networks and communities of practice, online and offline communities, public discourses, and finance and participation. It discusses the development of democratic participation, with objectives to implement a shared responsibility to identify values, define priorities, and manage heritage-led projects.

## Content Development and Training Modalities—The Heritage Educational Portal

The E-Archaeology Heritage Content Repository is first and foremost designed for providing access to new content out of available didactic materials. This process can be compared with how the computer's editorial function works. The transfer of any selected element into a newly created content is made by a simple drag-and-drop operation. It means that content authoring is simple and straightforward and does not require IT competence.

However, creating e-learning–tailored content in the form of a module or curriculum requires a precise defining of the needs and expectation of a group of trainees and constructing the materials that can meet them. As soon as these needs are specified, it is necessary to find suitable didactic materials by searching the resources from the E-Archaeology Heritage Content Repository (see also J. Marciniak 2012). In this process, two types of data are displayed: (1) repository properties, and (2) metadata descriptions. They both are set to help the prospective trainer choose appropriate materials available in the Repository. The repository properties refer to basic information about the didactic content, such as the title, author, didactic categories, SCORM-type element, and rights to the displayed element. The metadata describe the content in the following way: educational difficulty, age range, interactivity level, and copyright information. There have been approximately 100 metadata attributes used to describe the content in the Repository.

Another important functionality of the E-Archaeology Heritage Content Repository involves the possibility of uploading new modules and curricula, assuming these are recorded in the SCORM standard. This is granted to users who have been given appropriate access rights. Following the uploading of new modules or curricula into the Content Repository, all their components must be tagged according to the specified rules.

The authored e-learning course can then be downloaded in the form of a SCORM package. The system makes it possible to download different categories of material, such as curricula, modules, and units. Such ready-to-use packages can then be uploaded to any LMS-compatible platform to run the training. Hence the Repository, along with a coherent methodology of building up potentially endless e-learning modules and curricula out of the stored materials, is the ultimate resource for the production of a wide range of e-learning courses targeting different audiences.

The authored e-learning courses designed for different training groups are made available through the Heritage Educational Portal (HEP), which is a gateway to all training activities. It is in the form of a MOOC and is designed to provide an easy access to a number of courses in the domain of heritage.[7] It is currently available in six languages: Dutch, English, Italian, Polish, Portuguese, and Spanish. The HEP offers support to the educational process, including expanding and strengthening a group of teachers/trainers and different didactic bodies responsible for delivering vocational training in archaeological heritage, as well as providing training to different end users based upon courses in the E-Archaeology Heritage Content Repository. Its integral element comprises a methodology of building up a potentially endless number of e-learning modules and curricula out of the stored didactic materials to meet the requirements and expectations of different end users.

The training materials prepared to meet the individual needs of a target group are then used in the didactic process in the distance learning environment (see J. Marciniak 2009, 2012). The process is carried out through the assisted e-learning model in which the source of knowledge is the e-learning content, not the teacher, and the role of teachers is to support and monitor learning. The e-learning content is presented in the form of multimedia and interactive solutions. The Heritage Educational Portal recommends five major forms of distance learning: (1) scheduled course sessions with instruction and certification, with content and examination available on an e-learning platform and sessions delivered according to a fixed schedule; (2) certification sessions with exams for certification, and available according to a fixed schedule; (3) open access to didactic materials on an e-learning platform, which is in the form of community learning with no expert present, but with discussion forums with facilitators; (4) e-mentoring involving consultation with an expert available online through a chat room, Skype, or other synchronous or asynchronous tool; and (5) self-paced learning from didactic material available online on a website with no control or tracking/reporting on learners' activity and no human support for learners.

Distance learning activities in the first four methods of training take place on the e-learning platform available in the LMS/LCMS system, such as Blackboard, Moodle, Dokeos, or Edumatic. The modules created in the E-Archaeology Heritage Content Repository and produced in the form of SCORM can be uploaded in any of such learning management systems. The LMS/LCMS system is set to support the organization and conduct of all elements of the distance didactic process. In particular, it facilitates (1) flexible mechanisms for course organization by meeting the demands of individual trainees; (2) building, managing, and publishing the didactic content; (3) managing the didactic process and monitoring the progress; and (4) providing tools for communication between trainees and trainers.

In order to facilitate efficient completion of training, the course syllabus needs to be produced and delivered to the trainee prior to the course's beginning. It aims to describe the rules of participation in the training and support trainees and trainers alike. In particular, the syllabus is set to clarify the following issues: (1) aims of the course, (2) course organization, (3) course timetable, (4) participation requirements, (5) rules in the course participation, and (6) contact information.

The course is made of a selected number of multimedia modules, as specified by the trainer. Depending upon the selected method of training, it can be supplemented by discussion forums, essays, and other forms of collective and individual work. The system also provides efficient tools for knowledge verification, including self-testing of knowledge and managing homework.

In the training conducted in a fully asynchronous mode, the trainees are given the possibility of working in the available time and in a convenient place. The major activity in the training comprises individual work on successive modules. Availability of individual modules and other resources is to be specified according to the character of training and needs of the trainees. While working on subsequent modules, the trainees are given access to a number of auxiliary materials. They are available in an electronic format, such as Word or PDF files. Access to the forum set to accompany the course section is only available after trainees acquire some knowledge by studying the modules.

The LMS/LCMS system makes it possible to support management of the entire didactic process and monitor the progress of the trainees. It facilitates tracking their progress, participation in forums (which can be measured by a number of entries to the course/module/forum), time spent in subsequent learning objects and modules, date of the first entry, date of the last entry, and so on. These details are made available in the form of customized reports. The LMS/LCMS system also facilitates communication between trainers and their trainees in the form of chat, electronic mail, and calendar.

## The Distance Learning Environment for Archaeological Heritage and Its Social and Economic Relevance

Adoption of a new pedagogical strategy aimed at building Intelligent Tutoring Systems (ITS) immersed in e-learning content repositories was of unquestionable social and economic relevance. This adoption resulted in the development of a coherent vocational training system in the domain of archaeological heritage, along with the production of a rich body of didactic materials addressing the most pertinent issues of European archaeological heritage policy and practice, which were prepared by competent specialists in their respective fields. The system aimed at developing and upgrading vocational skills of archaeological heritage professionals, enhancing cooperation between archaeological and natural heritage specialists, addressing significance and relevance of archaeological heritage in many realms of contemporary life beyond the heritage sector itself, as well as facilitating sustainable development of graduate and extramural students.

The integrated vocational training system of archaeological heritage can be a boon to professionals in the sector of archaeological heritage protection and management. The knowledge acquired during the training could later be efficiently implemented in their professional practice. This is particularly relevant to professionals whose knowledge might no longer be relevant to meet the newly emerging challenges, especially if they received their academic training before the recent period of unprecedented transformation in the domain of archaeological heritage. Moreover, the group is largely dispersed, as many of these practitioners are employed in local branches of the heritage sector located in provincial capitals and smaller cities. Understandably, their access to the newest knowledge in the field may be varied. At the same time, they want to remain professionally active. Hence, the methods of vocational training need to combine efficiency of the learning process with their obvious time constraints.

The vocational training system discussed above is also designed to enhance and facilitate closer cooperation between professionals from archaeological and natural heritage sectors. One of the most efficient strategies for meeting these objectives is to enhance the competencies of professionals in both domains, which can be achieved by developing and upgrading vocational skills in the sector of protection and management of archaeological and natural heritage. The pedagogical materials available in the E-Archaeology Heritage Content Repository are directly relevant to meet these challenges, as they explicitly address the nature of prospective cooperation between both sectors along with their intertwined relations.

As archaeological heritage is becoming increasingly important and relevant in many domains of contemporary life, the decision-making process affecting its assets is often taking place outside the realm of the heritage profession, which is formally responsible for their protection and management. Hence, a comprehensive understanding of archaeological heritage by the groups that have to deal with its various aspects in their professional work is crucial. The training system in archaeological heritage discussed here is designed to enhance competencies of different potential users from a range of sectors interested in this field of expertise. These include museum staff, school teachers, administrative staff, planners, architects, civil engineers, forest rangers, and teachers, among others. They can get to know the significance of archaeological heritage for city planning, landscape policies, sustainable development, construction of regional identities, and the like.

The vocational training system in archaeological heritage also serves the needs of graduate and extramural students. They can gain access to a body of knowledge produced by leading European experts in the field, making it possible to recognize the most appealing issues in the domain of protection and management of archaeological heritage across Europe. This would considerably enhance their qualifications on the job market. This is especially important as archaeological heritage is becoming the backbone of contemporary archaeology, and the broadly understood heritage sector creates the majority of archaeological jobs across Europe today.

## Concluding Remarks

The vocational training system of archaeological heritage in the distance learning environment involves a complex scheme for production and maintenance of a comprehensive set of didactic content and varied methods of training delivery. Its first major component comprises the E-archaeology Heritage Content Repository, a database for handling didactic materials available in different formats. The adopted solutions make it possible to author didactic content in response to the different needs of diverse target groups. The content of any training curriculum can easily be constructed from the database of didactic materials available in the form of learning objects. These can then be uploaded in the form of ready-to-use SCORM packages. The training can be carried out in diverse educational contexts and on different e-learning platforms, according to the resources available to the training providers. The second integral element of the vocational training system is the Heritage Educational Portal. It aims to support an entire educational process by hosting complete e-learning courses covering different aspects of archaeological heritage, offering courses directed for different end users, supporting the didactic process as well as strengthening a group of trainers and different didactic bodies.

The developers of this vocational training system in archaeological heritage believe that e-learning in the form of Web-based training is the most efficient method of vocational training for users in the European context. It has a range of advantages, including flexibility, ease in reaching geographically dispersed trainees, availability of materials in the most convenient time, and adjustment to the individual demands of trainees. It provides a nonsequential use that facilitates navigation of its content in different ways, allows access to the course structure before getting into details, and provides constant access to reference and revision material. It has to be emphasized, however, that learning at a distance requires self-discipline and good personal time management.

## Notes

1. http://www.coe.int/en/web/culture-and-heritage/valletta-convention, http://www.coe.int/en/web/landscape/home.

2. http://e-archaeology.org/teaching-heritage/e-archaeology-content-repository.

3. These ten modules were produced in the Leonardo da Vinci project "E-learning as a tool of knowledge transfer in the field of protection and management of archaeological heritage."

4. These six modules were produced in the Leonardo da Vinci project "Vocational training in archaeological heritage based upon e-learning."

5. These two modules were produced in the Leonardo da Vinci project "Archaeology and Construction Engineering Skills."

6. These eight modules were produced in the Erasmus Plus project "Innovative format of education and training of the integrated archaeological and natural heritage."

7. hep.e-archaeology.org.

## References Cited

Carliner, Saul
2002    *Designing E-learning.* ASTD Press, Alexandria, Virginia.
Collison, George, Bonnie Elbaum, Sarah Haavind, and Robert Tinker
2000    *Facilitating Online Learning, Effective Strategies for Moderators.* Atwood, Madison, Wisconsin.
Fellbaum, Christiane
2012    *WordNet. The Encyclopedia of Applied Linguistics.* Wiley, Hoboken, New Jersey.
Horton, William
2012    *E-learning by Design,* 2nd ed. Wiley, San Francisco, California.
Horton, William, and Katherine Horton
2003    *E-learning Tools and Technologies.* Wiley, Indianapolis, Indiana.
Kok, Marjolijn, Heleen van Londen, and Arkadiusz Marciniak (editors)
2012    *E-Learning Archaeology. Heritage Handbook.* University of Amsterdam Press, Amsterdam.
Marciniak, Arkadiusz
2009    E-learning in Archaeological Heritage. An Example of "Archaeological Heritage in Contemporary Europe," a Distance Learning Course. In *E-learning Archaeology,* edited by Heleen van Londen, Marjolijn Kok, and Arkadiusz Marciniak, pp. 41–55. University of Amsterdam Press, Amsterdam.
2012    E-learning Resources in the Vocational Training System in Archaeological Heritage. In *E-Learning Archaeology. Heritage Handbook,* edited by Marjolijn Kok,

Heleen van Londen, and Arkadiusz Marciniak, pp. 7–15. University of Amsterdam Press, Amsterdam.

Marciniak, Jacek

2009    Methodology and E-learning Solutions. "Archaeological Heritage in Contemporary Europe," a Distance Learning Course. In *E-learning Archaeology*, edited by Heleen van Londen, Marjolijn S. M. Kok, and Arkadiusz Marciniak, pp. 56–89. University of Amsterdam Press, Amsterdam.

2011    Enhancing Tagging Systems by Wordnet Based Ontologies. In *Proceedings of 5th Language and Technology Conference, November 25–27*, edited by Zygmunt Vetulani. Adam Mickiewicz University, Poznań, Poland.

2012    Organizing Effective Distance Learning Training, Using E-learning Content and the Content Repository. In *E-Learning Archaeology. Heritage Handbook*, edited by Marjolijn Kok, Heleen van Londen, and Arkadiusz Marciniak, pp. 16–24. University of Amsterdam Press, Amsterdam.

2014    Creating Pedagogical Strategies for Personalization in Intelligent Tutoring Systems Active in E-learning Content Repositories. In *EDULEARN14 Proceedings, 6th International Conference on Education and New Learning Technologies July 7th–9th*, Barcelona, Spain, edited by Luis Gómez Chova, A. López Martínez, and I. Candel Torres, pp. 2053–2062. IATED Academy, Valencia, Spain.

McGill, Alicia Ebbitt

2019    Assessing Student Learning in Heritage Studies: What Does It Mean for Students to "Understand" Archaeological Ethics? In *Pedagogy and Practice in Heritage Studies*, edited by Susan J. Bender and Phyllis Mauch Messenger, pp. 50–71. University Press of Florida, Gainesville.

Moe, Jeanne M.

2019    Archaeology in School: Student Learning Outcomes. In *Pedagogy and Practice in Heritage Studies*, edited by Susan J. Bender and Phyllis Mauch Messenger, pp. 9–29. University Press of Florida, Gainesville.

Politis, Dionysios (editor)

2008    *E-learning Methodologies and Computer Applications in Archaeology*. Information Science Reference, Hershey, Pennsylvania.

Schlanger, Nathan, and Kenneth Aitchison (editors)

2010    *Archaeology and the Global Economic Crisis. Multiple Impacts, Possible Solutions*. Culture Lab Editions, Tervuren, Belgium.

Willems, Willem

1998    Archaeology and Heritage Management in Europe. Trends and Developments. *European Journal of Archaeology* 1(3): 293–311.

2008    Archaeological Resource Management and Preservation. In *Preserving Archaeological Remains In Situ. Proceedings of the 3rd Conference, December 7–9, 2006, Amsterdam*, edited by Henk Kars and Robert M. van Heeringen, pp. 283–289. Geoarchaeological and Bioarchaeological Studies 10, VU University Amsterdam, Amsterdam.

# 13

# Help Needed!

## Reflections on a Critical Pedagogy of Heritage

LARRY J. ZIMMERMAN

The core elements of this essay stem from two education sessions at Society for American Archaeology (SAA) meetings. I was afforded an opportunity to serve as a discussant for "Lessons from the Trenches II: New Pedagogies of Archaeology and Heritage," a session organized for the 2013 SAA annual meeting. Having recently learned some valuable lessons from a special topics class on Issues in Cultural Heritage, co-taught with Elizabeth Kryder-Reid (see Kryder-Reid 2019), I eagerly agreed. The presentations, many of which developed into chapters in this book and its companion volume (Bender and Messenger 2019), were excellent and fun presentations about archaeology education projects on which colleagues had been working, but I found myself at the time, and even after reading many of them for this volume, wondering where the *new* pedagogies were and whether or how the projects were related to heritage.

Two years later I was privileged to be invited by Jeanne Moe (see Moe 2019) to be one of several discussants for a session commemorating the twenty-fifth anniversary of *Project Archaeology,* the most carefully developed and successfully evaluated public archaeology curriculum in American archaeology. Developers, national partners, and teachers in *Project Archaeology* have every right to be proud of what they have accomplished, exposing the many *thousands* of 4th- to 7th-grade students, for whom the program is structured, to what archaeologists do, how they think, and the ways they interpret the past. Listening to the presentations and to the other discussants, I was surprised and bothered by the profoundly small percentage of students involved over the twenty-five-year life of the program compared to the number of 4th- to 7th-grade students in the United States every year, estimated to be about 14 *million* in the 2010 census (Bauman and Davis 2013: 3), information I quickly looked up on my smartphone. Having heard nothing but praise for the program and its successes, I wanted to turn those numbers into a challenge for the program's future, but unfortunately let my inner curmudgeon overwhelm what was intended as a celebration. My challenge seemed to be taken as a criticism of *Project Archaeology*. My intention, however, was to say that, as a profession, archaeology can't be doing everything right if we engage so relatively few students and teachers in what is arguably America's most well-designed program. Thinking about the matter later, I puzzled about why just about every nonarchaeologist I know seems to be interested in heritage, while relatively few—even those with some exposure to excellent archaeology education—show any long-term, serious interest in archaeology. Interest in heritage is certainly cross-cultural, maybe even universal, but for some, archaeology and the knowledge it generates apparently seem boring or, at worst, a waste of time and money. I suppose I shouldn't be puzzled that they think archaeology doesn't matter all that much.

For most nonarchaeologists, archaeology has little to do with their daily lives; some—particularly Indigenous people—even see archaeology as anathema (see Deloria 1995 for one example). Heritage, on the other hand, is actually central to identity, to self-esteem, and to daily life. Most archaeologists—myself included—unfortunately and indiscriminately conflate archaeology with the pasts they study (Holtorf 2007: v) and those pasts, with heritage. Doing so has a profound impact on how we create and promote archaeology's "brand." Unfortunately, archaeology's brand confuses our approaches to archaeology and heritage pedagogy, which hints at where this reflection will drift.

Archaeologists need to recognize this divide between relatively low public interest in archaeology and the publics' nearly universal interest in heritage (compare Carman 2002: 11–20; Lowenthal 1996: 1–30; Smith and Waterton 2009: 138–142), figure out why the divide exists, and develop some ways to reduce the distance. To do that, archaeology needs to become a partner with other heritage disciplines, which in many ways share similar problems in theorizing a critical pedagogy of heritage (for example, Hayes et al., this volume). In this chapter, I will try to follow some logical steps to suggest how archaeology might accomplish this, starting with most archaeologists' and, very likely, most other kinds of heritage specialists' lack of teaching experience, which is exacerbated by almost no study of pedagogy. Then I'll move on to more complicated, but related, concerns about how archaeologists might contribute to theorizing a critical heritage of pedagogy. Be warned that I also intend to keep the style of these reflections mostly conversational, not scholarly, which is something you quickly learn to do if you do much public archaeology education.[1] Finally, theorizing need not be complicated, nor does whatever theory might come from the process. Theorizing often just reflects systematically developed, organized common sense.

## Archaeologists and (Not) Teaching

I suspect that I am like many other senior, primarily academic, archaeologists who have taught archaeology to a wide range of audiences. During my fifty years in the discipline, I taught archaeology and heritage-focused classes at university; won teaching awards; worked on educational programs at three museums and one state historical society; worked with 6th-grade teachers, co-developing an engaging curriculum (Zimmerman et al. 1994); organized and supervised numerous public archaeology events; completed multiple cultural resources management (CRM) contracts that included reports for the public; developed archaeology websites for the general public; wrote several text and trade books; and presented and published several papers on teaching archaeology. My self-esteem tells me that I have done a mostly good job teaching about archaeology, but the reality is that only near the end of my career have I come to recognize that I usually confused archaeology with heritage in all my teaching; I was just teaching archaeology.

That's a whole paragraph about my teaching experiences, yet I have never taken a course on how to teach. I actually have gone out of my way to avoid reading education literature.[2] I suspect that, as with me, most archaeologists have had very little formal training in how to teach.[3] Many of us joke that we learned how to teach by seeing bad examples from our own professors and from our own miserable failures or occasional successes in the classroom. Those in cultural resources management/cultural heritage management, our discipline's heroes on the frontlines of public archaeology, probably have had even less formal education training. Yet we successfully engage our students and our publics with seat-of-our-pants passion, trying to translate our excitement about archaeology into activities that entice visitors to our excavations or public archaeology events. We slip into the comfortable (and fun!) routines of hands-on demonstrations of atlatls, flint-knapping, artifact identification, simulated digs, and tours of real or virtual sites. A very few even get involved in production of video. We enjoy the feedback from audiences when we give public lectures about our discoveries.

We emphasize a few key points about what archaeologists do and something of what we find and interpret. Whether academic or CRM archaeologists, we get by primarily on our native inventiveness, then build on what went right or wrong. With rare exception (such as in *Project Archaeology*; see also McGill 2019, Moe 2019, White 2019; Cobb and Croucher, this volume) do we work closely with teachers or do evaluation, and *pedagogy* truly is an uncommon word in our field. We know that pedagogy has to do with teaching, but most of us can be little more specific unless we Google it. The result is that we may think about our teaching, but we rarely think about real pedagogy, let alone try to theorize a critical pedagogy of either archaeology or heritage.

Don't get me wrong! Archaeologists have gotten darn good at teaching about archaeology and have proven to be skilled developers of curricula to teach archaeological methods and the discipline's interpretations of the past. Many who wrote chapters for this and numerous other volumes and papers use fascinating tools in their teaching, especially new media, and a few explicitly discuss pedagogical methods (see Franklin, Marciniak, and Sievert et al., this volume; McGill 2019). That archaeologists do this well should not surprise because we always have been adept borrowers of new tools, methodologies, or theoretical models, but we often do so uncritically, unaware of pitfalls already discovered by other scholars and disciplines. None of this detracts from the enthusiasm that most archaeologists display for their discipline or their desire to share what they do or discover with their publics,[4] but we might ask what people really take home when they leave our events, websites, hands-on activities, classes, or lectures. More importantly, what do we want them to take home? In other words, how do we present archaeology content within a context of learning strategies that connect to a cognitive process (compare Moe 2019)? Put a simpler way, what do we want people to learn or think about archaeology, what effective strategies can we use to get that across to them, and, once we have done so, what do we want them to take away that might make a real difference in their lives?

Some may recognize these questions as a ragged definition of archaeology pedagogy. Archaeologists do moderately well with the first part, especially if we emphasize methods and culture history; with the strategies part, we are magnificent, but on the cognitive processes—what we want people to get out of archaeology—we fall far short. We usually fail to answer that ultimate brute question: "So what?" Our answers rarely go beyond vagaries—that archaeology can fill in gaps in the historical record, that it can provide perspective on human cultural change over time, that the past is public heritage that must be protected, ad nauseam—but hardly anything that will matter much to more than a few of them. Yet providing better answers—heritage-centered, not archaeology-centered, answers—is where the payoff will be. Along the way, the public will come to understand that archaeology really can matter.

## Archaeology Is Really Cool, but Can Archaeology Really Matter?

Some archaeologists may be happy to get *any* attention or to inspire a few members of the public to read more or even to participate in paraprofessional avocational pursuits,[5] but for much of the public, archaeology serves as little more than a hobby, an interesting subject to read about, or a documentary to watch. When children want to go to university to become archaeologists, parents ask how they will make a living at it; or when a newly discovered site delays or halts construction citizens want to see built, archaeology becomes an "enemy of progress." There is nothing particularly wrong with sending people away happy and excited about archaeology, but we may be reinforcing impressions that archaeology is *just* fun or fascinating, but probably of little real use in their daily lives and mostly not related to their own heritage. How often, after all, will most need to know how to lay in a grid, use a total station or an atlatl, or even the fact that Mississippian tradition peoples built truncated temple mounds or made shell-tempered pottery?

We don't seem to realize that we market our brand in ways that support the public's opinion that archaeology is esoteric and romantic and, by doing so, we undercut archaeology's potential. The very name of the discipline—archaeology—says that we study old stuff; that is what many of us believe and what our publics most definitely believe. "Old" is what we emphasize in our pedagogy, one of three hooks we use to engage our publics. Skim just about any popular magazine or website with archaeology content and read only the title or lead sentence of news items and stories. Time-loaded words such as *first, oldest,* and *earliest* appear surprisingly often. "Discover" is another hook that by its very definition—unexpectedly finding something missing or hidden—generates a level of excitement and interest. Our third hook is archaeology's "mystery" words—*rare, mysterious, unexplainable, vanished, abandoned,* and the like—which are powerful enticements to most people's imaginations. Combined, these hooks sell magazines, tickets to museum exhibits, novels, films, and, unfortunately, even pseudoarchaeology cable television programming. As archaeologists, many of us readily use the hooks to interest reporters, magazine editors, and media producers, but we also use them in our teaching. We try to make archaeology "sexy" by trying to seduce our publics with the "romance of archaeology." This "gets them in the door," but once inside many quickly get bored when they find out that archaeology can be tedious hard work, with exceedingly infrequent fantastic discoveries, and producing nearly unreadable, jargon-larded reports.

Clearly, however, some archaeologists would desperately like the public to believe that archaeology matters beyond just providing perspectives about the past or being fun and fascinating, and there is growing evidence that archaeology really can be directly applicable to nagging social problems (Atalay et al. 2014; Little and Shackel 2014; Little and Zimmerman 2010; Rathje and Murphy 1992; Sabloff 2008; Stottman 2011). A few, such as Kryder-Reid (2019) describes, try to create curricular links or public programs between archaeological projects and a range of contemporary issues. Generally this kind of archaeology is being called "contemporary archaeology" or "archaeology of the contemporary" (see Gannon 2016 for a popular media discussion of the approach and several projects). Others have developed community-based participatory research programs (Atalay 2012), with projects that directly link archaeology and specific descendant communities, as in the multiple community initiatives of the Intellectual Property Issues in Cultural Heritage (IPinCH) project;[6] the "A Long Time Coming" project, a collaborative public history and archaeology Initiative of Higher Ground Intercultural and Heritage Association in the Setauket area in New York (Matthews 2013; for a discussion of issues, see Matthews et al. 2011 and Matthews and McDavid 2013; see also B. Clark, King, MacDonald, and Watkins, this volume). All engage very specific groups or communities and aspects of their own heritage. The projects demonstrate how the methods and interpretive power of archaeology can be applied directly to well-defined interests, projects, or social problems as determined by the community. For them, making the public understand that archaeology can be useful is crucial if archaeology is to matter. Fail this and archaeology remains an arcane and esoteric—albeit interesting—field. Reflecting on my career as an archaeologist and educator, I would include myself in most of what I've described here, and I certainly want archaeology to matter. To paraphrase Victor Buchli (2007: 14), I want archaeology to "earn its keep." However, no matter our good intentions for educating the public, we seem to struggle in showing the public what archaeology is really capable of doing and how it is related to their heritage.

## That Archaeology Is Not Heritage Is Probably a Good Thing

Archaeology can be a potent tool for heritage, but they should never be thought of as the same thing. Archaeology has an extremely powerful set of tools whose primary focus is the study of "stuff" and its contexts, not just time. The methods archaeologists use to recover stuff and analyze it may differ, and the archaeological toolkit constantly seems to shift and improve with technological change, but the questions archaeologists ask of "stuff"— who; what; when; how was it acquired, produced, modified, used, and disposed of; and what might it have meant?—are mostly the same, no matter where archaeologists recover it or how old it is (Zimmerman 2013: 336). How archaeologists interpret stuff depends heavily on theoretical models in vogue at the time, which certainly can be controversial; but fortunately, what comes from our work is different from the product of heritage studies. Heritage is vastly more complicated.

For something so powerful and at the core of cultural or individual identity, heritage is profoundly ill-defined and vaporous (compare Harrison 2010, 2013). Heritage can be a process or a set of values that relate to the past, which can be natural, cultural, tangible, intangible, dark, and of assorted other types. Depending on which type, heritage can raise or lower self-esteem, can be destructive or inspirational, can be powerful or benign, can be colonized and politically manipulated, can be a political act—the list could go on. Most people tend to associate it with history and the past in some way, but as Lowenthal (1996: x) points out, heritage is not history and "it is not an inquiry into the past, but a celebration of it . . . a profession of faith in a past tailored to present-day purposes." As Harrison (2010: 10) suggests, it is a "repackaging of the past for some purpose in the present."

A project on which I am a team member (Kryder-Reid et al. 2018: 756) suggests that the differences between archaeology and heritage are significant, and that heritage is where archaeology should focus its attention when it comes to pedagogy. The project involves two large archaeological clusters in Indiana: Mounds State Park and Strawtown Koteewi, a county nature center and park. Both have public archaeology education programs that represent Native American heritage at the sites, and both are currently embroiled in political controversy, the former over development of a reservoir that will harm archaeological sites, and the latter, over repatriation of human remains excavated at the sites on park land. Our project used interviews, focus groups, and surveys to study stakeholder-defined heritage and values that visitors attach to them at the two contested sites. One of the Native American interviewees, when asked what heritage means said, "I don't really use the word heritage . . . [I] Don't ever use the term—doesn't inform my thought process. If I had to give a stereotypical answer, I guess I would say the customs of a people, but I just don't ever use that word" (Kryder-Reid et al. 2018: 756). He sent an e-mail later detailing his concerns:

> I just thought of why I don't use "heritage." To me, it connotes a disconnect from a particular group's culture. If one labels things as "heritage," it makes those things abstract and easier to write off as novelty. At least in regards to Native American culture. When people talk about Native American heritage it's usually regarded as a spectacle, something to talk about for nostalgic reasons. But, that's no one particular person's fault, it's unfortunately just the way that we have been represented. Where some people say "heritage," I would say "way of life." The ancestors who made those sites still live through us today, and we gain strength through that.[7]

At the risk of my overinterpreting this e-mail, he reflects almost exactly what Lowenthal and Harrison wrote in the quotations above, that heritage is not history and that the past is repackaged for some purpose in the present. The author expresses his disdain for what he thinks of as the usual definitions of heritage. As has happened with many colonized and marginalized people, he is alienated from a heritage defined and represented by others, reduced to spectacle, nostalgia, or social problem. As heritage is so often defined, it is an artifact of the past, with little value in the present. As expressed in the e-mail, however, the author sees it and the places or sites where it is represented as a "way of life," lived by the ancestors, lived through their descendants today, and that gives them strength. Outsiders see his people as if they are barely visible or have disappeared, with a heritage that archaeology helped create, a heritage that connotes the disconnect he feels.

## Critical Archaeology, Public Archaeology, or Community Archaeology: Does It Matter?

In this instance, for a change, archaeology isn't directly blamed, but certainly is a participant in what the e-mail author considers a social injustice by misrepresenting the lifeways of his people. This pushes assessment of both archaeology and heritage into the realm of critical social theory. Where traditional social theory is oriented primarily to explaining or understanding society and culture, critical social theory has a specific practical purpose in that it seeks to critique and change society. The notion of being practical in a distinctly moral sense, rather than in just an instrumental sense, is aimed at identifying and confronting historical, social, and ideological forces and structures that constrain cultures.[8] The detail of how and why archaeology moved toward a critical archeology is best left for history of archaeology texts,[9] but there were hints of an incipient critical social theory emerging in archaeology as early as the 1950s suggesting that an applied archaeology was possible (see Kleindienst and Watson 1956).

Oversimplified, the difference between an archaeology that conflates the pasts it creates with a people's heritage and a critical archaeology is that the latter sees archaeology as a tool to explore, extend, explain, and challenge a heritage with which people identify, which they seek to clarify, which they reject in some way, or which they hope to use in some way. Critical archaeology is far from being objective and is inherently political (see McGuire 2008). By recognizing archaeology's political nature, the discipline can challenge colonial and class struggle legacies, but also can work with communities to develop meaningful representations of their pasts (see B. Clark, King, Sievert et al., and Watkins, this volume; Elia et al. 2019; Pluckhahn 2019). If we want people to be interested in archaeology and care about it, we need to recognize and freely admit that "it is what it is," a powerful, useful, and political tool for communities to deploy as they try to understand and represent their own heritage. Put another way, archaeology doesn't do heritage, people do!

Critical archaeology has slowly been morphing into public archaeology, Indigenous archaeology, and community archaeology in archaeology's exploration of critical theory and its efforts to make archaeology matter. Archaeologists still have lots of questions, such as how we define community, whether and how archaeology can create community, whether communities have a pre-existing identity, and how any of these relate to heritage (see Carman 2011 for an excellent summary of these issues). How we respond underpins archaeology's role in theorizing a critical pedagogy of heritage.

An important question, for which I have no real answer, might be whether theorizing a critical pedagogy of heritage is necessary or even possible. Lots of definitions of theory say roughly the same things.[10] A theory is a system of ideas containing both contemplative and rational types of abstract or generalized thinking, the goal of which is a simplification of reality. Theory can be normative and prescriptive, suggesting what goals, norms, or standards ought to exist or be considered, and it can also be a body of knowledge associated with particular modes of explanation. We have given scant attention to theory—goals, norms, and standards—and how to understand and explain heritage, let alone how to teach about it. Theory is usually contrasted with practice, but pedagogy is about both theory and practice, so theorizing it seems redundant. However, doing so adds to the body of knowledge about it and might be useful.

## From Archaeology Pedagogy to a Critical Pedagogy of Heritage

Pedagogy[11] might be essentialized as figuring out how best to teach, to whom, what their characteristics are (their prior knowledge, experience, and current situation), and what their and your learning goals might be. In terms of archaeology pedagogy, as I commented earlier, archaeologists have gotten very good at it. However, archaeology pedagogy mostly reflects a brand we've created that presents archaeology in simplistic terms and undersells its potential. Critical pedagogy involves the same elements as pedagogy generally, but doesn't consider the validity of specific belief claims,[12] which is more the realm of traditional archaeology's epistemology. Rather, it considers such claims to be parts of belief systems and action related to the power structures in society and who benefits from them, then how to transform inequitable institutions and power relations that create or support social injustice (compare Burbles and Berk 1999: 47). Paulo Freire (1970) was probably the leading advocate for critical pedagogy, which he elaborated on in *Pedagogy of the Oppressed*, and which sets up an oppressors–oppressed dichotomy.[13] Oppressors need to be willing to reflect and to rethink their way of life and their role in oppression, and the oppressed must play a role in their liberation by serving as their own example in their struggle for redemption.[14] In other words, critical pedagogy works only if it is bidirectional.

Deploying critical pedagogy would be difficult for a traditional archaeology that claims objectivity and for the types of heritages it creates, which primarily benefit mainstream society and support its master narratives, as well as the archaeologists and other heritage specialists producing them. These issues are evident in the complaint of the Native American's concern in the e-mail discussed above and what numerous other Indigenous people have told archaeologists for a long time: we do not need your past (for several examples, see Zimmerman 2001: 173, 176).

A warning is needed here, however, one that both oppressors and the oppressed should heed: no individual or group has a monopoly on truth about either themselves or others. As I tell my students about archaeology, there are always other stories—new ones, not-yet-heard ones, and ones not meant for your ears. The validity of the stories changes based on current contexts, but the fundamental truths revealed by the stories remain the same. If archaeologists need to reflect on what their role is, and marginalized people need to sense and use their own agency, both need to recognize that the other can be useful. They will sometimes have mutually exclusive truths; they must recognize each other's needs and limits; they must set research agendas together; and they must understand that their stories may differ and assessment of their validity may be challenged. They must become partners and collaborators, not oppressor and oppressed. They need to persuade each other, not demand or dictate terms of the collaboration. If we hope to theorize a critical pedagogy of heritage, these are surely a starting point. They are not complicated; the tough part is letting go of preconceived ideas about the roles each plays and figuring out where to go next.

However, because archaeologists are often cast in the role of oppressors, archaeologists may need to "let go" first to establish trust (compare Zimmerman 2012).

Freire's critical pedagogy, as summarized by Precey (2014: 1048), includes instructive strategies in correlation with "the instructor's own philosophical beliefs of instruction [that] are harbored and governed by the pupil's background knowledge and experience, situation, and environment, as well as learning goals set by the student and teacher." His proposed methodology is to work with communities to become familiar with and to understand the themes that are important in their lives, generating objects for study including a wide range of media. His is a problem-solving education in which the teacher and student become partners in a dialogue both to identify and come to conclusions about problems. Students and teachers learn from each other. This should sound familiar to those who practice critical archaeology of some variety, but one difference may seem to contradict Freire's notions about partnership. Some communities are so oppressed by and so marginalized by dominant society narratives that they may be unable to identify or in any way specify a heritage, so will need assistance. In such instances, archaeologists and other heritage specialists may need to become activists who provide clues or themes that guide community members in an exploration of what the heritage is and sometimes even identify or suggest which problems need solutions.[15] For the moment, as archaeologists and teachers, the more important concern is how we identify what it is that we want from ourselves and our students. Doing so is where help in theorizing a critical pedagogy of heritage is really needed.

## An Approach to Theorizing a Critical Pedagogy of Heritage

Following Freire, how do we, as instructors, identify "our own philosophical beliefs of instruction"? I have no easy answers here except to say that if you are interested in critical archaeology or critical heritage studies, you likely have some interest in social justice issues and in betterment of society. You probably practice social sciences and humanities research seeking to learn how cultures became what they are, why social injustices occur, and what possibilities for improvement of such situations have been tried or might be possible. Why do you think any culture needs to know what you offer them? Why do you think you are the appropriate person to teach them? What gives you the right even to offer collaboration with them? Your answers are matters for honest self-reflection. If you believe that you have any answers before you directly interact with possible collaborators or that you believe you know best, you probably are not ready for critical pedagogy.

Assessing whether or not they are interested in working with you, and just how interested, is a key element of understanding the attributes—knowledge and experience, situation, and environment—that potential students, communities, or stakeholders bring to your interaction with them. Asking them might seem the obvious answer and is an important part of the process. However, for them to articulate what they wish to know about their heritage or why may be as difficult as you telling them why you are asking. There may be ways of estimating probable interest, associated goals, and teaching questions that are hierarchical as much as anything.

### A Trial Hierarchy of Heritage Awareness and Intensity of Interest

I offer the structure that follows simply to demonstrate how heritage theory can be translated into practice as part of a critical pedagogy of heritage (see Figure 13.1).

The guiding assumptions for building such a structure should be understood first, followed by a classification of intensity of heritage interest, then a series of questions that help clarify each "level" in the hierarchy in terms of goals, practice, and related issues. Although lengthy debates in the literature argue the assumptions, they are not intended to be part of this discussion, nor are they necessary. The same is true for any detailed definition of terms, all of which are relatively common in the literature.[16]

### Guiding Assumptions That Underlie This Trial Hierarchy

1. All heritage—even intangible heritage—is spatially bound.
2. Spatial boundaries may be real or conceptual at any level in the hierarchy.
3. All heritage is local first and often associated with specific objects and places (compare Lowenthal 1996: 31).
4. Passion/intensity of interest for heritage decreases as spatial boundaries increase.
5. Numbers of individuals and possible stakeholders increase as spatial boundaries increase.

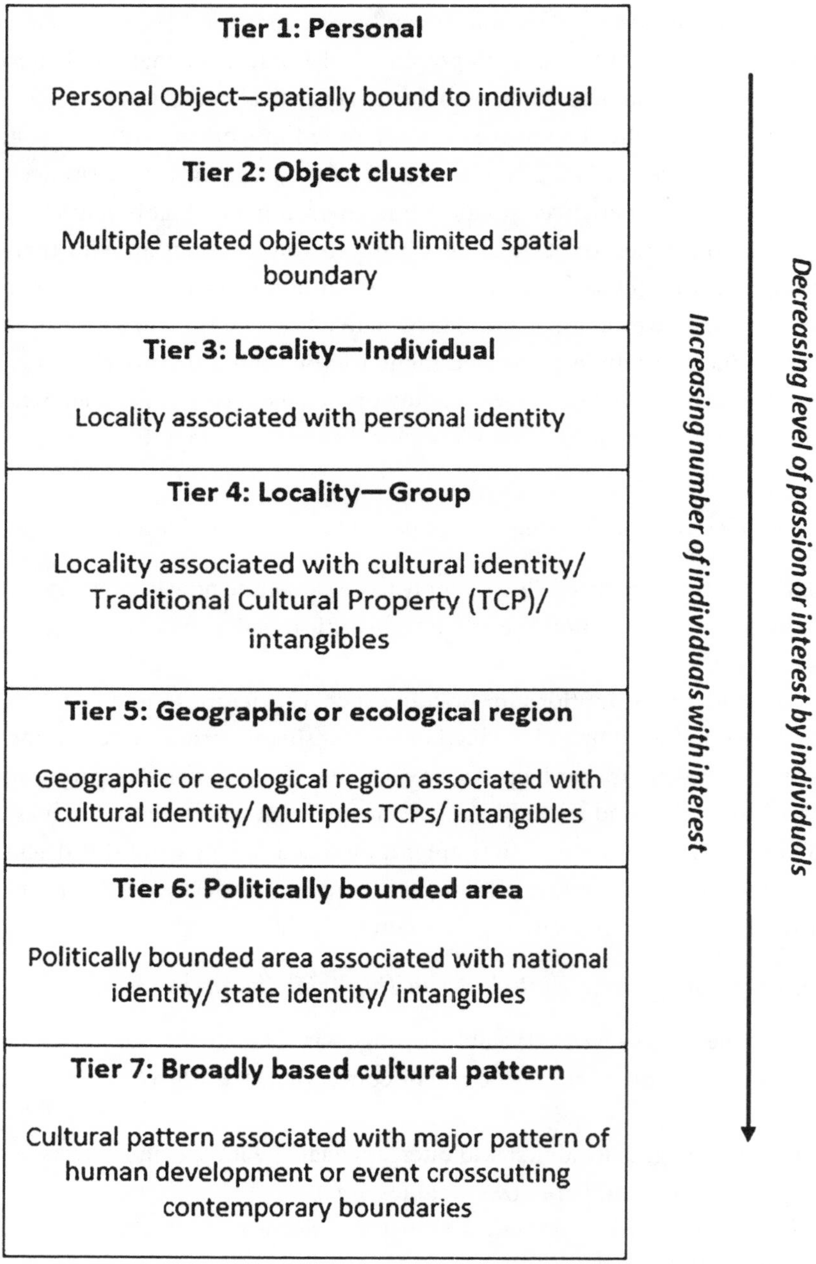

| Tier 1: Personal |
|:---:|
| Personal Object—spatially bound to individual |
| **Tier 2: Object cluster** |
| Multiple related objects with limited spatial boundary |
| **Tier 3: Locality—Individual** |
| Locality associated with personal identity |
| **Tier 4: Locality—Group** |
| Locality associated with cultural identity/ Traditional Cultural Property (TCP)/ intangibles |
| **Tier 5: Geographic or ecological region** |
| Geographic or ecological region associated with cultural identity/ Multiples TCPs/ intangibles |
| **Tier 6: Politically bounded area** |
| Politically bounded area associated with national identity/ state identity/ intangibles |
| **Tier 7: Broadly based cultural pattern** |
| Cultural pattern associated with major pattern of human development or event crosscutting contemporary boundaries |

*Increasing number of individuals with interest*

*Decreasing level of passion or interest by individuals*

Figure 13.1. A trial hierarchy of heritage awareness and intensity of interest.

6. Detailed characteristics of passion and interest are ill-defined and are initially unnecessary.

7. Levels are not mutually exclusive and are on a continuum.

*Questions Related to Heritage Pedagogy*

1. What are key heritage pedagogy goals or learning outcomes for each level?

2. How—and working with whom—are goals determined and vetted?

3. What is the most efficient strategy to reach the greatest number of people in each level?
   - Who is (are) the mostly likely educator(s) to "teach" any level?
   - What is the most efficient (time, money, other resources) medium (face to face, video, demonstration, other) to reach any level?
   - Which medium or educator will be most inspirational or motivating within each level?

4. What dangers (poor quality or superficial Authorized Heritage Discourse [AHD], hidden or overt political agendas, alienation of audience, creation of nostalgia or "phony" heritage, other)[17] exist for each educator or media type?
   - What methods or tools are available to counter dangers and how effective are they likely to be?

5. How can achievement of goals/learning outcomes be evaluated?

These heritage pedagogy questions combine many standard pedagogical questions with those of critical pedagogy, the latter most evident in question 4, which get at concerns about oppression, how to help people understand how it came to be, and how to address it. Theorizing a critical pedagogy of heritage hinges on answers to question 4, but is contingent on a wider range of issues within a general pedagogy.

In spite of Freire's and others' insistence on a critical pedagogy, sometimes people just want to know who was where, when, with what, and why? Sometimes they may not wish to identify with a particular heritage at all, for reasons they already know, because the heritage with which they now identify provides better options for day-to-day life (see Breglia 2006 for an example). The point is that all heritage pedagogy does not need to challenge a heritage status quo unless individuals, community members, and stakeholders want it to. That is their decision, not ours as heritage profession-als. Sometimes, however, they don't know the background of their heritage, the epistemological foundations of their heritage, or that they even have a heritage with which they might identify. These situations are where critical heritage research and pedagogy may improve well-being and contribute to a higher quality of life.

Where Should Archaeology Fit?

I began this chapter by trying to explain why our publics have a mostly simplistic understanding of archaeology and what it is capable of, usually thinking of it as interesting, but not really all that important to their day-to-day lives. We have become very good at teaching people about archaeol-ogy, but in a superficial way that undersells our "brand" by failing to show how it can be relevant. Part of the problem is that archaeologists have very little training in educational practice, and so they might benefit from pay-ing closer attention to pedagogy. Since people usually seem to be heavily invested in their heritage, to make archaeology matter, a better approach might be a pedagogy that shows how archaeology can help them identify elements of their heritage about which they may have questions that can be addressed by material culture study. Similarly, they may see the benefit of an archaeology that allows them to challenge deeply rooted, not necessarily positive or accurate, narratives about their heritage.

Critical archaeology, community archaeology, Indigenous archaeology, and similar variants have moved archaeology toward this approach, all of them employing elements of a critical pedagogy of heritage. In many ways, they have already tackled many of the steps necessary to theorizing a criti-cal heritage pedagogy. Most directly enlist community members in the technical aspects of archaeology field and laboratory methods, much as tra-ditional archaeology pedagogy has been doing for decades with volunteer programs, archaeology events, and the like. The difference is that in critical archaeology, people work on projects they helped design that are related to their own heritage. They provide detailed information on aspects of mate-rial culture, sometimes basic functional information about what some arti-fact is, but often more complex interpretations about meaning, which helps to create richer versions of their past at least partly in their own voices (see Kiddey et al. 2015 for an excellent example of all of these). Lots of these projects are now in the literature, but few address matters of moving from critical archaeology toward critical heritage, and how to help communities learn the processes of translating archaeological epistemology and interpretation to practical elements that will help their communities. Doing this should help communities and archaeologists who work with them to take the next step, which is learning how to craft meaningful public policies relating to heritage that move beyond protecting archaeological sites or repatriation, and make archaeology matter in their lives.

## Notes

1. Also be warned that my perspectives are primarily from North American archaeology, but many of the matters relating to critical heritage theory, especially when it comes to discussions of making archaeology relevant to contemporary life, are more international in scope.

2. I am not particularly proud of this, but as with archaeology theory, I have seen too much of the rush toward new theory and method by education school faculty members, much of it with little evaluation and critical reflection, and often had the education pedagogy *du jour* shoved down my throat at the university curriculum committee level. I suppose the same thing happens in most disciplines, if all the irritated complaining I have heard about it means much.

3. I recognize the dangers of generalizing from one's self to the whole, but doing so can be central to self-reflection. Experience is rarely systematically assessed and is usually anecdotal, which many of my reflections here will be.

4. In the United States, for example, the SAA has codified this into its Principles of Archaeological Ethics, particularly Principle 4, Public Education and Outreach, http://www.saa.org/AbouttheSociety/PrinciplesofArchaeologicalEthics/tabid/203/Default.aspx.

5. Some may find this to be adequate; maybe it is, and maybe it does build a level of public support for archaeology. But can't archaeology do and be more?

6. The IPinCH project website is a product of a multi-national group of researchers that includes many archaeologists, lawyers, Indigenous communities, and other research partners that deal with issues of intellectual property in Indigenous communities. A seven-year project funded by the Social Science and Humanities Council of Canada, IPinCH sponsored 18 community initiatives (http://www.sfu.ca/ipinch/project-components/community-based-initiatives/), 11 of them directly concerned with archaeology, but all of them in a context of contemporary heritage issues identified by the community. See the IPinCH Resources base for a list of materials generated by IPinCH activities.

7. This long quotation is directly taken from an e-mail and used with its original form, punctuation, and word use without editorial protest. Doing so better transmits the conversational, nonacademic tone and emotional content expressed by the e-mail's author.

8. This is an outrageously simplistic explanation of critical theory but should suffice for the purposes of this chapter. For a more thorough history and discussion of the approach, see philosopher James Bohman's (2016) summary.

9. For American archaeology, and historical archaeology in particular, see the *Current Anthropology* article by Leone et al. (1987), as well as the reviewer critiques included at the end of the article. 10. This paragraph is summarized from the Wikipedia entry for Theory, so if you want the unaltered, formal version of it, see https://en.wikipedia.org/wiki/Theory. Near the end, you will find a listing for Education with a link that will take you to Critical Pedagogy Theory, which will take you to more than you probably want to know about Paulo Freire.

11. For what it's worth, pedagogy applies to children (the *ped* part), so the education literature has also been debating since the early 1800s about whether teaching for adults might be different. Andragogy, as it has been labeled, has been claimed to require more emphasis on helping learners acquire information and skills. For a summary of the history and whether being concerned about child-vs.-adult learning is a false dichotomy, see Holmes and Abington-Cooper (2000).

12. In other words, what matters is what people believe, not what can be demonstrated by data and argumentation to be "true." I discuss this elsewhere in more detail (Zimmerman 2008: 58–60).

13. I really do not like the oppressor/oppressed dichotomy, which seems to imply intentionality on the part of the oppressor and a complete lack of agency for the oppressed. The terms hinder collaboration and critical pedagogy. Freire also describes a third category, the liberated, which has its own set of problems; the liberated can become the new oppressor (Freire 1970: 37). I have been around anthropology and archaeology for a lot of years, and most anthropological archaeologists I know have been bewildered by having someone call them an oppressor. When Inhanktonwan (Yankton Sioux) scholar Vine Deloria, Jr. (1969), published his "Anthropologists and Other Friends" chapter in *Custer Died for Your Sins*, many of my professors were utterly taken aback, puzzled by how Deloria could say such horrible things when anthropologists had done so much for Native Americans. The only time I would agree that archaeologists truly were oppressors was when some completely rejected repatriation and reburial, attacked oral tradition, accused Indigenous people of playing identity politics, and refused to listen to anything Native Americans were telling them (see Zimmerman 2001).

14. Critical pedagogy is much more than can be presented here, but the model fits reasonably well for what we can see in the development of critical archaeology and critical heritage.

15. See, for specific examples, recent uses of archaeology to address wellness among homeless people (Kiddey 2017) and among the Stó:lō–Coast Salish people of southwestern British Columbia and northwestern Washington by using community-based archaeology to promote health by connecting community members with their territories and both their tangible and intangible heritage (Schaepe et al. 2017).

16. Heritage and heritage theory are complicated; theorizing a critical pedagogy of heritage—not so much. Theorizing is essentially playing and can be translational, which in the sense used here, implies taking the results of basic research and translating them into meaningful outcomes that promote well-being.

17. These terms have variable meanings, and examples of each are rife. See Chilton's discussion of "official heritage" as "top down" (this volume) and its links to Smith's (2006: 4) AHD, which "privileges expert values and knowledge about the past and its material

manifestation, and dominates and regulates professional heritage practices." For more detailed discussion and critique of AHD see Smith (2006: 29–34) and Harrison 2013: 110–112). For a lengthy discussion of various forms of nostalgia and its problems, see Lowenthal (1985: 3–13). As for hidden or overt political agendas, the classic example is Hitler's use of archaeology to create a phony heritage to justify the Third Reich and its actions (Arnold 1990, 2006), but such agendas are evident even in disputes in the United States over removal of Civil War statues commemorating Confederate military and political leaders (see a blog by archaeologist Paul Mullins at https://paulmullins.wordpress.com/2017/06/16/memory-monuments-and-confederate-things-contesting-the-21st-century-confederacy/ (accessed January 21, 2018).

## References Cited

Arnold, Bettina

1990    The Past as Propaganda: Totalitarian Archaeology in Nazi Germany. *Antiquity* 64(244): 464–478.

2006    Pseudoarchaeology and Nationalism. In *Archaeological Fantasies: How Pseudoarchaeology Misrepresents the Past and Misleads the Public*, edited by Garrett G. Fagan, pp. 154–179. Routledge, London.

Atalay, Sonya

2012    *Community-Based Archaeology: Research with, by, and for Indigenous and Local Communities*. University of California Press, Berkeley.

Atalay, Sonya, Lee Rains Clauss, Randall H. McGuire, and John Welch (editors)

2014    *Transforming Archaeology: Activist Practices and Prospects*. Left Coast Press, Walnut Creek, California.

Bauman, Kurt, and Jessica Davis

2013    Estimates of School Enrollment by Grade in the American Community Survey, the Current Population Survey, and the Common Core of Data. *SEHSD Working Paper 2014-7.* U.S. Census Bureau, Washington, D.C. Electronic document, https://www.census.gov/hhes/school/files/ACS-CPS-CCD_02-18-14.pdf. Accessed January 27, 2017.

Bender, Susan J., and Phyllis Mauch Messenger (editors)

2019    *Pedagogy and Practice in Heritage Studies*. University Press of Florida, Gainesville.

Bohman, James

2016    Critical Theory. In *The Stanford Encyclopedia of Philosophy*, edited by Edward N. Zalta. Electronic document, https://plato.stanford.edu/archives/fall2016/entries/critical-theory/. Accessed January 27, 2017.

Breglia, Lisa C.

2006    *Monumental Ambivalence: The Politics of Heritage*. University of Texas Press, Austin.

Buchli, Victor

2007    Opinion. *Conservation Bulletin* 56: 14.

Burbules, Nicholas C., and Rupert Berk

1999      Critical Thinking and Critical Pedagogy: Relations, Differences, and Limits. In *Critical Theories in Education: Changing Terrains of Knowledge and Politics*, edited by Thomas S. Popkewitz and Lynn Fendler, pp. 45–66. Routledge, New York.

Carman, John

2002      *Archaeology and Heritage: An Introduction*. Continuum, London.

2011      Stories We Tell: Myths at the Heart of "Community Archaeology." *Archaeologies: Journal of the World Archaeological Congress* 7(3): 490–501.

Deloria, Vine, Jr.

1969      *Custer Died for Your Sins: An Indian Manifesto*. University of Oklahoma Press, Norman.

1995      *Red Earth, White Lies: Native Americans and the Myth of Scientific Fact*. Fulcrum, Golden, Colorado.

Elia, Ricardo J., Amalia Pérez-Juez, and Meredith Anderson

2019      Teaching Heritage in the Field: An Example from Menorca, Spain. In *Pedagogy and Practice in Heritage Studies*, edited by Susan J. Bender and Phyllis Mauch Messenger, pp. 94–111. University Press of Florida, Gainesville.

Freire, Paulo

1970      *Pedagogy of the Oppressed*. Continuum, New York.

Gannon, Megan

2016      Archaeologists Digging into the Here and Now. *UnDark: Truth Beauty Science*. Electronic document, http://undark.org/article/archaeologists-digging-into-the-here-and-now/. Accessed January 27, 2017.

Harrison, Rodney

2010      What is Heritage? In *Understanding the Politics of Heritage*, edited by Rodney Harrison, pp. 5–42. Manchester University Press, Manchester, UK.

2013      *Heritage: Critical Approaches*. Routledge, New York.

Holmes, Geraldine, and Michele Abington-Cooper

2000      Pedagogy vs. Andragogy: A False Dichotomy? *Journal of Technology Studies* 26(2): 50–55.

Holtorf, Cornelius

2007      *Archaeology Is a Brand: The Meaning of Archaeology in Contemporary Popular Culture*. Left Coast Press, Walnut Creek, California.

Kiddey, Rachael

2017      *Homeless Heritage: Collaborative Social Archaeology as Therapeutic Practice*. Oxford University Press, Oxford.

Kiddey, Rachael, Andrew Dafnis, and Jane Hallam

2015      Journeys in the City: Homeless Archaeologists, or Archaeologies of Homelessness. *Journal of Contemporary Archaeology* 2(2): 235–244.

Kleindienst, Maxine R., and Patty Jo Watson

1956      Action Archaeology: The Archaeological Inventory of a Living Community. *Anthropology Tomorrow* 5: 75–78.

Kryder-Reid, Elizabeth

2019      Do the Homeless Have Heritage? Archaeology and the Pedagogy of Discomfort.

In *Pedagogy and Practice in Heritage Studies*, edited by Susan J. Bender and Phyllis Mauch Messenger, pp. 129–147. University Press of Florida, Gainesville.

Kryder-Reid, Elizabeth, Jeremy Foutz, Elee Wood, and Larry J. Zimmerman

2018    "I just don't ever use that word": Investigating Stakeholders' Understanding of Heritage. *International Journal of Heritage Studies* 24(7): 743–763.

Leone, Mark P., Parker B. Potter, Jr., and Paul A. Shackel

1987    Toward a Critical Archaeology. *Current Anthropology* 28(3): 283–302.

Little, Barbara J., and Paul A. Shackel

2014    *Archaeology, Heritage, and Civic Engagement: Working toward the Public Good.* Left Coast Press, Walnut Creek, California.

Little, Barbara J., and Larry J. Zimmerman

2010    In the Public Interest: Creating a More Activist, Civically-Engaged Archaeology. In *Voices in American Archaeology,* edited by Wendy Ashmore, Dorothy Lippert, and Barbara Mills, pp. 131–159. Society for American Archaeology Press, Washington, D.C.

Lowenthal, David

1985    *The Past is a Foreign Country.* Cambridge University Press, Cambridge.

1996    *Possessed by the Past: The Heritage Crusade and the Spoils of History.* Free Press, New York.

Matthews, Christopher N.

2013    Unconventional Archaeologies in Setauket, New York. *Anthropology Now* 5(2): 26–34.

Matthews, Christopher N., and Carol McDavid

2013    Community Archaeology. *Oxford Companion to Archaeology,* 2nd ed., pp. 336–340. Oxford University Press, Oxford.

Matthews, Christopher N., Carol McDavid, and Patrice L. Jeppson

2011    Dyamics of Inclusion in Public Archaeology: An Introduction. *Archaeologies: Journal of the World Archaeological Congress* 7(3): 482–489.

McGill, Alicia Ebbitt

2019    Assessing Student Learning in Heritage Studies: What Does It Mean for Students to "Understand" Archaeological Ethics? In *Pedagogy and Practice in Heritage Studies,* edited by Susan J. Bender and Phyllis Mauch Messenger, pp. 50–71. University Press of Florida, Gainesville.

McGuire, Randall H.

2008    *Archaeology as Political Action.* University of California Press, Oakland.

Moe, Jeanne M.

2019    Archaeology in School: Student Learning Outcomes. In *Pedagogy and Practice in Heritage Studies,* edited by Susan J. Bender and Phyllis Mauch Messenger, pp. 9–29. University Press of Florida, Gainesville.

Pluckhahn, Thomas

2019    The Challenges of Curriculum Change and the Pedagogy of Public Archaeology and CRM at the University of South Florida. In *Pedagogy and Practice in Heritage Studies,* edited by Susan J. Bender and Phyllis Mauch Messenger, pp. 72–93. University Press of Florida, Gainesville.

Precey, Robin

2014    Frozen in Time, Left out in the Cold: Teacher Training and Development and the Role of the Head Teacher—Considering Alternatives. In *Human Factors of a Global Society: A System of Systems Perspective*, edited by Tadeusz Marek, Waldemar Karwowski, Marek Frankowicz, Jussi Kantola, and Pavel Zgaga, pp. 1045–1056. CRC Press, Boca Raton, Florida.

Rathje, William, and Cullen Murphy

1992    *Rubbish! The Archaeology of Garbage*. HarperCollins, New York.

Sabloff, Jeremy

2008    *Archaeology Matters: Action Archaeology in the Modern World*. Left Coast Press, Walnut Creek, California.

Schaepe, David M., Bill Angelback, David Snook, and John R. Welch

2017    Archaeology as Therapy: Connecting Belongings, Knowledge, Time, Place, and Well-Being. *Current Anthropology* 58(4): 502–533.

Smith, Laurajane

2006    *Uses of Heritage*. Routledge, Abingdon, Oxon.

Smith, Laurajane, and Emma Waterton

2009    *Heritage, Communities, and Archaeology*. Bloomsbury, London.

Stottman, M. Jay (editor)

2011    *Archaeologists as Activists: Can Archaeologists Change the World?* University of Alabama Press, Tuscaloosa.

White, Charles S.

2019    Archaeology in School: Tapping into Histories and Historical Inquiry. In *Pedagogy and Practice in Heritage Studies*, edited by Susan J. Bender and Phyllis Mauch Messenger, pp. 30–49. University Press of Florida, Gainesville.

Zimmerman, Larry J.

2001    Usurping Native American Voice. In *The Future of the Past: Archaeologists, Native Americans, and Repatriation*, edited by Tamara Bray, pp. 196–184. Garland, New York.

2008    Unusual or "Extreme" Beliefs about the Past, Community Identity, and Dealing with the Fringe. In *Collaboration in Archaeological Practice: Engaging Descendent Communities*, edited by Chip Colwell-Chanthaphonh and T. J. Ferguson, pp. 55–86. AltaMira Press, Lanham, Maryland.

2012    On Archaeological Ethics and Letting Go. In *Appropriating the Past: Philosophical Perspectives on the Practice of Archaeology II*, co-edited by Geoffrey Scarre and Robin Cunningham, pp. 98–118. Cambridge University Press, Cambridge.

2013    Homelessness. In *The Oxford Handbook of the Archaeology of the Contemporary World*, edited by Paul Graves-Brown, Rodney Harrison, and Angela Piccini, pp. 336–350. Oxford University Press, Oxford.

Zimmerman, Larry J., Steve Dasovich, Mary Engstrom, and Lawrence E. Bradley

1994    Listening to the Teachers: Warnings about the Use of the Archaeological Agenda in the Classroom. In *The Presented Past: Archaeology, Museums and Public Education, edited by* Peter Stone and Brian Molyneaux, pp. 359–374. Routledge, London.

# Contributors

Susan J. Bender is professor emerita at Skidmore College and served as research director of the South Park (Colorado) Archaeology Project. She has contributed to the Society for American Archaeology's initiative to reform the undergraduate curriculum for the twenty-first century and worked collaboratively with the South Park National Heritage Area as part of her research interests in hunter-gatherer settlements in mountainous regions of the American West.

Elizabeth S. Chilton is professor of anthropology and dean of Harpur College of Arts & Sciences at Binghamton University (New York). She is the founder and former director of the Center for Heritage & Society at the University of Massachusetts–Amherst and served as the coeditor of the journal *Heritage & Society* from 2011 to 2016. Her research, publications, and teaching focus on heritage management, the archaeology of New England, the origins of agriculture, and ceramic ecology.

Bonnie J. Clark serves as associate professor of anthropology at the University of Denver (DU), as well as the Curator for Archaeology of the DU Museum of Anthropology. Since 2005, she has led the DU Amache Project, a collaborative endeavor committed to preserving, researching, and interpreting Amache, the World War II Japanese American incarceration camp in Colorado. In 2011, Dr. Clark's work was recognized by her peers with the University of Denver's Teacher/Scholar of the Year award. Other publications include *On the Edge of Purgatory: An Archaeology of Place in Hispanic Colorado* and the coedited volume *Archaeological Landscapes on the High Plains*.

Kate Clark is professor of heritage valuation at the University of Suffolk and an industrial archaeologist with over thirty years of experience in working with heritage.

Hannah Cobb is senior lecturer in archaeology at the University of Manchester, UK. Her research focuses on both contemporary archaeological practice and the British Mesolithic. In both areas, her research is informed by a New Materialist approach. Hannah chairs the Chartered Institute for Archaeologists Equality and Diversity Group. Since 2006 she has codirected the multiperiod Ardnamurchan Transitions Project. She is coauthor, with Karina Croucher, of *Archaeology: A Relational Approach to Teaching, Practice and Research* and is an editor of *Reconsidering Archaeological Fieldwork*. She has also worked for the Higher Education Academy's Subject Centre for History, Classics and Archaeology.

Karina Croucher is lecturer in archaeology at the University of Bradford, UK, and a senior fellow of the Higher Education Academy. She has previously taught archaeology at the Universities of Manchester and Liverpool. Her research focuses on mortuary practices and funerary archaeology, predominantly of the Neolithic Period of Southwest Asia. She has worked for the University of Manchester's Widening Participation Team and for the Higher Education Academy's Subject Centre for History, Classics and Archaeology (based at Liverpool University), where she researched and worked on topics including diversity and inclusivity, fieldwork, employability and enterprise, and sustainability.

Greg Donofrio teaches historic preservation in the School of Architecture at the University of Minnesota. His teaching and research interests include the historic preservation history, theory, and policy in the United States, as well as community engagement to advance diversity and inclusion in historic preservation practice. He is coeditor of the journal *Preservation Education & Research*.

Patricia Emerson has been conducting archaeological and historical research in the Upper Midwest for forty years. Currently she is director of archaeology for the Minnesota Historical Society. Her interests include place-based studies, public education, and digital archaeology.

M. Elaine Franklin (formerly Davis) is director of the Kenan Fellows Program for Teacher Leadership at North Carolina State University. She has extensive experience in STEM education and teacher professional development and specializes in archaeology education and inquiry learning. Franklin is a former director of education at the Crow Canyon Archaeological Center and has directed five National Endowment for the Humanities Summer Institutes for Teachers. She is author of *How Students Understand the Past: From Theory to Practice* and, with Marjorie Connolly, editor of *Windows into the Past: Crow Canyon Archaeological Center's Guide for Teachers*.

Katherine Hayes is trained as a historical archaeologist of North America, with a research focus on the contexts and ongoing outcomes of settler colonialism in New England and Minnesota. Her current research examines the history, archaeology, and contemporary heritage interpretations at the site of Fort Snelling to provide more inclusive perspectives on its 125-year history as an active military installation. She is associate professor of anthropology and former chair of the Department of American Indian Studies at the University of Minnesota.

Tim Hoogland is instructor of history at the University of Minnesota, Twin Cities. He holds an MA in history from the University of Minnesota and is a graduate of the Seminar for Historical Administration. For the past thirty years he has directed history education, curriculum development, and teacher professional development programs in Minnesota—most notably the National History Day program. In 1998, Mr. Hoogland was recognized with the History Channel Outstanding History Educator Award, and in 2016 he was awarded the University of Minnesota's Outstanding Community Service Award for his efforts to build public history partnerships and campus connections to K-12 schools.

Eleanor M. King is associate professor in the Department of Sociology and Criminology at Howard University. A specialist in Maya archaeology, she has also investigated the Apaches and the Buffalo Soldiers in the Southwest United States. Research and advocacy interests include heritage studies, precollegiate education in archaeology, and the underrepresentation of minorities and other groups in anthropology. She is the cofounder, with Carol Ellick, of The Heritage Education Network (THEN), http://theheritageeducationnetwork.org, an online alliance for those who use, manage, teach, or create information about past or present peoples and cultures.

Robert I. MacDonald, PhD, RPA, is managing partner of Archaeological Services, Inc. He holds adjunct appointments as assistant professor in the Department of Anthropology at the University of Waterloo and as a member of the anthropology graduate faculty at Trent University.

Arkadiusz Marciniak is professor of archaeology at Adam Mickiewicz University in Poznań, Poland. His expertise is in the development of early farming communities in western Asia and central Europe and their progression to complex societies. He has been directing a project at the Late Neolithic settlement at Çatalhöyük East in Turkey. His other interests comprise archaeological heritage and the political context of practicing archaeology as well as the zooarchaeology of farming communities. He is an initiator of the E-Archaeology Heritage Content Repository—an interactive database for uploading, storing, and producing training materials in the domain of archaeological heritage and associated fields—and the Heritage Educational Portal—a platform offering a wide range of online courses in the domains of cultural and natural heritage for professionals and the public.

Phyllis Mauch Messenger, RPA, holds a master's in anthropology and a doctorate in education and has worked on archaeological projects in Mexico, Honduras, and the United States. She is grants consultant for the Institute for Advanced Study (IAS) at the University of Minnesota, an editor of the university's online journal *Open Rivers*, and was founding director of the Center for Anthropology and Cultural Heritage Education at Hamline University. She has edited several volumes, including *The Ethics of Collecting Cultural Property*; *Cultural Heritage Management*; and *Heritage Values in Contemporary Society*.

Kevin P. Murphy is professor of history at the University of Minnesota. His research focuses on public history, the history of gender and sexuality, and urban history. He is on the steering committee of the Humanities Action Lab and on the editorial board of the *Public Historian*.

Teresa Nichols is the grant and program manager for the Center for the Study of Global Change at Indiana University and acted as the project manager of the NSF-funded "Learning NAGPRA" project. She has conducted research in Mongolia and in the United States on cultural heritage policy, Indigenous rights, and professional ethics.

Patrick Nunnally is coordinator of River Life, a program at the Institute for Advanced Study, University of Minnesota. He holds a PhD in American studies from the University of Iowa and is editor of *Open Rivers: Rethinking Water, Place & Community*, a digital journal of interdisciplinary scholarship and community expertise.

K. Anne Pyburn is Provost's Professor of Anthropology at Indiana University. She does research in Belize and Kyrgyzstan and writes about archaeological research ethics, gender issues in archaeology, and archaeology and development. Recent publications include *Collision or Collaboration: Archaeology Encounters Economic Development (Series: One World Archaeology)*; "Preservation as 'Disaster Capitalism': The Downside of Site Rescue and the Complexity of Community Engagement," in *Public Archaeology*; and "Activating Archaeology," in *Transforming Archaeology: Activist Practices and Prospects*.

Paul A. Shackel is professor of anthropology and director of the Center for Heritage Studies at the University of Maryland. His research projects have focused on the role of archaeology in civic engagement activities related to race and labor. A sample of his work on this topic includes *New Philadelphia: An Archaeology of Race in the Heartland* and a coauthored volume with Barbara Little: *Archaeology, Heritage and Civic Engagement: Working toward the Public Good*. He is currently engaged in a project that focuses on labor and migration in the northern Appalachia region of the United States. This work focuses on issues of class, race, and labor; the foundation for the project can be found in his book *Remembering Lattimer: Migration, Labor, and Race in Pennsylvania Anthracite Country*.

April Sievert is senior lecturer in anthropology, director of the Glenn A. Black Laboratory of Archaeology at Indiana University, and lead PI on the NSF-funded "Learning NAGPRA" project. Her work centers on archaeological and industrial heritage in North America, repatriation, and the scholarship of teaching and learning.

Chris Taylor is the chief inclusion officer at the Minnesota Historical Society (MNHS). He is responsible for creating an inclusive work culture within the organization and assisting staff in developing inclusive work practices within the various functions of MNHS.

Jayne-Leigh Thomas is director of the Office of the Native American Graves Protection and Repatriation Act (NAGPRA) at Indiana University. She is the lead author on the *International Journal of Osteoarchaeology* article, "Violence and Trophy Taking: A Case Study of Head and Neck Trauma in Two Individuals from the Gant Site (3MS11)." Her research interests are human osteology, cremation studies, NAGPRA, repatriation, mortuary studies, and ethics.

Joe Watkins, a member of the Choctaw Nation of Oklahoma, currently works for the Archaeological and Cultural Education Consultants (The ACE Consultants) in Tucson, Arizona. He was the American Indian liaison officer, supervisory cultural anthropologist, and chief of the Tribal Relations and American Cultures Program of the National Park Service in Washington, D.C., from May 2013 to May 2018; the director of the Native American Studies Program at the University of Oklahoma from 2007 to 2013; and associate professor of anthropology at the University of New Mexico from 2003 to 2007. Watkins has served on numerous committees of international, national, and regional anthropological organizations and was elected president of the Society for American Archaeology for 2019–2021. His study interests concern the ethical practice of anthropology and the study of anthropology's relationships with descendant communities and populations, including American Indians, Australian Aboriginals, New Zealand Maori, and the Japanese Ainu.

Anduin Wilhide is a public historian and a PhD candidate in the Department of History at the University of Minnesota. Her research explores histories of immigration and refugee resettlement in Minnesota through collaborative digital humanities projects.

Larry J. Zimmerman is professor emeritus of anthropology and museum studies at Indiana University–Purdue University Indianapolis (IUPUI) and public scholar of Native American representation at the Eiteljorg Museum of American Indian and Western Art. He has served as both secretary and vice president of the World Archaeological Congress, which in 2008 awarded him the inaugural Peter J. Ucko Medal for his contributions to world archaeology. His research and publications focus on North American archaeology, repatriation, Native American representation, ethics, and the use of archaeology to understand contemporary homelessness.

# Index

Page numbers followed by the letters *f* and *t* indicate figures and tables.

NAGPRA (Native American Graves Protection and Repatriation Act), 40, 60, 87–88, 131; benefits and harms, 97–98; biological anthropologists and, 93; compliance, 91; conflicts over, 68; learning about, 101–102; "Learning NAGPRA" project, 94, 101; NAGPRA Collegium, 94–96, 95f; repatriation, 89–90; working on, 99–100

Nara Document on Authenticity, 27

National Register of Historic Places, 19, 134

National Science Foundation (NSF): funding for "Learning NAGPRA" project, 94; grant for "Making Archaeology Teaching Relevant in the XXIst Century" (MATRIX), 108; Research Experiences for Undergraduates, 76

Native American(s): biological anthropologists and, 92–93; engaged in archaeology, 113–114; heritage, 222, 224; relations between archaeologists and, 112; scholars, 96; scholars and research, 91–92; students, 109; studies program, 112–113; working *with and for*, 89–90. *See also* American Indian(s); NAGPRA; Repatriation

Official heritage. *See* Heritage

Outstanding Universal Value (OUV), 26–27, 89

Patrimony: objects of cultural, 88; *patrimoine*, or "that which is inherited," 24. *See also* Cultural heritage; Heritage

Pedagogic practice: resisting neoliberalism in, 186–187

Pedagogic research: in archaeology, 183; assemblage theory valuable in transforming, 187; funding in the UK, 182, 183; momentum for, 191

Piaget, Jean: and disruptive innovation models, 34; saw perturbations as central to learning, 33

Principles of Archaeological Ethics, SAA's: accountability, 116; "circular" communication in the development of, 110; SAA's ethic of stewardship, 110; "Safe Educational and Workplace Environments," 45

*Project Archaeology*, 79, 215, 216. *See also* Warriors Project Archaeology

Public anthropology, 155; applied anthropology defined as, 159; six formal programs in in North America, 156. *See also* Public issues anthropology

Public archaeology, 3, 6, 50, 217; Bohemian Flats project, 139; critical archaeology morphing into, 224; curriculum, 215; education, 217, 222; events, 218, 222; module, 203t, 205; museums as critical locations of, 176; new pedagogies in, 33. *See also* Archaeology education

Public history: creating a program, 136; definitions, 134–135; emerged from New Social History movement, 135; heritage approaches rooted in, 133; interest from faculty and students, 129; projects, 139, 220; rise of the movement, 130. *See also* Heritage Studies and Public History; Teaching Heritage Collaborative

Public issues anthropology, 5; addressing the heritage concerns of First Nations through, 160; approaching cultural heritage through, 158; case study in, 160–163; University of Waterloo graduate program in, 156–157

Quasi Autonomous Nongovernmental Organization (QUANGO), 182

Repatriation, 4, 6; consultation, 99, 101; critical heritage and, 231; ethical principles and, 87; false dichotomy between science and religion, 89, 93; how taught and learned, 94–95, 102; of human remains to First Nations, 163; as part of heritage, 25; political controversy over, 222; repatriation as a threat to science, 96–97; tribal professionals, 96, 100. *See also* NAGPRA; Native American(s)

Research Excellence Framework (REF), 181–184, 186

Research in Archaeological Education (RAE), 183

Silo mentality, 136

Social injustice(s), 223, 225; research on why they occur, 226; understanding the root causes of, 14. *See also* Social justice

Social justice, 2, 14, 32; centering programs on, 79; civic engagement and, 100;

CPSIA information can be obtained
at www.ICGtesting.com
Printed in the USA
BVHW031453170720
583896BV00009B/50